Archaeologists

EXPLORERS OF THE HUMAN PAST

Archaeologists

EXPLORERS OF THE HUMAN PAST

BRIAN FAGAN

OXFORD

UNIVERSITY PRESS

This book is for would-be archaeologists everywhere

OXFORD
UNIVERSITY PRESS

Oxford New York
Auckland Bangkok Buenos Aires Cape Town
Chennai Dar es Salaam Delhi Hong Kong Istanbul Karachi
Kolkata Kuala Lumpur Madrid Melbourne Mexico City Mumbai
Nairobi São Paulo Shanghai Singapore Taipei Tokyo Toronto

Copyright © 2003 by Brian Fagan
Published by Oxford University Press, Inc.
198 Madison Avenue, New York, New York 10016
www.oup.com

Library of Congress Cataloging-in-Publication Data:

Fagan, Brian
Archaeologists : explorers of the human past / Brian Fagan.
p. cm. — (Oxford profiles)
Includes bibliographical references (p.) and index.
ISBN 0-19-511946-0 (alk. paper)
1. Archaeologists—Biography. 2. Archaeology—History.
I. Title. II. Series.
CC110.F34   2002
2002006293

9 8 7 6 5 4 3 2 1
Printed in the United States of America
on acid-free paper

On the cover: Earthen pot; *inset* (clockwise from left) Raymond Dart, Kathleen Kenyon, John Evans

Frontispiece: Excavations at Koster, Illinois by the Center for American Archaeology and Northwestern University, 1968–1979.

Design: Sandy Kaufman
Layout: Loraine Machlin
Picture research: Lisa Barnett

Contents

Preface 7

Maps 10
North America 10
Central and South America 10
Egypt and the Nile Valley 11
Africa 11
Great Britain 12
Europe and North Africa 12
Asia 13
Southwest Asia 13
Greece 13

Part 1. Searching for Human Antiquity 15
William Stukeley 18
Johann Joachim Winckelmann 22
Christian Jurgensen Thomsen .26
Giovanni Battista Belzoni 29
John Evans 33
Jacob Jens A. Worsaae 37
More Archaeologists to Remember 41

Part 2. Finding Lost Civilizations 45
John Lloyd Stephens 48
Austen Henry Layard 51
Henry Creswicke Rawlinson 55
Auguste Mariette 58
Charles Warren 61
Heinrich Schliemann 64
More Archaeologists to Remember 67

Part 3. The Birth of Scientific Archaeology 71
Augustus Lane Fox Pitt-Rivers 74
William Matthew Flinders Petrie 78
Gertrude Bell 82
Henri Breuil 86
Howard Carter 90
Arthur John Evans 94
Harriet Boyd Hawes 98
Alfred Vincent Kidder 102
Oscar Montelius 106

Sylvanus Griswold Morley 109
Aurel Stein 113
Leonard Woolley 117
Vere Gordon Childe 121
More Archaeologists to Remember 125

Part 4. Great Fieldworkers .129
Gertrude Caton-Thompson 132
Dorothy Garrod 136
Kathleen Kenyon 140
Mortimer Wheeler 144
Louis and Mary Leakey 148
Grahame Clark 153
John Desmond Clark 157
Gordon R. Willey 160
More Archaeologists to Remember 163

Part 5. Team Players 167
Some Prominent Archaeologists of Our Time 170

Major Events in the History of Archaeology . . .174

Major Events in Prehistoric Times 176

Glossary of Archaeological Sites and Terms . . .178

Further Reading and Websites 183

Index 187

Preface

Archaeologist—the word conjures up images of eccentric professors and bold adventurers searching for lost cities and gold-laden burial sites. Hollywood movies like the Indiana Jones sagas and *The Mummy* spring to mind. The earliest archaeologists were indeed adventurers and, sometimes, treasure hunters. Today's popular stereotype has at least some basis in history but is far from reality. Modern-day archaeologists are highly trained scientists who study every aspect of ancient human behavior, from that of the earliest humans over 2.5 million years ago to modern industrial sites. But they share one characteristic with their predecessors—a deep and passionate curiosity about the human past.

Archaeology began as little more than treasure hunting, a frenzied search for lost civilizations and spectacular artifacts. Along Africa's Nile River, in northeast Africa, generations of adventurers excavated and looted ancient Egyptian temples and sepulchers. During the 1940s, Englishman Austen Henry Layard and Frenchman Paul Emile Botta discovered the spectacular palaces of Assyrian kings in Iraq, in the Near East. During the same decade, American traveler John Lloyd Stephens and artist Frederick Catherwood revealed the glories of the Central American Maya civilization to the outside world.

Serious archaeology, which keeps detailed records of the past, began in 1859 with the discovery of human-manufactured stone tools in the same layers as long-extinct animals. The discovery coincided with the publication of Charles Darwin's momentous essay, *Origin of Species*, in the same year. For the first time, the human past had an unlimited time scale, far longer than the mere 6,000 years assigned to all our existence in the Old Testament. When the biologist Thomas Huxley proclaimed in 1863 that humans' closest relatives were chimpanzees, he caused furious controversy between scientists and the religious community. He also started a scientific search for human origins which continues to this day.

The 19th century was the century of archaeological adventure and spectacular discoveries, such as the tombs of pharaohs surrounded by gold, and lost civilizations. German businessman-turned-archaeologist Heinrich Schliemann dug deep into ancient Troy (Hissarlik), with the help of engineers who had dug the Suez Canal in Egypt. This was archaeology on a grand scale, with relatively little concern for science. But by the 1870s, times were changing. German archaeologists at Olympia and other well-known Greek sites began to stress recording and conservation over magnificent finds. In England, General Augustus Lane Fox Pitt-Rivers developed excavation methods at sites on his extensive estates that were to serve as models for modern-day techniques.

Archaeology came of age in the 20th century. At that time, a few archaeologists, like Egyptologist Flinders Petrie, were using the newest scientific methods to study such unspectacular finds as potsherds and beads. In the United States, Alfred Kidder developed the Direct Historical Method at Pecos, New Mexico. His approach worked back from known historic sites with careful observation of occupation layers into the remote past, tracking changes in human societies through their evolving pottery styles. This approach is one of the foundations of modern American archaeology. British and German archaeologists refined Flinders Petrie's methods in the 1930s and developed the precise excavation methods of today. They were also the first to use photography to look at archaeological sites from the air, many of them invisible on the surface.

The greatest scientific advances came in the post–World War II era, when archaeology formed a lasting marriage with high-technology science. The

Ole Worm's Museum of Curiosities was a popular attraction in 17th-century Copenhagen, Denmark. An early prototype for the modern museum, Ole Worm's displayed all manner of exhibits, including geological samples and fossils, skeletons and skins of exotic Arctic and tropical animals, and artifacts from Africa and Asia.

physicist Willard Libby developed radiocarbon dating in 1949, the first truly reliable method for dating 40,000 years of the past in any part of the world. Simultaneously, some archaeologists in Europe and the Near East began taking teams of specialist scientists with them on their excavations, to study such important topics and changing local environments and the origins of agriculture more than 10,000 years ago.

Computers, new methods of studying ancient climate change, tree-ring dating, and numerous other scientific methods all helped revolutionize archaeology from a somewhat casual science into the highly specialized academic discipline and profession that it is today. At the same time, the simple explanations of the past and how human societies changed that were widely accepted in the 1920s and 1930s gave way to new, much more sophisticated theories. These involved systems theory, which argued that human societies were part of much wider ecosystems and changed constantly to maintain a dynamic relationship with their surroundings. In recent years, the search for explanations of the past has gone in new directions as scholars have looked more closely at ancient human behavior, religious beliefs, and other variables that generate change in human societies, yet are hard to detect in archaeological finds.

Since the 1950s, archaeologists have become increasingly concerned about the continuous destruction of archaeological sites. Such destruction stems from many causes—huge dams, which flood river valleys and the archaeological sites located there; urban expansion; highway construction; deep plowing; and mining, to mention only a few. Individuals have done their part, too, looting and digging up priceless sites to sell their contents on the open market. So have archaeologists, by digging sites but then not publishing information about their finds. Unlike forests or many other natural resources, the priceless archives of the human past in the form of artifacts and sites cannot be replaced or regrown. All archaeological excavation is destruction—which makes the technical skills of the archaeologist all-important and makes looting an immoral pastime. Amateur archaeologists, working with professionals and through local archaeological societies, have an important role to play in preserving and studying the past.

In recent years, much federal and state legislation in North America has tried to stem the destruction by establishing legal requirements for anyone developing or disturbing publicly owned land (private land is subject to different rules in the United States). Most archaeology in North America today—both surveys and excavations—is devoted to ensuring compliance with existing laws. These field projects come under the label of Cultural Resource Management (CRM), something very different from academic archaeology, which is concerned only with intellectual issues and basic research. CRM involves many legal issues and is often carried out by private archaeological businesses as well as by archaeologists who also have professional training in the many legal and related skills needed to carry out such projects.

Despite a huge volume of CRM research, looting and destruction continue. Thousands of archaeological sites have vanished in recent years, not only in urban, but in rural areas. Less than 5 percent of all the archaeological sites in Los Angeles County have not been disturbed. The figure is even lower in many areas. Such great destruction means that all of us, whether archaeologist or member of the public, must live ethically and responsibly with the past, and with archaeological sites and artifacts. If we do not, vast amounts of information about the development of humanity will vanish forever.

The ethics of archaeology for all of us are simple. Report all archaeological discoveries to the proper authorities. Do not disturb archaeological sites without professional training, and above all, do not collect artifacts for yourself either for the pleasure of owning them or for profit. Respect native peoples' burial grounds and sacred places. Above all, treat the past in all its forms as a finite resource that we hold in trust for future generations. The finds of archaeology in all their forms, whether a humble stone chopper, an early farming village, a great city, or a vast pyramid, are part of the common cultural heritage of all humanity. As such, it is our responsibility to look after it for future, still unborn generations.

On the following pages you will meet a wide variety of archaeologists who have been prominent in the study of the past. In chronological order, 33 archaeologists are profiled in extended essays; many others are identified in the section called "More Archaeologists to Remember" that follows each of parts 1–4 of this book. If you want to find out more about some of the archaeologists, consult the books in the Further Reading list at the end of each person's profile. There is also another Further Reading list in the back of the book that includes more books and articles about individuals, archaeology, and the past that may be available at your school or local library.

Devout Christians search for the relics of St. Etienne in an 11th-century manuscript illustration. Priests valued saints' relics as ways of attracting pilgrims (and money) to a church, and tomb robbing was a way of acquiring the relics.

The stories in this book focus on archaeologists between the 17th century and about 1960. Since then, the number of archaeologists in the world has increased dramatically. At the same time, archaeology has become a team science, where few scholars achieve the kind of prominence enjoyed by such earlier archaeologists as Howard Carter, who discovered the tomb of the Egyptian pharaoh Tutankhamun. For this reason, the book ends in Part 5 with a brief survey of developments since 1960, accompanied by short notes on 27 well-known archaeologists of today.

Of course, this book cannot tell the story of every archaeologist who has ever lived; there are thousands of them. Today, the growing concern over the destruction of the past has led to the creation of many new archaeological jobs. Many of them are held by professionals who work at protecting the finite records of human life and activity throughout the ages. Amateur archaeologists also play an important role in caring for the past for the benefit of future generations. At a time when archaeological sites everywhere are threatened with destruction by looters, treasure hunters, and industrial activity, we need an abundance of archaeologists and interested people to care for our past.

Brian Fagan

NORTH AMERICA

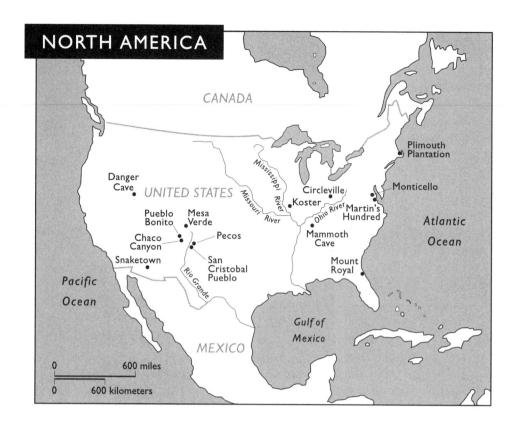

CANADA

UNITED STATES

Danger Cave

Pueblo Bonito
Mesa Verde
Chaco Canyon
Pecos
Snaketown
San Cristobal Pueblo

Mississippi River
Missouri River
Ohio River
Rio Grande

Circleville
Koster
Martin's Hundred
Mammoth Cave

Plimouth Plantation
Monticello
Mount Royal

Atlantic Ocean

Pacific Ocean

Gulf of Mexico

MEXICO

0   600 miles

0   600 kilometers

CENTRAL AND SOUTH AMERICA

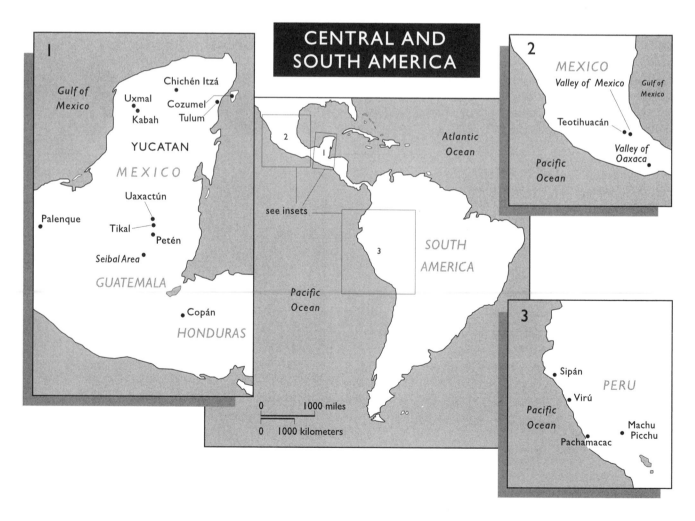

1

Gulf of Mexico

Uxmal
Kabah

Chichén Itzá
Cozumel
Tulum

YUCATAN

MEXICO

Palenque

Uaxactún
Tikal
Petén
Seibal Area

GUATEMALA

Copán

HONDURAS

see insets

Atlantic Ocean

SOUTH AMERICA

Pacific Ocean

0   1000 miles

0   1000 kilometers

2

MEXICO

Valley of Mexico

Teotihuacán

Valley of Oaxaca

Gulf of Mexico

Pacific Ocean

3

Sipán

Virú

PERU

Pacific Ocean

Machu Picchu

Pachamacac

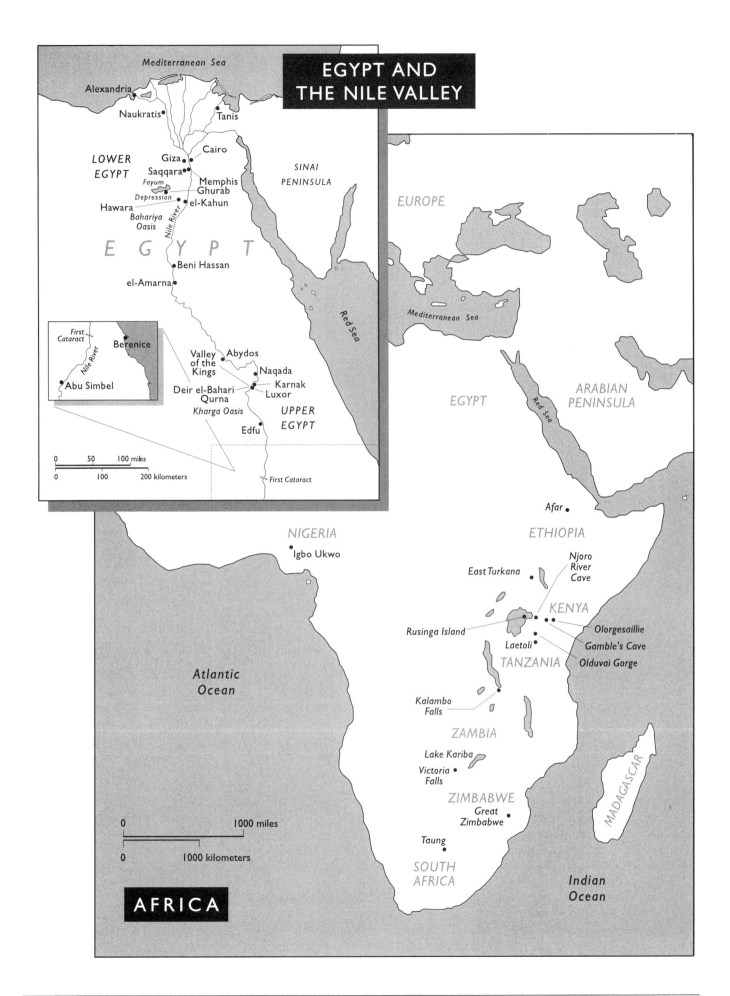

EGYPT AND THE NILE VALLEY

Mediterranean Sea

Alexandria

Naukratis

Tanis

LOWER EGYPT

Cairo

Giza

Saqqara

SINAI PENINSULA

Memphis
Ghurab

Fayum Depression

el-Kahun

Hawara

Bahariya Oasis

E G Y P T

Nile River

Beni Hassan

el-Amarna

Red Sea

First Cataract

Berenice

Nile River

Abu Simbel

Valley of the Kings

Abydos

Naqada

Deir el-Bahari
Qurna

Karnak
Luxor

Kharga Oasis

Edfu

UPPER EGYPT

0   50   100 miles

0   100   200 kilometers

First Cataract

EUROPE

Mediterranean Sea

EGYPT

ARABIAN PENINSULA

Red Sea

Afar

ETHIOPIA

NIGERIA

Igbo Ukwo

Njoro River Cave

East Turkana

KENYA

Rusinga Island

Olorgesaillie

Laetoli

Gamble's Cave

Olduvai Gorge

TANZANIA

Atlantic Ocean

Kalambo Falls

ZAMBIA

Lake Kariba

Victoria Falls

ZIMBABWE

Great Zimbabwe

MADAGASCAR

Taung

SOUTH AFRICA

Indian Ocean

0   1000 miles

0   1000 kilometers

AFRICA

GREAT BRITAIN

Skara Brae

SCOTLAND

Hadrian's Wall

Stanwick
Star Carr

IRELAND

ENGLAND

Leicester

Rollright Stones

WALES

Peacock's
Farm

London

Lydney

Avebury

Stonehenge

Cissbury Hill

Brixham Cave

Cranborne Chase

Maiden Castle

Le Cotte de
St. Brelade

NORWAY

SWEDEN

Meilgaard

Hvidegaard

Gronhojh

Baltic
Sea

North Sea

IRELAND

GREAT
BRITAIN

DENMARK

Neander
Valley

GERMANY

Atlantic
Ocean

Somme
Valley

Champigny

L'Angles-
sur-Anglin

FRANCE

La Chapelle-
aux-Saints

Les Eyzies

Grotte de
Chauvet

Font-de-Gaume

Les Combarelles

Le Moustier

ITALY

Altamira

Niaux

Rome

Herculaneum

Pompeii

SPAIN

Devil's Tower,
Gibraltar

Mediterranean Sea

Carthage

TUNISIA

0   300 miles

0   300 kilometers

EUROPE AND NORTH AFRICA

Sabratha

LIBYA

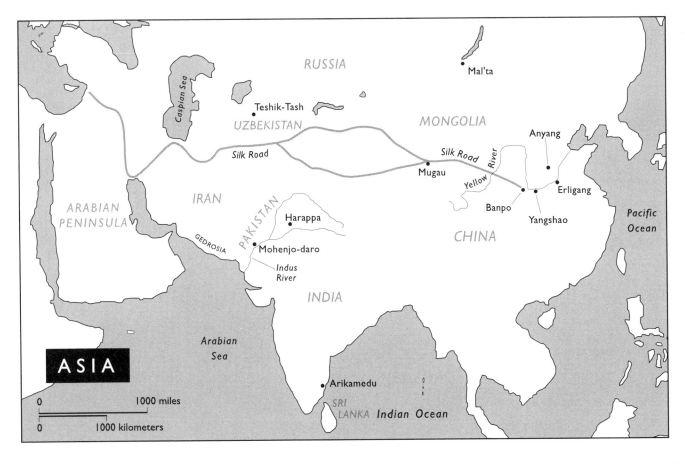

ASIA

RUSSIA

Mal'ta

Caspian Sea

Teshik-Tash

UZBEKISTAN

MONGOLIA

Anyang

Silk Road

Silk Road

Yellow River

Mugau

ARABIAN PENINSULA

IRAN

PAKISTAN

Harappa

Banpo

Erligang

Yangshao

CHINA

Pacific Ocean

GEDROSIA

Mohenjo-daro

Indus River

INDIA

Arabian Sea

Arikamedu

SRI LANKA

Indian Ocean

0   1000 miles

0   1000 kilometers

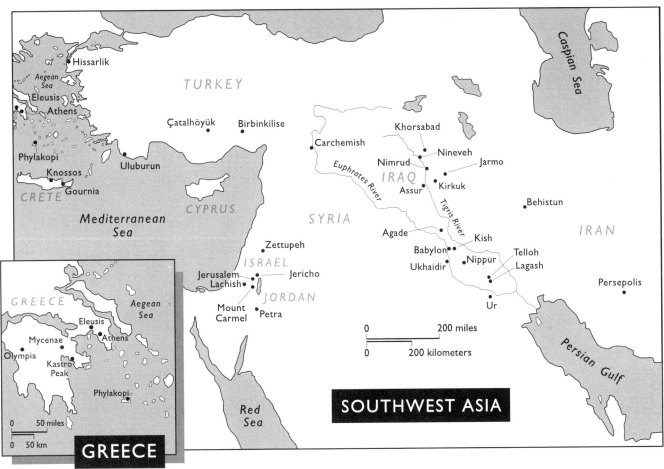

SOUTHWEST ASIA

Hissarlik

Aegean Sea

TURKEY

Caspian Sea

Eleusis

Athens

Çatalhöyük

Birbinkilise

Khorsabad

Carchemish

Nineveh

Phylakopi

Knossos

Uluburun

Nimrud

Jarmo

CRETE

Gournia

CYPRUS

Euphrates River

IRAQ

Kirkuk

Assur

Mediterranean Sea

SYRIA

Behistun

Tigris River

Agade

Kish

IRAN

Zettupeh

Babylon

Telloh

ISRAEL

Ukhaidir

Nippur

Lagash

Jerusalem

Jericho

Lachish

JORDAN

Persepolis

Mount Carmel

Petra

Ur

0   200 miles

0   200 kilometers

Red Sea

Persian Gulf

GREECE

GREECE

Aegean Sea

Eleusis

Mycenae

Athens

Olympia

Kastro Peak

Phylakopi

0   50 miles

0   50 km

Per tota ista planitie puto Troya ampliabat usq dadanellu.

S. PI.

Darda nellus.

CAE.

Oriens.

p totu fl uinee

Meridies

A sketch of the ruins of Troy from a 15th-century manuscript by the Florentine traveler Cristoforo Buondelmonti. Buondelmonti was a pioneering geographer who traveled extensively in search of antiquities.

1 Searching for Human Antiquity

People have speculated about human origins and the remote past since the beginnings of civilization more than 5,000 years ago. New Kingdom pharaohs of 1200 BC ordered the restoration of monuments like the already millennium-old Sphinx. As early as the 8th century BC, the Greek philosopher Hesiod speculated about a glorious, heroic past of kings and warriors. He described five great ages of history. The earliest was an Age of Gold, when people "dwelt in ease." The last was an Age of War, when everyone worked hard and suffered great miseries.

Two centuries later, when a torrential rainstorm cut a gully through a mound at Agade, near Babylon, and revealed the foundations of a long-forgotten shrine, the monarch Nabonidus ordered the finds from the temple displayed in his palace.

The Chinese, Greeks, and Romans puzzled over the origins of human society. As long ago as AD 52, Chinese scholars were speculating about ages of stone, bronze, and iron. Roman tourists flocked to the Nile to admire the pyramids and visit the great temples of Karnak and Luxor in Upper Egypt. Both the Greeks and Romans assumed that the institutions and priceless knowledge of civilization had originated with the ancient Egyptians. Nearly 2,000 years passed before archaeologists proved them only partially correct.

Despite Nabonidus's diggings in the distant past, early modern scholarly interest in human origins was little more than philosophical speculation. At the same time, the tight shackles of Christian doctrine taught that the biblical account of the Creation in Genesis, Chapter 1, in which God created the world in six days, was the literal historical truth. Humankind was created in the Garden of Eden, then cast out because of sin. To question Divine Will was heresy.

The biblical story of the Creation sufficed in a world where few people traveled widely and there were no archaeological discoveries to challenge Genesis. It was not until the Italian Renaissance of the 14th to 16th centuries that Europeans of leisure and wealth began to travel in Greece and Italy, studying antiquities and collecting examples of classical art. They acquired paintings, furniture, and classical statuary for their homes in a thoroughly unscientific manner. Soon it became fashionable to be an antiquary—a collector and student of ancient things.

While rich collectors made beelines for the Mediterranean, their less wealthy compatriots stayed at home. In England and France they found Roman coins as well as hoards of stone tools and bronze artifacts that seemed much

IN THIS PART

WILLIAM STUKELEY

JOHANN JOACHIM WINCKELMANN

CHRISTIAN JURGENSEN THOMSEN

GIOVANNI BATTISTA BELZONI

JOHN EVANS

JACOB JENS A. WORSAAE

older. There were burial mounds and mysterious stone circles, among them Stonehenge, a place where, in the words of a 12th-century text, "stones of wonderful size have been erected after the manner of doorways." Antiquaries such as Englishman William Camden traveled the countryside in search of the past, captivated by what he called "a back looking curiosity." In his great book *Britannia*, published in 1586, Camden described the British countryside and many archaeological sites, among them Stonehenge, which he dismissed as "weatherbeaten and decaied."

Camden was an observer, not a digger. So were his immediate successors, curious about "Antiquities . . . so exceeding old that no Bookes doe reach them," as Camden put it in *Britannia*. Prominent among them were John Aubrey, a 17th-century landowner who came across the prehistoric stone circles at Avebury in southern England while out foxhunting. A half-century later, the eccentric William Stukeley carried out the first surveys of Avebury and Stonehenge and dug into several nearby burial mounds. He was one of the first people to dig for evidence about the past rather than merely describe monuments and artifacts.

Serious archaeological excavation began in the 18th century. In 1738, Italy's King Charles III commissioned Spanish engineer Rocque Joaquin de Alcubierre to probe the depths of Herculaneum, the Roman town buried by a catastrophic eruption of Vesuvius in AD 79. The German antiquary Johann Joachim Winkelmann published finds from Herculaneum and nearby Pompeii in 1764. His book attracted much attention. Classical antiquities became the height of fashion. Interest reached fever pitch when Napoleon Bonaparte's scientists returned from Egypt in 1804 with thousands of artifacts and magnificent sketches of exotic pyramids, temples, and tombs along the Nile. After the Napoleonic wars ended in 1815, diplomats and tomb robbers competed for Egyptian artifacts, among them circus strongman turned grave robber Giovanni Belzoni, one of the most colorful figures ever to work in Egypt.

While ancient Egypt was being discovered—and looted—local antiquaries began excavating barrows, or burial mounds in Europe. The English wool merchant William Cunnington and landowner Sir Richard Colt Hoare opened 465 such mounds in southern England, sometimes as many as two or three a day. Their excavations, and those of many other antiquarians, produced an incredible jumble of stone artifacts, bronze axes, clay funerary urns, and iron objects. Colt Hoare was moved to remark of the mess of finds, "How Grand! How Wonderful! How Incomprehensible!"

Colt Hoare was not alone in his confusion. The Danish antiquary Rasmus Nyerup started a small museum and despaired of putting anything in a meaningful order. "Everything which had come down to us from Heathendom is wrapped in a thick fog," he complained. He was sure his artifacts were older than Christianity, but "whether by a couple of years or a couple of centuries, or even by more than a millennium, we can do no more than guess."

Nyerup's collections formed the nucleus of the National Museum of Denmark, which was founded in 1807. Its first curator was Christian Jurgensen Thomsen, a merchant's son with a passion for order. He adopted the ideas of Danish historians and philosophers and divided early Scandinavian cultures into three ages: a Stone Age, a Bronze Age, and an Iron Age. Then he arranged the prehistoric displays in the museum in three rooms, one for each age. Thus was born the Three Age System, the first scientific classification of the prehistoric past, still used to this day.

Thomsen knew that his cherished classification was mere theory. One of his assistants, a young law student named Jacob Jens A. Worsaae, was an experienced burial mound digger. He took the Three Age System out of the museum and applied it to archaeological sites. He proved that the three ages had followed one after the other through time, finding Stone Age artifacts in layers that were under layers of artifacts of Bronze Age and later Iron Age life in the same location. Toward the end of the 19th century, another Dane, Oscar Montelius, built on Worsaae's research. He studied prehistoric artifacts across Europe and linked the Scandinavian Three Age System to sites and cultures between the Balkans and Britain (see Part 3).

Part of the confusion over the classification of the prehistoric past came from the stifling influence of Christian theology. In the 17th century, Archbishop James Ussher of northern Ireland had studied the accounts in the Old Testament of the Bible listing how long succeeding generations had lived. Adding them up, he concluded that there were a mere 6,000 years for all human existence. By the late 18th century, scientists were becoming uncomfortable with the biblical theory. The new science of stratigraphic geology—the science of recording and analyzing information from the layers of the earth, which developed during the Industrial Revolution—led to the discovery of the fossil bones of long-extinct animals in layers that appeared to be much earlier than the 6,000 years of Creation. French paleontologist Jacques Cuvier, an expert on fossil mammals, promptly claimed that successive worlds and their animals had been wiped out by great floods, the last being the catastrophe for which Noah built an ark, according to the Bible. Then stone axes and other objects of indisputably human manufacture were found in the same levels as extinct European animals in caves, and notably river gravel in the Somme Valley in northern France.

An eccentric French customs officer, Boucher de Perthes, claimed in 1837 that humans and extinct animals had lived in France long before the biblical flood. He was ridiculed for his persistent claims until 1858, when a committee of the Geological Society of London excavated Brixham Cave in southwestern England. They found more than a dozen stone artifacts sealed in cave layers that also contained the bones of mammoths (Arctic elephants) and rhinoceroses.

A year later, biologist Charles Darwin published his *Origin of Species,* in which he laid out his theory of evolution and natural selection. His essay argued that living organisms developed one from another over long periods of time (evolution), through a process that saw the survival of those best adapted to change (natural selection). Darwin's essay provided a theoretical framework for a human prehistory much earlier than the mere 6,000 years Bishop Ussher had calculated from the Scriptures. A stream of English antiquaries and geologists, headed by a remarkable man, John Evans, crossed the English Channel to examine de Perthes' sites and finds. Evans himself proclaimed the Somme Valley discoveries proof of a great antiquity for humankind. One of his colleagues remarked that "The flint hatchets . . . seem to me as clearly works of art as any Sheffield whittle."

The serious study of archaeology dates from 1859, when the theory of evolution and the proof of the association of humans and extinct animals opened up a vast landscape of prehistoric time, subdivided by Thomsen into the three vast Stone, Bronze, and Iron ages of human development. A century and a half later, archaeologists have peopled this once unknown landscape with a myriad of long-forgotten cultures and civilizations.

The insights of Charles Darwin and his colleague, the biologist Thomas Henry Huxley, generated bitter controversy, both from devout Christians and from those who were horrified to learn that humans were descended from apes and from "brute-like" people like the brow-beetled Neanderthal man, discovered in the Neander Valley, Germany, in 1856. The controversies still echo in the background to this day, but the establishment of the antiquity of humankind set the stage for the momentous achievements of 19th-century archaeology.

William Stukeley

A MIXTURE OF SUPERSTITION AND ANTIQUARIANISM

William Stukeley was one of the founders of British archaeology and is famous for having eaten dinner atop one of Stonehenge's massive trilithons (arched stone uprights made from three stones). His observations and sketches of the famous prehistoric stone circles at Avebury and Stonehenge in southern England were years ahead of their time and are of priceless value to modern archaeologists. His theories about these famous sites and about the mysterious Druid cults of the ancient Britons influenced historical, literary, and religious thought for generations.

Stukeley was born at Holbeach, Lincolnshire, in eastern England, in 1687. From an early age he was intensely curious about the workings of the natural world and the heavenly bodies. He wandered for hours in surrounding forests observing animals and collecting plants. His endless curiosity about the world around him also came from reading and collecting rare trinkets like coins and some antiquities while still a child. In 1703 he was admitted to Trinity College, Cambridge, where he studied botany and human anatomy. He was an enthusiastic student who was known to steal and dissect dogs, even bodies of the homeless, to satisfy his anatomical curiosity. He went on to study and practice medicine in

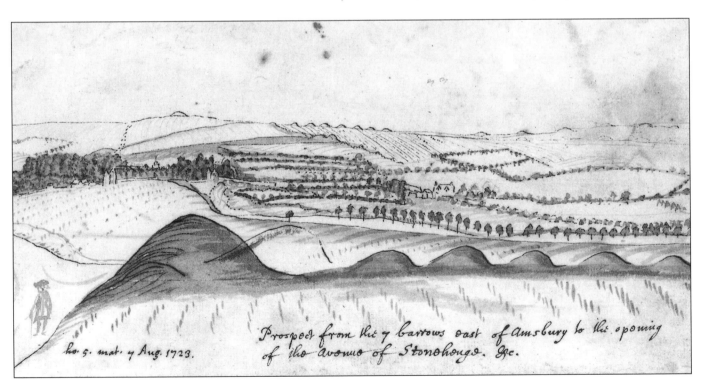

Archaelogy before the time of photography relied heavily on hand-drawn sketches and field notes of excavation sites. In this sketch made on August 7, 1723, William Stukeley notes the compostition of a barrow excavated near Stonehenge, the first such record in British archaeology.

London in 1705, under physician Richard Mead, who encouraged his interest in natural history.Stukeley eventually graduated from Cambridge University with an M.D. in 1708.

The young physician had been interested in antiquities since his undergraduate days. He was soon well known in London scientific circles, welcomed on account of his broad interests. Stukeley was soon elected a Fellow of the Royal Society, England's most important and prestigious scientific organization. He counted the physicist Isaac Newton and the astronomer Edmund Halley among his friends in the scientific elite.

Stukeley thrived in the company of fellow scientists and wrote learned articles on earthquakes and flute music, the origin of card games, water turbines, and Queen Anne's alleged descent from the biblical Noah. But his lifelong passion was British antiquities and the ancient Britons, a subject of intense interest at the Royal Society. Many of the society's fellows were studying the countryside and describing archaeological sites, ancient coins, fossils, and other curiosities. Stukeley was also one of the founders in 1717 of the Society of Antiquaries of London, still the premier archaeological society in Britain.

In 1710 Stukeley began a tradition of making an annual excursion on horseback across England, studying architecture, visiting gardens, and examining archaeological sites. These rides provided the raw material for his scientific investigations. On his first such trip, Stukeley admired the 4,500-year-old Rollright Stones in Oxfordshire, a stone circle on a low hilltop with stones "corroded like worm-eaten wood by the harsh Jaws of Time." Stukeley was an ardent supporter of classical romanticism and described the circle as a "heathen temple of our ancestors, perhaps in the Druids' time." In 1716 he saw a print of the circles of stone arches at Stonehenge in Wiltshire,

southern England, and resolved to make "an Exact Model" of the circles both as ruins and in their original state, an ambitious project for someone who had never visited the place.

Between 1720 and 1724 he made a series of visits to Wiltshire, where he mapped both the stone uprights at Stonehenge and the prehistoric earthen circles at Avebury in the same region. Stukeley was not the first scientist to investigate either of these famous sites, but he was the first to produce reasonably accurate plans of the stone and earthen circles at Avebury, which were some 4,500 years old. He also rode across the surrounding landscape and traced the celebrated Avenue, which links the great monument to an outlying sanctuary.

Likewise, at Stonehenge, Stukeley observed the association between the stone circles and nearby burial mounds. He was the first antiquarian to link a major monument with its surrounding landscape, a major concern of modern-day archaeologists working at both Avebury and Stonehenge. Stukeley's careful survey oriented the Stonehenge circles to the cardinal directions of the compass. Being a skilled astronomer, he also checked with a compass to see if they were aligned with any heavenly bodies, paying careful attention to the rising and setting of the sun. He wrote: "What would be more probable . . . than that unlettered man in his first worship and reverence would direct his attention to that glorious luminary, the Sun." On the longest day of the year, June 21, the summer solstice, he observed how the rising sun shone into the center of the circles, which had been carefully aligned by the builders with this important moment in the passing of the seasons. Every modern scholar accepts this astronomical interpretation of the alignment.

Stukeley has left us memorable descriptions of his fieldwork at both sites. In his book *Itinerarium Curiosum*,

ARCHAEOLOGISTS

William Stukeley

BORN
November 7, 1687
Holbeach, Lincolnshire, England

DIED
March 3, 1765
London, England

EDUCATION
Cambridge University (M.D. 1708)

ACCOMPLISHMENTS
Mapped Avebury and Stonehenge accurately for the first time and founded a tradition of landscape archaeology in Britain; first scientist to observe astronomical alignments at Stonehenge; influenced generations of writers and scholars with his theories about Druids. Wrote *Itinerarium Curiosum* (1724); *Stonehenge, A Temple Restored to the British Druids* (1740); *Avebury, A Temple of British Druids, Described* (1743).

A page of Stukeley's field notes, made at Avebury in May 1740. The passage includes references to Silbury Hill (the significance of which is still a mystery) and also to wildflowers and earthworks.

near the stone circles, where they found "chippings of the stones of the temple. So that probably the interr'd was one of the builders."

In 1740, Stukeley published a monograph titled *Stonehenge*, and three years later another, titled *Avebury*. These books set a new standard for field archaeology and remained definitive works for many years. In writing them, he was strongly influenced by the work of his predecessor, the antiquary John Aubrey, who had proclaimed Avebury to be the work of ancient British priests, the Druids described by Roman general Julius Caesar in 55 BC. Stukeley accepted Aubrey's Druidical conclusions with enthusiasm. He became convinced that the two great monuments were constructed by the Druids for their sacred rituals. He thought of the Druids as ancient British philosophers and priests who were the founders of ancestor worship.

Carried away by his enthusiasm, Stukeley shaped his landscape maps to accommodate his fantasies. At Avebury, he mapped a row of stone alignments to create a serpent's tail and changed a nearby ancient circle to an oval so it resembled the snake's head. While these obsessions reduced the value of Stukeley's researches, his observations and plans provide modern scholars with a unique picture of Avebury and Stonehenge before the surrounding landscapes were disturbed by modern industrial agriculture. At the time, the stone alignments and other features were much more complete than today. Destruction already was in progress during his visit to Avebury. He watched as the local villagers levered and cracked ancient standing stones for building material. His records of the now-vanished stones are priceless today.

Stukeley's last long antiquarian journey, in 1725, took him and his

printed in 1724, he describes how he and his patron, Lord Pembroke, put together "a most accurate description" of Stonehenge with "nice plans and perspectives." They took the time to dine on top of one of the archlike trilithons, where he found space enough "for a steady head and nimble heels to dance a minuet." The two men also dug into several burial mounds

friend Roger Gale across remote areas of northern England. They rode along part of Hadrian's Wall, the outermost frontier of the Roman Empire, built between AD 122 and 130. Stukeley was so overcome by the sight of the wall following the contours of steep hillsides that he announced his intention to preserve and resurrect the glory of the Roman Empire. But his obsessions with Druid lore gripped his mind even more strongly and he never visited the ancient wall again. He decided to take holy orders and became the vicar of Stamford, Lincolnshire, in 1730, a position he held until 1747. In that year, he became rector of St. George's Church in London, a post he held until his death.

In later life, Stukeley became increasingly obsessed with the Druids. His work shifted from sober observation to subjective theorizing. He lived at a time when romanticism flourished, when classical allusions and romantic views of simpler societies were in fashion. Stukeley embraced the Druids as his own, even building a Druidlike temple in his garden and considering himself an "arch-Druid" named Chydonax. He became increasingly eccentric, his life a collage of oddities and infatuations. His lengthy sermons were famous for their diversions into obscure topics of natural history and astronomy. On one occasion he delayed a service for an hour so that the entire congregation could witness a solar eclipse. His friend and contemporary, Bishop Warburton, remarked, "There was in him such a mixture of simplicity, drollery, absurdity, ingenuity, superstition, and antiquarianism . . . a compound of things never meant to go together." Stukeley died of a stroke in 1765 and was buried, at his request, in an unmarked grave in the churchyard of East Ham, Essex.

> *"There is as much of it [Stonehenge] undemolished, as enables us sufficiently to recover its form, when it was in its most perfect state. There is enough of every part to preserve the idea of the whole."*
>
> —William Stukeley, *Itinerarium Curiosum* (1724)

For all his eccentricities, William Stukeley was a shrewd observer whose plans of Avebury and Stonehenge were a model for generations. His astronomical observations at Stonehenge were the foundation for all subsequent research into the significance of this remarkable monument. As archaeologist Christopher Chippindale has remarked, "Stonehenge has never fully recovered from the Reverend Stukeley's vision." Every Midsummer's Day, modern-day Druids act out their bizarre rituals in the heart of the stone circles, even if archaeologists have shown that Stonehenge predates the Druids by thousands of years. We should look beyond Stukeley's fantasies about ancient religious practices, for he was the founder of a tradition of landscape archaeology in Britain that survives and flourishes to this day.

FURTHER READING

Chippindale, Christopher. *Stonehenge Complete*. London: Thames and Hudson, 1994.

Malone, Caroline, and Nancy Stone Bernard. *Stonehenge*. New York: Oxford University Press, 2002.

Piggott, Stuart. *The Druids*. London: Thames and Hudson, 1985.

———. *William Stukeley*. Rev. ed. London: Thames and Hudson, 1985.

Johann Joachim Winckelmann

PIONEER OF CLASSICAL ARCHAEOLOGY

"I came to Rome to open the eyes of those who will come after me," wrote Johann Joachim Winckelmann in a letter to a friend in 1756. He succeeded with a vengeance, using Greek art to proclaim that Beauty was the sister of Liberty. Winckelmann achieved archaeological immortality through his visionary studies at the Roman towns of Herculaneum and Pompeii, buried intact by a volcanic eruption of Mount Vesuvius in August AD 79. Thanks to his researches, artifacts from classical sites became not just art objects, but precious sources of knowledge about our forebears.

A cobbler's son, Winckelmann was born in Stendal, Prussia. He was a successful student and became a private Latin tutor at the age of 18. From 1738 to 1741, he attended the University of Halle as a theological student, intending to become a minister. Winckelmann was an indifferent theologian, and dabbled in medicine before taking a series of jobs as a tutor. He also read every book he could get his hands on, which kindled a lifelong passion for knowledge. At the

Johann Joachim Winkelmann was a library scholar, not an excavator. By visiting museums and private collections, he acquired an encyclopedic knowledge of classical art.

age of 26 and penniless, he found a job as the senior assistant master at a grammar school in Seehausen. He referred to the next five years as his "slave years," when he labored for a meager salary. But he was obsessed with learning and taught himself English, French, and Italian to add to his already impressive knowledge of Greek and Latin. He also steeped himself in classical literature, which was hard to come by in a small town like Seehausen. His greatest passion was classical art, an obscure subject two centuries ago.

In 1748, Winckelmann received a major career break when he left Prussia, which he called a "despotic land," for the more congenial atmosphere of Dresden. There he became the librarian for Count Bunau of Saxony, a post that allowed him to visit other art libraries and museums. His seven years as a librarian gave him plenty of time for private research. During these years, he labored on two great works, *Reflections on the Imitation of Greek Works in Painting and Sculpture,* published in 1755, and a lengthy monograph on art in antiquity. The book caused considerable interest, as stories of spectacular art discoveries from excavations at nearby Herculaneum and Pompeii were circulating through learned circles in Europe. Winckelmann developed an increasing preoccupation with Italy and specifically with the Roman town of Pompeii.

As Winckelmann's reputation as a brilliant antiquary rose, Italy drew him like a magnet. In 1755 he became librarian to Count Alberigo Archinto, Papal Nuncio to the Count of Saxony, and became a Catholic, much to the disapproval of his Protestant friends. He left Germany for Rome in 1758, when he became librarian to Cardinal Albani, whose collection of classical art was famous throughout Europe. Five years later he was appointed supervisor of the Cardinal's antiquities collection and placed in charge of new

acquisitions. He resolved to make a study of Herculaneum and Pompeii.

In 1738, Italy's King Charles III had commissioned Spanish engineer Rocque Joaquin de Alcubierre to probe the depths of Herculaneum. Alcubierre used gunpowder and miners to tunnel into the city, recovering jewelry and statues of eminent citizens. The king insisted on secrecy, but rumors of the discoveries had spread through Europe. Only a few distinguished visitors were allowed belowground, and the finds were taken to adorn the king's palace. The king's secrecy shocked Winckelmann, who was reluctantly allowed into the king's museum but was forbidden access to the excavations. This was hardly surprising, for he had strong views on the proper way to excavate archaeological sites and was not afraid to express them.

Winckelmann's impressive credentials intimidated Italian scholars. The excavators also were afraid that Winckelmann would publish pictures or descriptions of the works of art before they had had their turn to evaluate them. He angered local experts by accusing them of being little more than treasure hunters with no respect for antiquities. He railed against the ignorant royal court, which supervised the Pompeii excavations. Senior officials insisted that nude statues of mythological figures be locked away because of their "lewdness."

Fortunately, during his stay in Dresden Winckelmann had learned how to draw under a gifted artist named Adam Friedreich Oeser. He managed to sketch some of the relics brought back to the museum by the excavators and occasionally bribed the excavation foremen to show him recent finds. He became increasingly frustrated by the restrictive atmosphere surrounding the excavations. "Without seeing the plan of the excavations one cannot form a distinct impression," he wrote. "One is confounded by the

Johann Joachim Winckelmann

BORN
December 9, 1717
Stendal, Prussia

DIED
June 8, 1768
Trieste, Italy

EDUCATION
University of Halle (theology degree, 1741)

ACCOMPLISHMENTS
One of the first scholars to take a systematic approach to classical archaeology and art, and to recognize that artifacts and their contexts could yield vital social information about ancient societies; produced some of the first scientific descriptions of classical art, using finds from Roman Pompeii and Herculaneum. His *History of the Art of Antiquity* (1767) was the first volume on the subject.

This page of Johann Winckelmann's notes describes the Palazzo Massimi in Rome, built by architect Baldassare Peruzzi in 1535. He notes Greek and Latin inscriptions and the rounded corner of the rectangular building, shaped to accommodate a roadway.

Palais Massimi   37   73

Caput Theophrasti Philos. cum inscript.

ΘΕΟΦΡΑΣΤΟΣ
ΜΕΛΑΝΤΑ
ΕΡΕΣΙΟΣ

ap. Gronov. Antiq. Gr. Tom. II. n. 92.

Caput Xenocratis c. inscr.

ΣΕΝΟΚΡΑΤΗΣ
ΚΑΛΚΑΔΟΝΙΟΣ   ΚΑΛΚΗΔΟΝΙΟΣ apud Spon Misc
Sect. IV. qui de Typum capitis
vid. Ibid. n. 91.

Ara sepulcralis mit der Inschrift

P. SCANTIVS
PHILETVS
FECIT SIBI ET
SCANTIAE
NICE LIB.
REQVIETORIVM
AMICI BENE FACERE
SEMPER STVDIOSVS
FVI.

Spon Miscell. Sect. IV. p. 122.

tunnels and coming and goings by which one passes underground."

On a second visit to Italy in 1762, he was greeted more warmly, because even his enemies recognized the accuracy and scholarly nature of his writings. He was allowed to examine some excavations at first hand and to review architectural plans of the major buildings. As a result, Winckelmann took a novel approach. He was the first scholar to examine the Herculaneum artifacts in their original contexts in the site, which allowed him to draw social information from the artifacts. For example, he studied the placement of statuaries, such as those of household gods, in buried Herculaneum residences, trying to reconstruct what part they placed in daily life. To Winckelmann, the finds from Herculaneum and Pompeii were far more than museum specimens or trophies displayed by antiquarians. They were vital sources of information about daily existence in Roman times. Winckelmann published

> *"In the design of the constitution and government of Greece it is freedom that is the most distinguished reason for the superiority of its art."*
>
> —Johann Joachim Winckelmann, *History of the Art of Antiquity* (1767)

his masterpiece, *History of the Art of Antiquity,* in 1767. It contained the first systematic descriptions of Greek and Roman art based in part on the finds from the two buried cities.

Winckelmann continued to study the Pompeii finds and describe them until June 1768, when he was robbed and fatally stabbed for some gold coins in his hotel room while waiting for a ship in Trieste. His murderer was a man named Francisco Arcangeli, a criminal and former cook, whom Winckelmann had unwisely befriended at his hotel.

Unfortunately, Winkelmann never had a chance to confirm his theories with his own excavations. Not that his discoveries caused the excavators of the two towns to change their ways. Chaotic treasure hunting continued for another century as successive generations of diggers removed frescoes, stripped ancient buildings of their contents, and left the exposed buildings to decay. The situation improved only in 1860, when King Victor Emmanuel II began to encourage scientific excavations at Pompeii as a matter of national prestige. It was his excavator, Giuseppi Fiorelli, who first recorded Pompeii block by block. And it was Fiorelli who first noticed cavities in the hardened volcanic ash that appeared to have human shapes. He filled them with liquid plaster, which hardened in place, and recovered casts of the bodies of fleeing citizens suffocated by falling ash.

Johann Joachim Winckelmann was not an excavator, nor did he discover any lost civilizations. But the authority and accuracy of his classical scholarship placed the study of ancient Rome and Pompeii on a new footing. He was the first archaeologist to show that every artifact, however humble, has a story to tell—about daily life, religious practices, warfare, for example—if it is studied in its proper context in the earth. His brilliant books and painstaking analyses set Roman archaeology on a new course that came to fruition in the late 19th and the 20th centuries.

FURTHER READING

Ceram, C. W. *Gods, Graves, & Scholars.* New York: Knopf, 1951.

Leppman, Wolfgang. *Winckelmann.* New York: Knopf, 1970.

Winckelmann, Johann Joachim. *History of the Art of Antiquity.* Trans. G. Henry Lodge, 1767. Reprint, New York: Ungar, 1969.

———. *Reflections on the Imitation of Greek Works in Painting and Sculpture.* Trans. Elfriede Heyer and Roger C. Norton, 1755. Reprint, La Salle, Ill.: Open Court, 1987.

Christian Jurgensen Thomsen

THE THREE
AGE SYSTEM

Christian Jurgensen Thomsen used a museum to bring order to a chaotic jumble of prehistoric artifacts, and to human antiquity. As curator of the National Museum of Denmark, he sorted through the disorganized storerooms and laid out three galleries coinciding with three eras of human history. One showed artifacts from the Stone Age, a second from the Bronze Age, and a third from the Iron Age. Thomsen was a master at classifying prehistoric artifacts. His museum displays produced the first chronological framework for the remote human past, known as the Three Age System.

Born in Copenhagen, Denmark, the son of a wealthy merchant, Thomsen developed an enthusiasm for numismatics, the study of ancient coins, at an early age. He soon became an amateur scientist of varied accomplishment, equally at home with Roman and Scandinavian coins and with art of all kinds. He was so enthusiastic about the past that he came to the notice of eminent scholars involved with the newly formed Danish Commission for Ancient Monuments, set up in 1806. The commission had come into being as a result of concerns over the destruction of archaeological

These objects were some of the artifacts used by Christian Jurgensen Thomsen to establish his Three Age classification of the past. Stone objects appear to the left, bronze artifacts in the middle, and iron specimens to the right.

and historic sites throughout Denmark. The commission's tasks included protecting sites, founding a scientific periodical, and planning for a future national museum.

The antiquary Professor Rasmus Nyerup of the University of Copenhagen was a leader in the commission's affairs. He had written much on archaeology and had lamented the confusion surrounding the prehistoric past. Thanks to Nyerup's lobbying, Thomsen was appointed to the commission in 1816, with the specific task of placing the Royal Museum of Nordic Antiquities' collections in order and displaying them to the public.

At the time, the museum's collections were stacked in a church loft with no one to look after them. The methodical and thoroughly practical Thomsen was the ideal scholar to bring order from chaos. He organized the collections like a business, entering new acquisitions in a ledger, cataloging them, and assigning them numbers. More than 500 specimens passed through his hands in a few months, so he soon became familiar with a wide range of prehistoric artifacts. He used his classification expertise with ancient coins to place the collection in order.

Once cataloged, the collections had to be made intelligible to the general public. Thomsen considered various options and decided to concentrate on the materials from which the tools were manufactured as a basis for classification. He divided prehistoric times into three subdivisions: a time when stone tools and weapons were used, followed by one with bronze and copper artifacts, and finally one marked by the use of iron objects. Thomsen based his new "Three Age" scheme entirely on the museum collections. He drew on Nyerup and other earlier writings about archaeology, and on artifacts, especially grave furniture, which typically was found as several objects of different type in the same sepulcher, and thus of the same age.

Christian Jurgensen Thomsen was a lively conversationalist and a prolific letter writer, although only one book, the museum catalog, came from his pen. As a result, the only public exposition of Thomsen's Three Age System was in the new National Museum's galleries, where the visitor found separate cases devoted to each of the three ages. Nevertheless, Thomsen's ideas spread widely, largely because he spent a great deal of time showing visitors around the museum, which opened at first for two hours a week, then for longer periods. Every Thursday between eleven and one o'clock, he would show visitors through the galleries, enchanting young people with his stories and down-to-earth enthusiasm. He would take the trouble to place a prehistoric gold necklace around a young girl's neck as a way of making the past come alive for her.

To Thomsen, the past was not just legend, but made up of material evidence. "A tumulus, a stone circle in the countryside, a stone tool, or a metal ornament unearthed from the sequestered burial chamber—all these afford us a more vivid picture of the prehistoric age," he wrote in his classic museum catalog, A Guide to the Northern Antiquities, published in 1836. What could have been an obscure Scandinavian work soon drew the attention of archaeologists elsewhere. In 1848, noted British archaeologist Sir John Lubbock translated Thomsen's slim volume into English, ensuring its circulation throughout Europe and North America. Within a few years the Three Age System had become the foundation of all attempts to subdivide and classify the prehistoric past in Europe.

Thomsen was a museum man above all else, who had little time for archaeological excavation. When he did dig, it was with meticulous care by

Christian Jurgensen Thomsen

BORN
December 29, 1788
Copenhagen, Denmark

DIED
May 21, 1865
Copenhagen, Denmark

EDUCATION
Private

ACCOMPLISHMENTS
Developed the Three Age System for classifying prehistoric artifacts, first used in the Royal Museum of Nordic Antiquities, Copenhagen, and soon adopted all over Europe, and later throughout much of the Old World. Wrote A Guide to the Northern Antiquities (1848).

> *"The Age of Stone, or that period when weapons and implements were made of stone, wood, bone, or some other material, during which very little or nothing at all was known of metals."*
>
> —Christian Jurgensen Thomsen, *A Guide to the Northern Antiquities* (1848)

the standards of the day. In 1845, he and four colleagues, one an anatomist, excavated a Bronze Age burial site at Hvidegaard, north of Copenhagen. The stone-lined tomb contained cremated bones, a fine array of textiles, and a leather pouch. The pouch contained seashells, a snake's tail, and other unusual, perhaps sacred, objects. The grave goods, which lay on an ox-skin, included a sheathed sword, a fine brooch, and a pair of simple pliers. Thomsen's excavation was unusual for its careful recording methods, and for the presence of an anatomist, who proclaimed the cremated bones those of a man. The grave goods were typical for a Bronze Age warrior.

Thomsen devoted his life to the National Museum, which was moved in 1832 from the unused church, to rooms at the Royal Palace at Christiansborg, thanks to King Christian VIII. During Thomsen's directorship, the museum collections expanded to more than 27,000 items. Funds were short, so he had to work closely with volunteers. Patiently and calmly, Thomsen persisted through financial shortage after shortage, working without salary himself, believing that concrete results and educational displays would ensure the survival of his beloved museum. The

Royal Museum for Nordic Antiquities eventually became Denmark's National Museum. Today it is one of the finest museums in Europe.

Few archaeologists have left such an enduring legacy. Christian Jurgen Thomsen had one of the essential gifts of an archaeologist—a sharp eye for form and ornamentation, for the small details of individual artifacts. The Three Age System was the result. With this simple, and now much elaborated, framework, the modern science of archaeology and archaeological classification was born. Later Scandinavian archaeologists, among them Jacob Jens A. Worsaae and Oscar Montelius, refined the classifications and provided more accurate dates for the three ages in Europe. However, to Thomsen alone goes the credit for placing the classification of prehistory on a sound basis.

The Three Age System still flourishes today, even if it is now little more than a broad framework for the past. During the early and mid-20th century, the Three Age System came into use in Africa and many parts of Asia, but increasingly as purely a technological label rather than a chronological subdivision of the past. But the Three Age System has never been used in the Americas, where copper and bronze were used only in a relatively small area.

FURTHER READING

Daniel, Glyn. *The Idea of Prehistory.* Cleveland: World, 1963.

Grayson, Donald K. *The Establishment of Human Antiquity.* Orlando: Academic Press, 1983.

Klindt-Jensen, Ole. A *History of Scandina-*

Giovanni Battista Belzoni

EGYPTIAN
ADVENTURER
EXTRAORDINAIRE

iovanni Battista Belzoni was a flamboyant circus strongman and tomb robber whose life story reads like a Hollywood movie. He spent many years as a theatrical and musical hall performer and muscle man, where he learned how to use gunpowder, levers, and weights. He migrated to Egypt, where he blasted and dug his way into royal tombs, pyramids, and temples with spectacular success.

Belzoni was born in Padua, Italy, in 1778, the son of a barber. He refused to enter his father's profession, lived for some time in Rome, then fled from Italy when Napoleon's armies invaded Italy. He made a living as a small-scale trader in Holland before crossing to England, where he became a performer in 1803. Belzoni was good-looking, with an imposing physique, towering more than 6 feet 6 inches tall, the ideal build for a theatrical strongman. He appeared at London's Sadler's Wells Theatre as the "Patagonian Samson," strutting around balancing 12 people on a massive

Giovanni Belzoni appears onstage in London, balancing fellow performers on an iron frame. Before taking up tomb raiding, Belzoni made his living as a theatrical performer and strongman. This experience allowed him to learn how to work with levers, weights, gunpowder, and other theatrical devices—skills that served him well as a tomb robber.

iron frame. Between 1804 and 1813 he performed in theaters throughout the British Isles and became a well-known figure on the circus and fair circuit. During these years Belzoni acquired an impressive expertise with levers, weights, and ingenious apparatuses for lifting heavy objects using water in spectacular theatrical displays, excellent training for a rough-and-ready archaeologist of the early 19th century.

In 1813, Belzoni, accompanied by his Irish wife, Sarah, left England. Belzoni performed for a while in Spain, then decided to make his way to the Sultan of Turkey's court at Constantinople. The couple spent six months on the island of Malta, where Belzoni met an agent of Mohammed Ali, the ruler of Egypt, who was trying to modernize his country. Ever on the lookout for a new opportunity, Belzoni came up with the idea of an ox-powered waterwheel for supplying Nile water to farmers' fields. The agent was sufficiently impressed to arrange for Belzoni to present his idea to Ali himself in Cairo. Belzoni landed in Alexandria, Egypt, in 1815.

During his stay in Alexandria he met his future archaeological nemesis, the French consul Bernardino Drovetti. The two men took an instant dislike to each other. Drovetti was collecting Egyptian antiquities to make a quick profit, using a gang of toughs who roamed up and down the Nile for the purpose. He seems to have sensed a potential rival, also out for fame and a profit, although at the time Belzoni had no interest in collecting. An intense rivalry did indeed develop as Belzoni became a collector a few months later. It is questionable who was the more ruthless, Drovetti with his gang or Belzoni with his inexhaustible ingenuity.

The Belzonis traveled on to Cairo, where Giovanni built his ox-driven waterwheel. Wily bureaucrats promptly sabotaged the ingenious machine because it threatened to undermine their hold over water supplies for farming. Penniless and without employment, Belzoni was hired by Henry Salt, the British consul in Cairo, to trans-port a half-buried, 9-ton head of the pharaoh Ramses II from its resting place in the pharaoh's mortuary temple on the east bank of the Nile at Luxor to the port of Alexandria on the Mediterranean Sea. From there, it would be shipped to the British Museum in London.

Most people, even Napoleon's soldiers, considered the task impossible. Belzoni simply applied the expertise learned during his circus days. He assembled some ropes and palm-tree trunks, levered the head out of the sand, loaded it on a crude wooden base, and employed dozens of men to drag the massive statue on rollers to the bank of the Nile River hundreds of yards away. When the local headman tried to make difficulties, Belzoni simply picked him up and shook him until he cooperated. Ramses's head is now on display in London's British Museum.

Belzoni had come to Egypt to build agricultural machinery. He now found himself a successful archaeologist of sorts, in a place with the potential for spectacular finds on every side. Drovetti's men were already digging at Luxor and in the rich burial grounds on the west bank of the Nile. Belzoni decided to see what he could find on his own account. While he waited for a boat to carry the head of Ramses II downstream, Belzoni dug in the temple of the sun god Amun at Karnak near Luxor and searched for mummies in the rocky caves near the village of Qurna on the east bank of the

Nile River. He soon realized that a great deal of money could be made by collecting and selling ancient Egyptian artifacts of all kinds. He was so successful that Drovetti accused him of working in areas where he had exclusive concessions to dig. Almost overnight, the two men became fierce, combative opponents, with no holds barred on either side.

Unlike his rival, Belzoni had a genius for making friends with the local people. He befriended the villagers of Qurna, who made their living by tomb robbing. In their company, he penetrated deep into narrow caves where hundreds of humbler ancient Egyptians were buried. He soon became used to the dust and filth, but received a rude shock when he paused for a moment's rest on what he thought was a rocky perch. His seat collapsed in a mass of bones and mummy bandages as he crashed to the floor, having sat on a dead Egyptian. The destruction and pillaging was widespread; the tomb robbers even used wooden mummy cases for firewood. Within a few months Belzoni had collected so many choice mummies and artifacts that Drovetti's agents were making life difficult for him with veiled threats of physical attack.

So Belzoni traveled far upstream, beyond the First Cataract at Aswan, the first set of rapids that interrupt navigation up the Nile. He then proceeded into what the Egyptians called Nubia, "Land of the Blacks," a region that today is part of Sudan and southeast Egypt. His destination was the great temple of Abu Simbel, with its enormous facade of seated figures of Ramses II overlooking the Nile River. Working almost single-handed among hostile local people, Belzoni cleared the sand from the long-hidden entrance and entered the shrine, hoping for

unimagined treasure. To his disappointment the temple was empty.

In August 1817, Belzoni returned to Qurna, where he started work in the Valley of the Kings, the burial place of Egypt's most celebrated rulers. By this time, he had developed an instinct for archaeological finds. Although the valley had been known as a royal burial place for 2,000 years, Belzoni soon found the tomb of a son of King Ramses II, and the sepulcher of Ramses XI. He also located the magnificently painted burial place of the great pharaoh Seti I, father of Ramses II, who died in 1278 BC.

Belzoni wanted to become rich, but above all famous. A fierce ambition and ego drove him. The antiquities and statuary he collected were worth enormous sums, but he collected them for another reason—so he could display them to an adoring public. He realized at once that Seti's tomb, with its fine rock paintings, was the key to a truly sensational exhibit. Unlike constructed tombs such as the pyramids, this one was cut into the rock and extended deep underground. It was empty except for a superb alabaster sarcophagus, or casket, with walls so thin that a candle on the inside shone through the sides. Belzoni spent the summer of 1818 making a complete copy of the sepulcher for display in London, using castings of wax mixed with dust and resin to copy wall statues, and copying the lavish paintings and hieroglyphic writing as faithfully as possible.

There was no limit to Belzoni's ambitions. While collecting the money to copy Seti's tomb, he returned to Cairo laden with artifacts of all kinds. Ever restless, he turned his talented excavator's mind to opening the huge pyramid of the pharaoh Kephren at Giza. The entrance was hidden under

Giovanni Battista Belzoni

BORN
November 5, 1778
Padua, Italy

DIED
December 3, 1823
Benin, West Africa

EDUCATION
Private

ACCOMPLISHMENTS
With tomb robbing and other aggressive forms of archaeology recovered thousands of antiquities from Egypt, opened the temple of Abu Simbel, discovered and copied the tomb of Seti I, and opened the Pyramid of Khephren at Giza. Created great popular interest in ancient Egypt at a time when little was known about early civilization on the Nile. Wrote *Narrative of the Operations and Recent Discoveries within the Pyramids, Temples, Tombs, and Excavations in Egypt and Nubia* (1822).

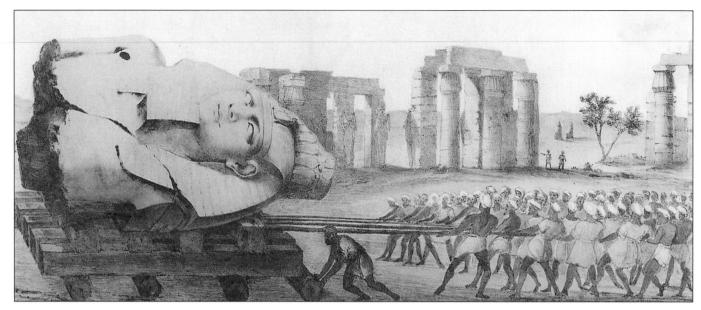

Belzoni's men haul the statue of Ramses II to the Nile. With brilliant improvisation, Belzoni used palm trunks to lever the heavy sculpture onto a wooden car mounted on rollers. Hundreds of men then hauled Ramses II to the bank of the Nile.

thick sand, a source of great frustration to the local people and to Drovetti, who believed fabulous treasure lay inside. Belzoni slipped away secretly to avoid his rivals, compared the position of the entrance of the Pyramid of Khufu with the base of the Kephren pyramid, and started digging. After a month's excavation with 80 men and the judicious use of gunpowder, Belzoni made his way into the burial chamber. Unfortunately, it was empty except for a large stone sarcophagus. The frustrated showman painted his name on the wall with soot, where it can be seen to this day.

By the time Belzoni had finished copying Seti I's tomb, the rivalry with Drovetti was so intense that there was a real danger of violence. After moving a fine obelisk from the Temple of Isis at Philae from under the very noses of Drovetti's agents, Belzoni was ambushed by his rival's gang at Karnak. Shots were fired. Belzoni escaped into the desert, and searched unsuccessfully for the ancient trading city of Berenice on the Red Sea.

Exhausted and in fear of his life, Belzoni left Egypt laden with treasure and returned to England in 1820. There he was in his element. "The

famous traveler Mr. Belzoni," so described by a London newspaper, charmed society with his good looks and broken English. He published a best-selling book on his discoveries and mounted a spectacular exhibition of Seti's tomb in London that was a popular sensation. The show did well in Paris also, and he became a famous man. But like all performers, he knew that celebrity was fleeting and that the public would soon turn its attention elsewhere.

As the Paris exhibition closed, he set off for West Africa in search of the source of the Niger River, one of the great geographical prizes of the day. This time his luck ran out. Giovanni Belzoni died of dysentery in Benin, in what is now Nigeria, only a week after landing in West Africa in December 1823. His lasting monument is the Egyptian Hall of the British Museum, where his finds can be seen to this day.

FURTHER READING

Fagan, Brian. *The Rape of the Nile*. Kingston, R.I.: Moyer Bell, 1992.

Mayes, Stanley. *The Great Belzoni*. New York: Walker, 1961.

John Evans

THE ANTIQUITY OF HUMANKIND

J ohn Evans was a remarkable man in a century filled with remarkable people. He was a self-taught scientist and archaeologist who thought nothing of working in his paper mill all day, then spending the evening searching for prehistoric artifacts in nearby plowed fields. Evans was a man of great energy. He was fond of saying that he believed in "peace, prosperity, and papermaking." He was one of the founders of modern prehistoric archaeology.

Born in 1823, at Burnham, Gloucester, in England, John Evans was the son of a parson and schoolteacher. At age 16 he went to work in his uncle John Dickinson's paper mill, learning the growing paper industry from the bottom up. He showed a natural aptitude for business. At the same time, he started to collect ancient coins.

In 1850, Evans married Harriet Dickinson and became a junior partner in his uncle's firm. Between 1850 and 1885, he turned John Dickinson and Company into one of the

By 1900, John Evans was an elder statesman of archaeology, revered for his vast knowledge of prehistoric artifacts. His beliefs were simple: "peace, prosperity, and papermaking." After all, peace and prosperity gave Evans an appropriate environment for his research.

John Evans acquired these bronze spear-heads in Ireland. They were a feature of his landmark study of prehistoric metal tools.

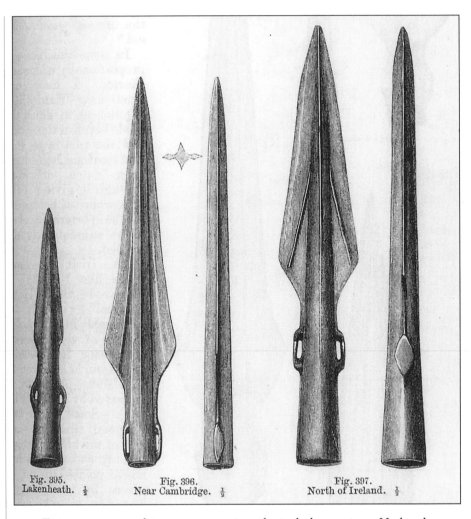

Fig. 395.
Lakenheath. ½

Fig. 396.
Near Cambridge. ½

Fig. 397.
North of Ireland. ½

great European papermaking companies of the 19th century. Evans had acquired an interest in science from his rambles through the countryside when a young man. By constant study and fieldwork squeezed between paper mill business, he became a respected and self-taught geologist and archaeologist who moved in the highest scientific circles.

John Evans was a collector in the finest sense of the word. During his long life he traveled extensively on papermaking business and used every opportunity to add to his collection, visit archaeological sites, and make geological observations. He lived a comfortable life in a house near his paper mills, assembling a magnificent collection of art, and above all, ancient artifacts of all periods. Evans became a noted coin expert who not only acquired coins, but studied their design and development. He also collected prehistoric artifacts, among them stone tools of all kinds; Bronze Age pins, brooches, and weapons; and pottery. He published two authoritative monographs on the stone and bronze artifacts of the British Isles, based almost entirely on his enormous collections.

By the 1850s, Evans was a respected member of the British scientific establishment at a time of momentous change in archaeology and geology. He was a friend of biologists Charles Darwin and Thomas Huxley, and of Sir Charles Lyell, a geologist who was the first to popularize stratigraphic geology—the systematic observation and analysis of the earth's geological layers formed through natural agencies like wind erosion and flooding. Lyell's geology helped Evans classify his stone tool collections and gave him an intellectual background for his most important research, which established that humans had lived on earth long before the 6,000 years allowed by Bishop Ussher's Old Testament calculations.

In the mid-19th century, great controversy surrounded what was commonly called "the antiquity of humankind." This debate pitted powerful Anglican church authorities against scientists in a fight over the age of the first humans. At the time, many people still believed that Genesis, Chapter 1, was historical truth and that the Creation had unfolded in 4004 BC. They refused to accept scientific finds which showed that humans had lived in Europe at the same time as long-extinct animals like the mammoth and woolly rhinoceros.

In 1858, John Evans served as a member of a special committee of the Royal Society, which commissioned excavations at Brixham Cave in southwestern England to resolve the scientific problem. Brixham Cave was important because the bones of extinct animals like Ice Age elephants had been found in its deposits in the same layer as human-manufactured stone tools. The finds lay under stalagmite, a layer of rock cemented by calcium carbonate and water into concretelike hardness. This layer had sealed off the animal remains and stone tools from becoming mixed with later deposits. The bones and tools had first been found during excavations in 1823 by a Catholic priest, Father James McEnery. The geologists of that time had explained the association of artifacts and animals by theorizing that the ancient inhabitants of the cave had dug pits for their tools into layers below the stalagmite layer. Evans and the committee supervised new excavations, which found no traces of ancient storage pits in the stalagmite. The scientists found no reason to doubt that the people who had made the Brixham Cave tools had lived at the same time as the extinct animals whose bones were found there.

The Brixham finds convinced most of the scientific establishment, Evans among them, that humans had flourished on earth much earlier than 6,000 years ago. As the committee was debating the Brixham discoveries, news of new associations of animal bones and stone artifacts came from Amiens in northern France. There, customs officer Boucher de Perthes, an amateur archaeologist, spent his free time combing the gravel quarries by the Somme River for fossil bones. Over many years, he found finely made stone axes in the same levels as elephant and hippopotamus bones, animals that had long vanished from northern France.

His scientific colleagues greeted his finds with scorn, but word of his discoveries reached England. In May

John Evans

BORN
November 17, 1823
London, England

DIED
May 31, 1908
Nash Mills, England

EDUCATION
Private

ACCOMPLISHMENTS
Most prominent 19th-century collector of and international authority on prehistoric and later artifacts of the 19th century; with geologist Joseph Prestwich, achieved scientific acceptance of the antiquity of humankind; Fellow of the Society of Antiquaries and Royal Society; received Copley Medal of the Royal Society, Gold Medal of the Society of Antiquaries. Wrote *The Ancient Stone Implements, Weapons, and Ornaments of Great Britain* (1872); *The Ancient Bronze Implements, Weapons, and Ornaments, of Great Britain and Ireland* (1881).

"This much appears established beyond doubt, that in a period of antiquity remote beyond any of which we have hitherto found traces, this portion of the globe was peopled by man."

—John Evans, *Archaeologia* (1859)

1859, John Evans and geologist Joseph Prestwich crossed the English Channel, examined de Perthes' collections, and visited the gravel quarries. Evans himself removed a stone axe from a bone-bearing bed. He was now convinced that humans and extinct animals had lived at this location long before 6,000 years ago. Back in London, the two scientists published a report of their findings, in which they publicly accepted the idea of the great antiquity of humankind. John Evans stated bluntly that humans and extinct animals had coexisted on earth much earlier than the Bible taught.

The scientific establishment was convinced by Evans's words, which came soon after the publication of Charles Darwin's *Origin of Species* in the same year. Darwin's great essay provided a theoretical explanation as to how animals, including humans, had changed their forms gradually over immensely long periods of time. John Evans's observations established the long antiquity of humankind, and since then have provided a practical foundation for all scientific study of the human past. Despite strong opposition from within the church, the science of prehistoric archaeology came into being soon afterward.

Evans himself continued his archaeological researches for the rest of his life and published two authoritative reports on stone and bronze artifacts, which were a yardstick for future generations of archaeologists. One of his greatest legacies came from his youngest son, Arthur John Evans, who learned about antiquities at his father's knee. From an early age, Arthur developed a passion for art and artifacts, especially for brooches and seals from Mediterranean lands. In his old age, John Evans watched with pride as his son discovered, then excavated, the Palace of Minos at Knossos on Crete in 1900. "Dies Creta Notanda" (a joyful day for Crete) he telegraphed to Arthur, sending him £500 to help finance the excavations, an enormous sum in those days. John Evans was able to visit the excavations and see the Minoan civilization firsthand before he died in 1908.

John Evans was one of the last Renaissance men of archaeology. His knowledge and field experience spanned the entire spectrum of the past. He was not an excavator, but an artifact man, whose collections survive in Oxford University's Ashmolean Museum for modern generations of scholars to use in their research. He was one of the first archaeologists who had the vision to look far back into the past, to link Darwin's theory of evolution and natural selection with an enormously long, and little-known human prehistory. It is only now, a century after his death, that we can begin to appreciate the enormous complexity of the human past, something even more complex than the visionary John Evans realized.

FURTHER READING

Evans, Joan. *Time and Chance*. London: Longmans, 1943.

Jacob Jens A. Worsaae

THE THREE AGES PROVED

Jacob Jens A. Worsaae nearly killed himself on his first excavation, which would have deprived archaeology of one of its seminal figures. In 1837, he and an army officer friend investigated a 4,000-year-old Stone Age tomb at Gronhojh, near Horsens, Denmark. The excavation almost ended in disaster. The soldiers doing the heavy work shifted the massive stone roof, which collapsed. Worsaae scrambled out of the way just in time and lived to become the leading figure in Danish archaeology in the mid-19th century. Through excavation rather than museum work, this energetic and charismatic archaeologist proved with stratigraphic, or layer-analysis, geology that the Three Age System accurately reflected the physical record of prehistoric development.

Worsaae was born in Vejle, Denmark, in 1821. The son of a wealthy official, he developed an interest in archaeology while still a young man. In an amazingly short time he accumulated an extensive collection of prehistoric artifacts, some by purchase, others by excavating sites and visiting ancient monuments.

Worsaae arrived in Copenhagen in 1838 and immediately made himself known to Christian Jurgensen Thomsen, the director of the National Museum. He became a volunteer, but the cautious Thomsen was suspicious of the dynamic and enterprising young man. Unlike his superior, Worsaae was a fluent writer, and not afraid to criticize other archaeologists. Unfortunately, his father fell ill and his family experienced bad times. Worsaae asked for a salary from the money-conscious Thomsen, who refused the request although longer-serving volunteers received pay. His young assistant resigned immediately and found a new patron in King Christian VIII, who paid for his trip to a famous runic inscription at Runamo in Sweden. (Runes are an early European script of the 3rd century AD.) The 23-year-old Worsaae promptly showed that the "runes" were in fact natural cracks, much to the amusement of His Majesty. The king now asked him to write a short survey of the early history of Denmark. The result was a book titled *The Primeval Antiquities of Denmark*, first published in 1843 and translated into English in 1849.

This small but bold book began with a daring statement: "It is inconceivable that a nation which cares about itself and its independence could rest content without reflecting on its past." Lucidly, Worsaae discussed Thomsen's three ages in terms of Danish prehistory, described prehistoric burial mounds and artifacts, and summarized recent research. The arguments and conclusions of *Primeval Antiquities* expressed Worsaae's nationalistic conviction that the Danish nation

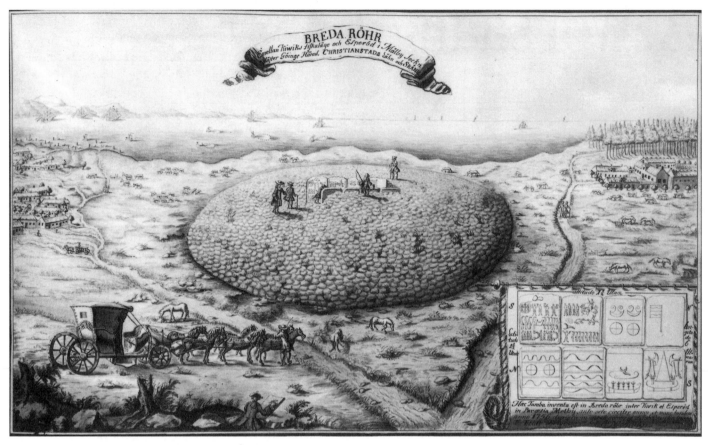

The Bronze Age burial mound at Kivik, Sweden, also called Breda Röhr, dates to about 1400 BC. It is one of Scandinavia's most celebrated prehistoric sites because of its excellent state of preservation. The central burial chamber bears rock carvings, which are enlarged at bottom right.

had deep roots in prehistory. The close ties with contemporary Danes evoked by Worsaae struck a sympathetic chord with the Danish public in the 1840s, as nationalist sentiments were running high in a tiny country engaged in a ferocious rivalry with a neighboring kingdom, Schleswig-Holstein. "The land can constantly remind us of the fact that our fathers, a free independent people, have dwelt from time immemorial in this country," Worsaae wrote in his book, which was brilliant propaganda for the young science of archaeology. He repeatedly linked ancient monuments and excavations with the major historical issues of the day.

King Christian VIII was impressed and sent his young protégé on a study tour of Viking sites in Britain and Ireland in 1846 and 1847. An acute

observer, Worsaae was struck by the strong similarities between Viking artifacts from the British Isles and those from Scandinavia. He acquired examples of closely similar artifacts and brought them back to Copenhagen for more direct comparison. From this research he wrote another book, *An Account of the Danes and the Norsemen in England, Scotland, and Ireland*, which appeared in 1852. This account of a vigorous and sophisticated culture that once flourished on both sides of the North Sea drew on an astonishing range of archaeological and historical sources.

Even before the book appeared, Worsaae's energetic researches were rewarded with a new post. He became Inspector for the Conservation of Antiquarian Monuments on his return from

Jacob Jens A. Worsaae

Britain in 1847. This demanding appointment involved making inventories of archaeological sites, attempting to save them from damage or loss by new construction, and directing the conservation of major monuments. The work kept him traveling constantly. He also excavated numerous burial mounds and other sites, many of them spectacular Stone Age and Bronze Age sepulchers where the dead lay with their finest possessions, including swords and shields, fine clay vessels, and clothing made from animal skin. Worsaae's many excavations provided new evidence from actual sites that validated Christian Jurgensen Thomsen's Three Age System, which until then had been based on museum collections alone.

As Inspector of Antiquarian Monuments, Worsaae also served as a member of a three-scientist commission responsible for investigating prehistoric mounds of empty mollusk shells accumulated by ancient shellfish-eating inhabitants along Danish coasts. Working with a geologist and a zoologist, Worsaae examined many such mounds, called shell middens, and excavated a large mound found during road-making near Meilgaard in east Jutland. He removed a large section of the midden, observing thick layers of oyster shells and mussels, where he also found antler spearheads, stone tools, hearths, and other traces of human occupation. Worsaae described the mounds as "some kind of eating place." They soon became called "kitchen middens" in contemporary scientific literature.

The simple antler and stone tools from the mounds were cruder than those from later Stone Age burial mounds, allowing Worsaae to divide the Danish Stone Age into two stages. The earlier period of the shell middens was a culture of simple hunters and fisherfolk, the later stage was marked by farming. His geological and zoological colleagues studied ancient climate changes using layers of peat bogs and the vegetable remains in them, animal bones, and shells. Zoologist Japetus Steenstrup was even able to use bird bones to establish in which seasons of the year the mounds were occupied. This research made Worsaae acutely aware of the importance of studying ancient environments a century before such approaches became commonplace in archaeology.

In 1855, Worsaae began teaching at the University of Copenhagen, the first professional teacher of prehistory in Scandinavia. He resigned in 1866 when he became Director of the National Museum of Denmark, while still retaining his inspector's position. He used his considerable diplomatic and administrative skills to obtain a government grant in 1873 for the systematic inspection and eventual protection of Danish antiquities. This survey was the first of this type ever carried out. An archaeologist and a draftsman were assigned to each area of the country. Their work produced a considerable body of valuable archaeological information from all parts of Denmark. Worsaae also proposed the establishment of a corps of regional inspectors that would assume responsibility for protecting monuments in all parts of the country. Unfortunately, this innovative proposal was never implemented, for it was far ahead of its day.

Worsaae remained a pivotal figure in Danish archaeology for the rest of his life. He reorganized the royal

BORN
March 14, 1821
Vejle, Denmark

DIED
August 15, 1885
Copenhagen, Denmark

EDUCATION
University of Copenhagen
(1738–41)

ACCOMPLISHMENTS
Established the validity of C. J. Thomsen's Three Age System through archaeological excavation and stratigraphic observation; linked the prehistory of Denmark and the Vikings to recent Danish history; established the basic stratigraphy of the Danish Stone Age; first teacher of archaeology in Denmark; director of the National Museum. Wrote *The Primeval Antiquities of Denmark* (1849); *An Account of the Danes and Norwegians in England, Scotland, and Ireland* (1852).

"The relics of prehistory strengthen our links to the Fatherland."
—Jacob Jens A. Worsae, *The Primeval Antiquities of Denmark* (1849)

collections and constantly rearranged the National Museum displays to reflect the latest scientific thinking. Under his directorship the museum was a lively place where many young students worked enthusiastically, united in a passion for archaeology, but with Worsaae's approval to disagree with one another. Worsaae's enormous comparative knowledge and lively imagination allowed him to put forward provocative theories for testing in the field. He had fingers in many pies. In 1874 and 1875 he served as Minster for Education and Ecclesiastical Affairs and displayed an unexpected flair for administration.

Unfortunately, this remarkable pioneer of European archaeology died suddenly in 1885, at the height of his powers. He left behind an extraordinary legacy of archaeological research that placed the prehistory of Scandinavia and much of northern Europe on its first scientific footing. Worsaae proved the scientific validity of the Three Age System and laid the foundations for the more detailed artifact studies of Oscar Montelius and others who followed in his footsteps (see Part 3).

FURTHER READING

Daniel, Glyn. *A Short History of Archaeology*. London: Thames and Hudson, 1981.

Fagan, Brian M. *The Adventure of Archaeology*. Washington, D.C.: National Geographic Society, 1985.

Klindt-Jensen, Ole. *A History of Scandinavian Archaeology*. London: Thames and Hudson, 1973.

More Archaeologists to Remember

Diego de Landa (1524–79) was a Franciscan friar who became bishop of the Yucatán territory in what was then New Spain. Notorious as a persecutor of the Indians there, he nevertheless admired ancient Maya ruins and attributed them to native Central Americans. He also studied the intricate Maya hieroglyphs and succeeded in deciphering some of them four centuries before modern scholars. His *Relacion de las Cosas de Yucatán* (unpublished until 1864) is a classic source of information on the ancient Maya.

William Camden (1551–1623) was a schoolmaster, antiquary, and historian. He spent much of his leisure time traveling through Britain describing the landscape and antiquities. His *Britannia*, published in 1586, was the first comprehensive topographic survey of the British Isles. Camden was

This engraving of Stonehenge from William Camden's *Britannia* (1609) is one of the earliest known illustrations of an excavation. It is probably not entirely accurate: at bottom left, diggers unearth what appears to be a giant's bones from a grave.

the first archaeologist to use telltale marks in growing crops to trace the buried streets of a Roman town, Calleva Atrebatum, near present-day Silchester, in Hampshire, England.

John Aubrey (1626–97), an English landowner and antiquary, made the first systematic examination of the Avebury stone circles in southern England. Aubrey considered Avebury to be the work of ancient Britons who were "two or three degrees less savage than the Americans." By "Americans" he meant Native Americans, whose exotic customs were the subject of intense curiosity at the time. The Avebury priests, he said, "were Druids."

William Hamilton (1730–1803), antiquarian and collector, served as British Ambassador to the Kingdoms of Naples and Sicily (the Two Sicilies) in 1764–1800. Hamilton was a man of many skills and was a well-known art collector. He accumulated two outstanding collections of Greek and Roman vases, including the celebrated Portland Vase, a Roman masterpiece, which is now in the British Museum. His books on such artifacts were influential and inspired the English potter Josiah Wedgwood.

Carsten Niebuhr (1733–1815), astronomer and mathematician, was appointed engineer-lieutenant of a Danish expedition to Arabia in 1761. He was the first Westerner to visit the remains of the ancient Persian city at Persepolis, burned by Alexander the Great. Niebuhr studied the wedgelike cuneiform inscriptions on the palace walls and brought some of the first examples of the script back to Europe. He was among the first foreigners to visit the ruins of Babylon and Nineveh.

William Bartram (1739–1823) was a Philadelphia botanist and nurseryman. From 1773 to 1777, he made a long journey through the southeastern United States, collecting botanical specimens and making detailed observations of Creek and Cherokee Native Americans. He also visited numerous earthworks, including the Mount Royal mound near the St. John's River in Florida. He wrote two books, an account of the Creek and Cherokee (1815) and *Travels* (1791), a remarkably accurate description of still-surviving Native American cultures and archaeological sites.

Thomas Jefferson (1743–1826), third President of the United States, achieved archaeological fame in 1781 when he excavated a Native American burial mound on his estate at Monticello, Virginia. Jefferson was one of the first excavators anywhere to observe and record stratified layers in an archaeological site. He noted the distinctive strata of human bones and concluded that burials had been deposited there by local Native Americans over many generations in the past.

William Cunnington (1754–1810) was a wool merchant with a passion for excavating burial mounds. Between 1803 and 1810 he excavated hundreds of such monuments in southern England, but was unable to make sense of his finds, as he lacked a means of classifying them. Cunnington's excavation methods were brutal at best, and he would sometimes open two or three mounds in a day.

Sir Richard Colt Hoare (1758–1838) was a banker and large landowner in southern England who became interested in antiquities after the tragic death of his wife and child. He financed William Cunnington's burial mound digs and studied the finds. His book *The Ancient History of Wiltshire* (1810) admitted defeat: he was unable to establish who had built the barrows around Stonehenge. He believed they were the work of "the first colonists of Britain." But the artifacts found in his burial records were a rich source of information for later investigators.

Rasmus Nyerup (1759–1829) was a Danish philosopher and natural scientist who held a professorship at the University of Copenhagen. He served as the Secretary of the Danish Antiquities Commission, established in 1806, and was responsible for the founding of the National Museum of Denmark in 1807. He was also well known for his writings on antiquities, in which he argued that prehistoric times had begun with a Stone Age, followed by Bronze and Iron ages. Nyerup's scheme was entirely theoretical, but laid the foundations for Christian Jurgensen Thomsen's Three Age System.

Caleb Atwater (1778–1867) became postmaster of Circleville, Ohio, in 1815. He devoted his leisure time to studying the mysterious earthworks and burial mounds in the Ohio Valley. Atwater's description of these sites, published by the American Antiquarian Society in 1820, was the first serious study of the North American mound builders. He falsely attributed most of them not to Native Americans, but to a numerous population of shepherds and farmers from India and China.

Claudius Rich (1787–1831) was appointed British Resident, the official British diplomatic representative, in Baghdad at age 22. Rich was the first to make a systematic map of biblical King Nebuchadnezzar's Babylon. In 1820 he spent five months examining and mapping the ruins of biblical Nineveh, where he recovered cuneiform-inscribed bricks and heard stories of fine stone relief carvings of people and

animals. His work laid the foundations for major discoveries a generation later.

Jacques Boucher de Perthes (1788–1868) served as a customs officer at Abbeville in northern France. He spent his spare time searching the quarries in the nearby Somme River gravel for human artifacts and fossil animal bones. His claims that the two occurred in the same gravel layers and were evidence for the antiquity of humankind were ignored until validated by English scientists John Evans and Joseph Prestwich in 1859.

Thomas Henry Huxley (1825–95), was a major British biologist and teacher who championed Charles Darwin's theories of evolution and natural selection. He was responsible for the first scientific description of the prehistoric skull with a large, overhanging brow found in Germany's Neander Valley in 1856, from which the classification Neanderthal Man derives. In his *Man's Place in Nature* (1863), Huxley compared the Neanderthal remains to the skeletons of apes and modern humans. He recognized that chimpanzees were our closest living primate ancestors.

Richard Colt Hoare and William Cunnington supervise the excavation of a mound on Salisbury Plain, England. The two excavators worked with lightning speed, opening two or three barrows a day.

When Napoleon Bonaparte and his troops landed in Egypt in 1798, Napoleon sought to learn as much as possible about the country. His explorations uncovered the Rosetta Stone, which enabled scholars to decipher hieroglyphics, a form of ancient Egyptian writing.

2 Finding Lost Civilizations

The 19th century was an era of romantic discovery and high adventure in pursuit of long-forgotten civilizations. If ever there was a living rather than fictional Indiana Jones, he flourished during the time when the Assyrians, the Maya, and other ancient civilizations were revealed to an astonished world.

IN THIS PART

JOHN LLOYD STEPHENS

AUSTEN HENRY LAYARD

HENRY CRESWICKE RAWLINSON

AUGUSTE MARIETTE

CHARLES WARREN

HEINRICH SCHLIEMANN

When General Napoleon Bonaparte invaded Egypt in 1798, he took 40 scientists with his army, with instructions to study this little-known country, ancient and modern. The scientists returned with the Rosetta Stone, which enabled the deciphering of the mysterious ancient Egyptian picturelike writing called hieroglyphics, and a myriad of lesser finds. The great book of their scientific reports, *Description de l'Egypte*, published in several volumes between 1809 and 1821, revealed an exotic, totally unfamiliar civilization. A passion for things Egyptian led both Britain and France to appoint consuls to Egypt, who were instructed to collect as much as they could for museums at home. Tomb robbers Giovanni Belzoni, Bernardino Drovetti, and others rampaged through Egypt's temples and tombs and did incalculable damage. Fortunately for science, Frenchman Jean François Champollion deciphered the Egyptian hieroglyphs in 1822, which set the stage for the serious study of ancient Egypt. Soon, a handful of scholars worked alongside the treasure hunters, among them Englishman John Gardner Wilkinson, who worked for years deciphering inscriptions while living in ancient tombs. He wrote the first popular account of daily life among the ancient Egyptians. Later in the 19th century, the first full-time Egyptologists worked along the Nile, among them the Frenchman Auguste Mariette and the German scholar Karl Richard Lepsius, who led a major expedition to Egypt from 1842 to 1845.

In 1840, the French government, anxious to repeat its triumphs in Egypt, appointed Paul Emile Botta its consul in the remote town of Mosul on the Tigris River in what is now northern Iraq. The community had one claim to fame— it lay across the river from what was thought to be ancient Nineveh. Two years after his arrival, Botta dug into Nineveh without success. In 1843, one of his workers reported the discovery of carved figures at Khorsabad a short distance upstream. Within a few days, Botta unearthed the remains of a palace with walls adorned with bearded men in long gowns, armies, and exotic animals. Botta announced that he had found Nineveh, when he had, in fact, discovered the palace of the Assyrian King Sargon II, who reigned from 721 to 701 BC. The Assyrians were known from the Second Book of Kings in the Old Testament as a fierce people who had attacked Israel. Botta's discoveries caused a sensation in Paris. A lavish expedition was mounted to dig at Khorsabad.

A young Englishman named Austen Henry Layard had visited Botta in 1842 while on his way by land from England to India. An adventurous and restless young man, Layard became fascinated by archaeology and desert life while in Mosul and Baghdad. He abandoned his journey, spent a year among the Bakhtiari nomads of highland Iran, then became a secret agent attached to the British Embassy in Constantinople. In 1845, Layard began excavations at the city of Nimrud (the biblical Calah) downstream of Mosul, where he found two Assyrian royal palaces. At first he thought Nimrud was Nineveh, but when he dug at the Kuyunjik mounds opposite Mosul, he discovered the real biblical city. Thanks to Botta and Layard, the Assyrians became a historical reality, not just a shadowy reference in the Scriptures. Layard was a gifted writer whose books on his excavations are still in print a century and a half later. He was helped in his interpretations by the cuneiform studies of Henry Rawlinson and others, who deciphered palace inscriptions and clay tablets for him. Layard was followed by his protégé Hormuzd Rassam, who carried out further excavations at Kuyunjik and elsewhere with important results.

Layard's most important discovery was the royal library of King Assurbanipal (668–627 BC) at Nineveh: thousands of cuneiform-inscribed clay tablets that he shoveled into baskets and sent to the British Museum in London. In 1872, George Smith, a young bank engraver with a passion for cuneiform, identified a legend remarkably similar to the biblical Noah's flood on one of the king's tablets. The find caused a sensation, for it seemed to prove the historical truth of the Scriptures.

The Bible and the Greek and Roman classics still drove much archaeological thinking in Layard's day. The popular obsession with the Scriptures led to the first investigations under the holy city of Jerusalem by engineer officer Charles Warren. These were hazardous excavations carried out in tunnels that traced the outline of much of the city walls. Warren was one of the founders of biblical archaeology, which flourishes to this day.

Ever since the first conquistadors landed in New Spain, scholars had speculated about the origins of the first Americans. Had they arrived by sea, or by land from Asia? The discovery of the Bering Strait by Vitus Bering in 1743 focused attention on an Asian ancestry for Native Americans. Meanwhile, speculations came fast and faster, especially after crowds of settlers crossed the Allegheny Mountains from the east and entered the Ohio and Mississippi valleys in the 1820s. They found themselves surrounded by mysterious earthworks, enclosures, and burial mounds. None other than Thomas Jefferson, future President of the United States, puzzled over the mounds, as did generations of antiquaries. The first serious inquiries came at the hands of the Circleville postmaster Caleb Atwater, then with the surveys of Ephraim Squier and Edwin Davis from 1845 to 1847.

Squier and Davis's report, published by the Smithsonian Institution in 1847, is still the only source of accurate plans of now-destroyed earthworks. The two men were convinced that Native Americans were incapable of such sophisticated construction, which they attributed to "Mound Builder peoples." A platoon of popular writers like Cornelius Mathew and Josiah Priest wrote epic stories of long-forgotten mound-builder civilizations that inhabited the Midwest long before Native Americans settled there. The books sold well, but were based on racist assumptions of white superiority.

Some scholars thought otherwise. In 1856, a wise and sober archaeologist named Samuel Haven pointed out that Native Americans had lived in their homeland for a very long time. Furthermore, they had Asian physical characteristics. But it was not until the 1890s that a massive campaign of excavation and survey headed by Cyrus Thomas of the Smithsonian's Bureau of American Ethnology proved beyond all doubt that the mounds were the work of Native Americans, the ancestors of recent tribal groups.

As speculation over the mound builders continued, an American traveler, John Lloyd Stephens, and Scottish artist Frederick Catherwood penetrated deep into the rainforests of the Yucatán Peninsula in Central America. They had heard rumors of ancient cities lost in the jungle from sporadic reports by returning travelers. Like Layard, Stephens was a brilliant writer, who entranced a wide public with accounts of his adventures. The two men traveled to the Maya city of Copán in 1839, then explored Palenque, Uxmal, and other Maya cities in this and a later journey. Both trips resulted in best-selling books, and separate folios of superb drawings by Catherwood of Maya sites and art works that were almost as accurate as photographs. Most important of all, Stephens proclaimed his newfound cities to be the work not of foreigners from across the Atlantic, but of the ancestors of the Maya people still living in the region in his day. All Maya research has proceeded from this assumption ever since.

Most educated people of the mid- to late 19th century received an education in the classics. These included the writings of the Greek poet Homer, who wrote his epics, the *Iliad* and the *Odyssey* in the 9th century B.C. But were these great adventure stories a true reflection of history? German businessman turned archaeologist Heinrich Schliemann was determined to find out. After making a fortune, he trained himself in archaeology and the classics. In 1871, he excavated the great mounds of Hissarlik in northwestern Turkey, which he believed to be the city of Troy besieged by the Greeks in the *Iliad*. Using huge gangs of laborers, he unearthed one city after another, declaring the sixth to be Homeric Troy. Schliemann was not entirely honest. He claimed to have found a single, fabulous treasure trove of rich golden ornaments, which he displayed on his lovely Greek wife, Sophia. In fact, the finds came from several levels of the site. After several seasons at Hissarlik, he turned his attention to the fortress and tombs at Mycenae in southern Greece. He soon found a series of magnificently decorated chieftain's burials adorned with gold face masks. These he proclaimed to be those of King Agamemnon and his compatriots from the *Iliad*. Later scholarship has shown that the Mycenae burials were much earlier than Homer's day.

Schliemann was the classic archaeological adventurer—single-minded, determined to find spectacular artifacts, and unconcerned about the damage he caused along the way. But archaeology was changing by the time he dug into Mycenae. A new generation of much more careful excavators was beginning to transform archaeology from a glorified treasure hunt into a meticulous science. When Schliemann resumed work at Hissarlik from 1882 to 1890, he had German archaeologist and architect Wilhelm Dorpfeld working alongside him to add scientific rigor to his excavations.

The last of the heroic discoveries came in 1912, when Yale historian turned archaeologist Hiram Bingham traveled up Peru's Urubamba River in search of the "Lost City of the Incas." He stumbled on the mountain ruins of Macchu Picchu, a well-preserved outlier center of Inca civilization. But his claim that this was the last Inca city has been proven wrong. Another stone-built settlement on the eastern side of the Andes Mountains was the last Inca refuge from Spanish conquistadors.

John Lloyd Stephens

CHRONICLER OF
THE ANCIENT MAYA

John Lloyd Stephens introduced the ancient Maya world to the people of the 19th century. Stephens had heard rumors of ruins deep in the Central American rainforest and set off on an expedition of discovery.

Not many archaeologists have revealed an entire ancient civilization to an astonished world. John Lloyd Stephens, archaeologist and traveler, had that opportunity, as well as the talent to write vivid tales about his experiences as well. He described long-forgotten Maya cities, where he walked through deserted plazas under the canopy of the rainforest, with the earthen heights of surrounding pyramids vanishing into the trees above.

Stephens was born in Shrewsbury, New Jersey, in 1805, the son of a wealthy New York merchant. He entered Columbia University in 1818, at the early age of 13, where he received an education in Greek and Latin and a sound grounding in literature. He graduated in 1821. Columbia gave him an endless curiosity about the world, which compelled him to pursue an active and adventure-filled life.

Stephens attended Tapping Reeves's Law School in Litchfield, Connecticut, graduating in 1824. But instead of being sworn in as a counselor at law, he took a long journey west to visit distant relatives in Illinois. At the time, this was frontier country, with thousands of people moving across the Allegheny Mountains into the Midwest in covered wagons. Stephens rode from Pittsburgh to Cincinnati, then went by steamer to Louisville before taking a trail to the tiny settlement of Carmi, Illinois. When he left Carmi he continued down the Mississippi River to New Orleans. The entire journey gave Stephens a taste of traveling in the wild. Now an experienced traveler, he returned to New York in 1825 and gained admittance to the bar, becoming involved in the family's Wall Street business. Stephens was a convincing and articulate speaker who soon became much in demand for political activities such as Andrew Jackson's presidential campaign of 1828. He developed a throat infection from excessive public speaking. The family doctor recommended an extended trip through Europe as a cure. Never enthusiastic about the law, Stephens left for his second long journey in 1835 and never practiced again.

Stephens passed rapidly through Paris and Rome, visiting the usual tourist spots. He next traveled to Greece, then across Russia to Moscow and St. Petersburg in a wagon, before returning to Paris through Poland. Browsing through a bookstall, he came across a book about the mysterious and little-known rock-cut city of Petra in distant Syria. He promptly decided to go there, first journeying up the Nile River by boat to visit ancient Egyptian ruins. By the time he returned to Cairo, he was an expert desert traveler, wearing Arab costume and going by the name of Abdul Hasis. This disguise enabled him to cross the Sinai Desert, where he nearly died of thirst, and to enter Petra unscathed after paying a large bribe to the local sheikh. Stephens was so entranced by Petra's temples that he developed a serious interest in archaeology almost overnight. He wrote in his book about these travels: "The first view of that superb facade must produce an effect which would never go away. Even [after I] returned to the pursuits and thought-engrossing incidents of a life in the busiest city in the world . . . I see before me the facade of that temple."

He went back to New York by way of Jerusalem, Alexandria, Egypt, and London, to find himself famous. Friends had published some of his letters in New York newspapers, which soon became his first book, *Incidents of Travel in Arabia Petraea*, published in 1837. *Incidents* was an immediate bestseller, with a vivid and easy style and a pleasing sense of humor that disguised thorough research and impressive scholarship. He promptly wrote a second book about his travels in Greece and Russia, which appeared in 1839 and enjoyed equal success. Stephens described 2,000 miles of bouncing travel in a wagon with no springs from Odessa on the Black Sea to Moscow. He was "obliged to strip naked" for customs examination.

While writing these books in New York, Stephens met the Scottish artist Frederick Catherwood, who shared his passion for ancient civilizations. Catherwood had traveled widely in Egypt and the Holy Land, and enjoyed a considerable reputation for his evocative drawings of ancient ruins. Catherwood drew Stephens' attention to some little-known publications that described mysterious ruins in Central America. Sensing a unique opportunity, Stephens wangled a Presidential appointment as American chargé d'affairs in Central America to give legitimacy to an expedition to the rainforests of Guatemala and Mexico.

In October 1839, Stephens and Catherwood sailed for Izabal in Guatemala, where they set off inland with five mules. After a difficult journey through rough country, they arrived at the remote village of Copán, where they saw well-preserved stone walls across the river. The next day they explored the overgrown Maya city, silent except for "monkeys moving along the tops of the trees." Few ancient cities have ever been described so eloquently. Stephens wrote: "The city was desolate. No remnant of this race hangs round the ruins. . . . It lay before us like a shattered bark in the midst of the ocean." Meanwhile, Catherwood stood copying the intricate carvings on the weathered stone columns set in Copán's great plaza. Stephens wanted to buy Copán and ship it back to New York piece by piece. However, the river was unsuitable for rafts, so he contented himself with buying the site for $50, the bargain of the century.

While Catherwood stayed behind to draw the ruins, Stephens traveled on to Guatemala City, where he found political chaos. He embarked on a 1,200-mile diplomatic journey to San Salvador and Costa Rica before rejoining Catherwood. The two men returned home across a huge area of Guatemala that took them a thousand miles northeastward to another great Maya city, Palenque. Virtually indistinguishable from the local people, with broad-brimmed hats and Spanish costume, they rode through rebel-infested country torn by civil war, finding their way with difficulty through thick forest. Palenque was worth the journey, despite heavy rain and thousands of mosquitoes.

They recorded details of the palace with its "spirited figures in bas-relief," made a plan of the site, and admired the fine art, which reminded them of ancient Egypt. It was then that Stephens realized that Palenque's art not only was unique, but was the

John Lloyd Stephens

BORN
November 28, 1805
Shrewsbury, New Jersey

DIED
October 12, 1852
New York, New York

EDUCATION
Columbia College, New York (B.A. 1821)
Tapping Reeve's Law School, Litchfield, Connecticut (L.L.D. 1824)

ACCOMPLISHMENTS
Became famous as a travel writer after extensive journeys in Europe and the eastern Mediterranean, including the city of Petra; traveled through Yucatán Peninsula and major Maya cities with Frederick Catherwood; was the first person to attribute Maya ruins to the ancestors of the modern native population of the region; brought ancient Maya civilization to a wide audience. Wrote *Incidents of Travel in Central America, Chiapas, and Yucatán* (1841); *Incidents of Travel in Yucatán* (1843).

> *"To men of leisure and fortune, jaded with rambling over the ruins of the Old World, a new country will be opened. After a journey on the Nile, a day in Petra, and a bath in the Euphrates, English and American travelers will be bitten by mosquitoes on the lake of Nicaragua."*
>
> —John Lloyd Stevens, *Incidents of Travel in Central America, Chiapas, and the Yucatán* (1841)

work of the ancestors of the local people. "It is a spectacle of a people originating and growing up here . . . having a distinct, separate, and indigenous existence," he wrote. All Maya archaeology is based on his carefully reasoned conclusion.

After a quick visit to the nearby Maya site at Uxmal, the explorers returned to New York in July 1840, after a 10-month journey. Nine months later, *Incidents of Travel in Central America, Chiapas, and Yucatán* appeared to great acclaim. More than 20,000 copies were sold in a few months. The book is still in print a century and a half later and is some of the finest writing about Maya ruins ever penned.

In September 1841, Stephens and Catherwood again set sail for the Yucatán Peninsula, this time with Samuel Cabot, a young physician. For six weeks they mapped and surveyed Uxmal, arguably the most magnificent of all Maya ceremonial centers. Catherwood's paintings and drawings of Uxmal were detailed enough to allow him to build a replica if he wished, and are deservedly admired. From Uxmal, the party traveled to Kabah and other Maya sites. They spent 18 days at Chichén Itzá in northeastern Yucatán. Stephens admired the Ball Court, which gave him another link between the ancient and modern Maya, for

historical records of ancient ball games survived. In these arenas, teams of players tried to shoot a rubber ball through a hoop on the wall. The losers were sacrificed to the gods.

Stephens noted the close links between Chichén Itzá and other Maya sites like Uxmal, Cozumel, and Tulum. In June 1842, Stephens returned to New York. Once again, just nine months later he published an account of the trip, *Incidents of Travel in Yucatán*, and once again he had produced a bestseller. Stephens declared that the ruins of the area were built by "the same races who inhabited the country at the time of the Spanish Conquest." Then he wrote: "I leave them with all their mystery around them." With these words, John Lloyd Stephens founded Maya archaeology. He never returned to the ruins, but became involved in a project to build a trans-Panama railroad in 1849. He died in New York in 1852, as a result of fever contracted in Central America.

John Lloyd Stephens brought ancient Maya civilization to the consciousness of the American public and kindled a lasting fascination with the subject that still entices thousands of visitors to Central America every year.

FURTHER READING

Stephens, John Lloyd. *Incidents of Travel in Central America, Chiapas, and Yucatán.* 1841. Reprint, Washington, D.C.: Smithsonian Institution, 1993.

von Hagen, Victor. *Frederick Catherwood, Architect.* New York: Oxford University Press, 1950.

————. *Maya Explorer.* Norman: University of Oklahoma Press, 1947.

Willey, Gordon R., and Jeremy A. Sabloff. *A History of American Archaeology.* San Francisco: Freeman, 1980.

Austen Henry Layard

EXCAVATOR OF NINEVEH

Austen Henry Layard had one of the shortest but most spectacular archaeological careers of all time. He became an archaeologist by accident, achieved world fame for his discoveries in Mesopotamia, then retired from archaeology at age 36. Almost single-handed, he unearthed the palaces of the Assyrian kings at biblical Nineveh, discovering a flamboyant civilization mentioned in the Old Testament.

Layard was born in Paris in 1817, five years before Jean François Champollion deciphered hieroglyphs, the writing system of ancient Egypt. He was the son of impoverished but genteel English parents who enjoyed living abroad. The family could not afford university fees, so Henry became a clerk in a relative's London law firm. For five years he lived a miserable existence. The dull and predictable career looming ahead of him filled his heart with gloom.

Salvation came in 1839 when his uncle Charles, a high British official in Ceylon (now Sri Lanka), suggested a law career on that remote island. Henry joined Edward Mitford, a 32-year-old businessman, on an overland journey from Europe to Constantinople, then through Syria, Jerusalem, and Baghdad to Persia, India, and on to Ceylon. In 1839 such a journey was an expedition into the hazardous unknown. Had Mitford not been chronically seasick, and elected to travel overland, Layard would never have found a lost civilization and would probably have led a life of respectable anonymity.

The two men set out in July 1839. By the time they arrived in Constantinople, Layard had fallen in love with the Middle East. They lived off beans, bread, and fish roe for about four shillings a day (39 cents in today's money) as they followed the centuries-old Roman route to Syria and Jerusalem. Leaving Mitford in Jerusalem, Layard hired two camels and rode across the desert to the remote rock-cut Roman caravan city at Petra in modern-day Jordan. He was attacked and robbed of all his possessions, then held as a hostage, but was eventually released unharmed.

In April 1841, Layard and Mitford reached Mosul on the Tigris River. Layard rode over the deserted mounds of the biblical city of Nineveh across the river. He wrote: "Desolation meets desolation. A feeling of awe succeeds to wonder." He was soon obsessed with the notion of digging into Iraq's ancient mounds. For two months, he stayed with Colonel James Taylor, the British consul in Baghdad, poring over clay tablets in the colonel's library that were covered with wedge-shaped cuneiform characters—the writing system of ancient Mesopotamian civilizations. Neither of them

Austen Henry Layard in Turkish nomad dress. Travelers often wore local dress so that they drew less attention to themselves. The flowing, loose-fitting robes were also much cooler and more comfortable than European clothes.

could decipher the tablets, but Layard became fascinated with archaeology.

By this time, Layard was addicted to adventure. He parted company from Mitford in Persia and spent a year among the fierce Bakhtiari nomads wandering with a chief whose son he cured of fever with quinine and a concoction called "Dr. Dover's Powder." He took part in their skirmishes and was captured by a cruel rival, but managed to escape and make his way to Baghdad dressed as a nomad.

For the next four years Layard served as an unpaid, confidential assistant to Sir Stratford Canning, the British ambassador to Constantinople, who respected his knowledge of local affairs. Layard relished his role as a secret agent, but never forgot the ruins of Nineveh. Eventually he persuaded Canning to put up the funds for two month's excavations at the biblical city of Calah (Nimrud), downstream of Mosul.

Nimrud consisted of a long line of narrow mounds covering 900 acres (365 hectares), dominated by a cone-like pyramid, once a mud-brick temple. Layard started work in November 1845. He chose a spot at random. Within a few days he had found two royal palaces. His first trenches entered the palace of the great Assyrian king Assurbanipal (883–859 BC). The Southwest Palace belonged to King Esarhaddon (680–669 BC), built on the ruins of yet a third royal residence constructed by King Tiglath-Pileser (774–727 BC). Layard concentrated on spectacular finds that would look good in museum displays, trenching along the walls of the palace rooms, where he found magnificent bas-reliefs—sculptures in which the figures project less than half their depth from the surface—depicting

military campaigns. He realized he had unearthed an ancient biblical civilization fully as important as that of the ancient Egyptians.

By May 1846 Layard had tunneled deep into Assurbanipal's palace. He found walls decorated with bas-reliefs of kings and horsemen, with servants and scenes of the chase. Human-headed stone lions guarded the gates of the palace. Working almost alone in temperatures as high as 117°F (47°C), he sketched each sculpture while his workmen sawed those he had already recorded out of the walls, transported them on buffalo carts to the nearby Tigris River, then loaded them on rafts supported by inflated goatskins for the long journey to Basra on the Persian Gulf. From there they went by steamer to the British Museum in London.

News of Layard's discoveries caused an immediate stir in England. "The portly figures of kings and viziers, were so lifelike, and carved in such true relief, that they might be imagined to be stepping from the walls," wrote journalist J. A. Longworth of the London *Morning Post*. The first loads of sculpture caused great excitement when they went on display in the British Museum on June 25, 1847. Meanwhile, Layard closed his Nimrud excavations and moved to the Kuyunjik mound opposite Mosul, which he suspected was the site of ancient Nineveh.

French diplomat Emile Botta had previously dug there, found nothing, and moved upstream to the Assyrian site at Khorsabad, which he had proclaimed to be Nineveh. Layard realized the Frenchman had not dug deep enough into the mound. After a month's hectic work, he uncovered nine rooms of a magnificent palace adorned with scenes of a city siege.

Austen Henry Layard

"Some who may hereafter tread on the spot when the grass again grows over the ruins of the Assyrian palaces, may indeed suspect that I have been relating a vision."

—Austen Henry Layard, *Nineveh and Its Remains* (1849)

BORN
March 5, 1817
Paris, France

DIED
July 5, 1894
Venice, Italy

EDUCATION
Private

ACCOMPLISHMENTS
Became an expert on Assyrian and Babylonian civilization, and western Asian and European art; excavated biblical Calah and Nineveh; unearthed historical evidence of the Assyrian civilization mentioned in the Old Testament; served as British ambassador to Madrid (1869–77) and Constantinople (1877–84). Wrote *Nineveh and Its Remains* (1849); *Discoveries in the Ruins of Nineveh and Babylon* (1853).

Heavily armed men attacked with ladders and ramps as the defenders threw stones and boiling oil on them, but to no avail. In the bas-reliefs the attackers overrun the beleagured city and kill and enslave the inhabitants in the presence of the king. Layard suspected he had found Nineveh, but proof could only come from still-undeciphered tablets.

Exhausted and suffering from malaria, Layard returned to London to find himself the hero of the day. He dined in great houses, lectured on his excavations, and wrote a "slight sketch," as he called it, of his excavations. The "sketch" was a book titled *Nineveh and Its Remains*, which appeared in early 1849 and became an instant bestseller. Layard was an enthusiastic and vivid writer. His excavations, and the ancient Assyrians themselves, came alive on every page of this remarkable travelogue, which remains in print to this day. No one challenged Layard's claim that he had revealed the "most convincing and lasting evidence of the magnificence, and power, which made Nineveh the wonder of the ancient world." Until then, the Assyrians had been known only from the Second Book of Kings in the Bible, fierce warriors who had conquered Israel and put the city of Lachish to the sword. Austen Henry Layard brought them out of historical oblivion.

The British Museum paid for more excavations at Khorsabad from 1849 to 1850. Layard commuted between Khorsabad and Nimrud, where he met Henry Creswicke Rawlinson, the brilliant cavalry officer and linguist who had deciphered Assyrian cuneiform. Rawlinson had originally told him Nimrud was Nineveh. Now he had deciphered the royal inscriptions, changed his mind, and identified it as biblical Calah. Kuyunjik was the true Nineveh, he said. Layard soon uncovered a huge ceremonial hall 124 feet long and 90 feet wide (38 by 27.5 meters) at Kuyunjik, guarded by statues of two human-headed bulls and adorned with bas-reliefs showing how fettered prisoners quarried, sculpted, and transported the bull-humans that guarded the palace. An inscription read: "Sennacherib, King of Assyria. The great figures of bulls . . . which were made for his royal palace at Nineveh." Sennacherib's "Palace Without a Rival" was built in 700 BC.

Layard excavated the 180-foot-long (55-meter) southeastern facade of Sennacherib's palace, also guarded by huge bulls and gigantic human figures and decorated with tales of the king's conquests. The limestone slabs of the entrances still bore ruts from Assyrian chariot wheels. Another large chamber bore scenes of the siege and capture of

Layard (on left horse) and a local chieftain oversee the moving of the human-headed bull from Nimrud (in the background) to the banks of the Tigris River. Hundreds of workers hauled the crude wagon and its precious load to the river, where the cargo was loaded onto a ship bound for London.

a heavily fortified city: The army camps before the walls, battering rams in place. The defenders put up a desperate resistance, but to no avail. Sennacherib himself sits in judgment over the captives. An inscription identified the city of Lachish, part of Sennacherib's campaign mentioned in II Kings 18:13 in the Bible. Huge bas-reliefs of the fish god Dagon guarded small rooms containing thousands of cuneiform tablets, the royal archives of King Ashurbanipal. Layard shoveled baskets of them into six crates, knowing they would place the scientific understanding of the Assyrians on a new footing. Cleaning and deciphering the tablets would take more than 50 years.

From Nineveh, Layard traveled to King Nebuchadnezzar's Babylon, a maze of dusty mounds and compacted, sun-dried mud brick. Layard's crude excavation methods were not up to the task of tracing buildings or individual levels in the mounds. He moved on to the ancient city of Nippur, also in the lowlands of the Euphrates River delta, but was equally unsuccessful. He returned to London in July 1851 to great popular acclaim, was elected a member of Parliament, and wrote a second bestseller, *Nineveh and Babylon*, which appeared two years later. This time he had the benefit of cuneiform inscriptions; these enabled him to write the first historical account of Assyrian civilization, which he called "a kind of confederation formed by many tributary states."

Austen Henry Layard gave up archaeology after the publication of *Nineveh and Babylon*. He enjoyed a long career as a politician and then a diplomat, becoming British ambassador to Constantinople and Madrid. Eventually he retired to Venice, where he indulged a lifelong passion for art. By the time he died in 1894, he ranked among the archaeological immortals.

His achievements were staggering. Without any formal training, with little money, and working almost single-handed without any special equipment, he unearthed a hitherto unknown civilization. He had a great archaeologist's instinct for the vital rather than the trivial, and a nose for discovery that led him unerringly to royal palaces and spectacular finds. His prodigious energy made up for his rough excavation methods, which ignored small finds and individual occupation levels. Unfortunately, no trained students stepped into Layard's shoes. Half a century passed before scientifically trained excavators worked in Mesopotamia.

FURTHER READING

Fagan, Brian M. *Return to Babylon*. Boston: Little, Brown, 1979.

Larsen, Mogens Trolle. *The Conquest of Assyria*. London: Routledge, 1994.

Lloyd, Seton. *Foundations in the Dust*. Rev. ed. London: Thames and Hudson, 1980.

Henry Creswicke Rawlinson

DECIPHERER OF
CUNEIFORM SCRIPT

Brilliant horseman, energetic Indian army officer, and highly gifted linguist: Henry Creswicke Rawlinson was a giant of 19th-century archaeology. He was one of a handful of scholars who deciphered the wedgelike cuneiform script of ancient Mesopotamia in the 1840s. As part of this work, he was the first to identify the biblical cities of Nineveh and Nimrud in present-day northern Iraq for what they were.

Like many eminent 19th-century scientists, Henry Rawlinson rose from a relatively ordinary background to international prominence, in his case as a cavalryman, diplomat, traveler, and respected scholar. He was born in Oxford, England, in 1810. His father Abraham was a well-known horse breeder, so it was no surprise that Henry became an excellent horseman at an early age. He was educated at Wrington and Ealing schools, where he excelled at both athletics and languages. His family background and intelligence made him a natural candidate for an officer's commission in the East India Company's service. He sailed for India in 1827 at the age of 17, and there showed immediate promise in his profession. Rawlinson led two lives, one as a carefree young officer who partied and engaged in sports of every kind, the other as a quiet scholar studying Asian languages in his spare time. His natural talents for local languages and infinite capacity for hard work soon qualified him as an interpreter, which gave him unusual opportunities for service on remote frontiers. At the same time, he was respected for his exceptional horsemanship. On one occasion, he rode 750 miles (1,200 kilometers) in 150 hours to warn the officer in charge of an isolated outpost of the presence of a Russian agent. Rawlinson's ride was the stuff of legend. For years, British sporting magazines called his epic gallop the ride of the century.

Rawlinson had an infinite curiosity about exotic lands and continued to study new dialects. Increasingly, he became involved in political issues and in 1835 was posted to Persia, where he explored the remote territory of Kurdistan. In 1838 he was awarded the Royal Geographical Society of London's gold medal for his explorations, reports of which were published by the society. During these travels, he visited the Great Rock at Behistun, a huge rock surface adorned with a vast ancient inscription commemorating Persian King Darius's victory over rebels in 522 BC. Rawlinson gazed 400 feet (150 meters) upward at the trilingual inscription in Old Persian, Elamite, and Babylonian. He knew that scholars could read many characters in Old Persian. If he could translate the Persian, then he would have the key for deciphering

Henry Creswicke Rawlinson at work deciphering cuneiform, the early Mesopotamian script. Rawlinson's brilliant deciphering skills enabled him to puzzle out the intricacies of the wedgelike script.

Babylonian cuneiform, at the time an untranslated writing system.

Soon he was devoting every spare moment to the difficult task of copying the Behistun inscriptions. The proclamation was set high above the ground, as it was addressed to the gods in heaven, not to mere mortals. The task of copying would have daunted even an expert mountaineer. Rawlinson scrambled all over the rock face during the next 12 years, using scaffolding and crude ladders. Once he almost plunged to his death when the ladder he was using to span a chasm collapsed. When only the most inaccessible lines of the inscription remained, he employed Kurdish climbers, among them a nimble boy with nerves of steel who copied the last few words "by hanging on with his toes and fingers."

In 1843 Rawlinson was appointed British consul in Baghdad, an ideal posting for a scholarly man who needed plenty of undisturbed time for research into ancient scripts. He labored on the Behistun inscription, beginning with the names of kings in the Old Persian script. Soon he compiled an alphabet, then translated entire sentences. In 1847 he published an important paper, "Persian Cuneiform Inscriptions at Behistun," in the *Journal of the Royal Asiatic Society,* which was widely accepted as a reliable translation. By this time Rawlinson was working on Babylonian cuneiform in cooperation with other experts, including an Irish parson named Edward Hincks, who was the first to identify syllables in cuneiform.

Once Rawlinson understood the polyphonic nature of cuneiform (the characters represented more than one syllable), he progressed rapidly. Soon he could read about 150 characters and understand the meaning of some 200 words of the language: Akkadian.

Rawlinson's Behistun work evoked great popular enthusiasm. His copies and translations were hailed as the "Rosetta Stone" of cuneiform. Any controversy about his translation was soon defused by the discovery of actual guides to Akkadian grammar on clay tablets in the Royal Library of Assyrian King Assurbanipal at Nineveh.

No cuneiform expert could engage in serious work without a steady stream of new inscriptions. Rawlinson's consular duties brought him in regular contact with both Paul Emile Botta and Austen Henry Layard, who were engaged in large-scale excavations at Khorsabad, Nimrud, and Nineveh. He corresponded with Layard, visited his excavations, and used inscriptions to identify the excavated cities and their palaces as Nineveh and biblical Calah (Nimrud). This identification took Botta and the French by surprise, for they had announced that Khorsa-bad, upstream of Mosul, was the true Nineveh.

It was Layard who, in 1850, unearthed a room filled with clay tablets in the library of King Assurbanipal. He promptly shoveled the priceless finds into wicker baskets for shipment to London. Rawlinson picked through the baskets, the first person able to read them in more than 2,500 years, and realized their historical value at once. He wrote in high excitement that they contained "the system of Assyrian writing, the distinction between phonetic (sound-based) and ideographic (idea-symbolizing) signs . . . grammar of the language, classification, and explanation of technical terms . . . A thorough examination of the fragments would lead to the most curious results."

By this time, Rawlinson was exhausted by the hot climate in Baghdad. He returned to England on leave to find himself a celebrity. In 1853 he resigned

Henry Creswicke Rawlinson

"The Babylonian translation of the records of Darius . . . is almost of equal value for the interpretation of the Assyrian inscriptions as is the Greek translation on the Rosetta Stone for the intelligence of the hieroglyphic scripts of Egypt."

—Henry Creswicke Rawlinson, from an 1852 lecture to the Society of Antiquaries of London

BORN
April 11, 1810
Oxford, England

DIED
March 9, 1895
London, England

EDUCATION
Wrington and Ealing schools

ACCOMPLISHMENTS
An expert on ancient Assyrian and Babylonian civilizations, Mesopotamian archaeology generally, and cuneiform; copied the Great Rock of Behistun inscriptions and deciphered cuneiform, two of the greatest scholarly feats of the 19th century; also had an exceptional career as a cavalry officer, horseman, and diplomat. Helped compile *The Cuneiform Inscriptions of Western Asia* (1861–84).

from Baghdad and was rewarded with a knighthood and a lucrative directorship of the East India Company.

Four years later, Rawlinson took part in a test of cuneiform decipherment devised by the Royal Asiatic Society, in which he, Edward Hincks, and a third expert, Frenchman Jules Oppert, were invited to submit independent translations of an unpublished, 810-line inscription of Assyrian King Tiglath-Pileser I (1115–1077 BC). Two months later, a five-man learned committee broke the seals of three envelopes and compared the translations. The close similarities between the three versions convinced even skeptics that cuneiform had been deciphered.

Following his retirement, Rawlinson devoted his life to public service. He became a member of Parliament and was actively involved in international diplomacy. He was to be seen around the Department of Oriental Antiquities at the British Museum in London. There he patiently worked on *The Cuneiform Inscriptions of Western Asia,* a compendium of accurate copies of cuneiform tablets. Generations of students benefited from his long experience and they refined the translations of the pioneers. He served as president of the Royal Asiatic and Royal Geographic societies and became a trustee of the British Museum. Rawlinson died

in 1895 at the age of 85, the epitome of a Victorian gentleman to the end.

Adventurer and dedicated scholar, Henry Creswicke Rawlinson was a loner who was often criticized for being secretive about his work. His work in deciphering cuneiform was the Mesopotamian equivalent of Frenchman Jean François Champollion's brilliant research on Egyptian hieroglyphs. "Lose no opportunity to be useful, whatever may be the affair which may happen to present the chance," Rawlinson once wrote. "Grasp at everything, and never yield an inch. Above all, never stand on trifles." By all accounts, he lived his life according to these rules.

FURTHER READING

Fagan, Brian M. *Return to Babylon.* Boston: Little, Brown, 1979.

Larsen, Mögens Trølle. *The Conquest of Assyria.* London: Routledge, 1994.

Rawlinson, George. *Memoir of Major General Sir Henry Rawlinson.* London: Longmans Green, 1898.

Rawlinson, Sir Henry Creswicke. *England and Russia in the East.* 1875. Reprint, New York: Praeger, 1970.

Waterfield, Gordon. *Layard of Nineveh.* London: John Murray, 1963.

Auguste Mariette

PRESERVING ANCIENT EGYPT FOR THE FUTURE

Auguste Mariette and his crew undertake excavations at Saqqara, Egypt. Mariette's digging methods were almost as brutal as those of the looters he battled. Sometimes, as here, he merely shored up walls and went on excavating.

Auguste Mariette came to Egypt to acquire manuscripts, but discovered a shrine full of mummified ancient Egyptian bulls instead. He was one of the earliest professional Egyptologists, founder of Egypt's Cairo Museum, and a passionate advocate for the preservation of ancient Egypt at a time when the looting of sites was commonplace along the Nile.

Mariette was born in Boulogne, France, in 1821 and educated at the College of Boulogne, where he achieved some distinction. However, lack of funds prevented Auguste from completing his education. At age 18 he went to England to teach French and art at a private London college, the Shakespeare Academy House, before returning home to complete his education. He then settled in as a teacher at a local college, but spent his spare time dabbling in popular journalism. In 1842, he received an interesting assignment. An artist named Nestor L' Hôte had accompanied hieroglyph expert Jean François Champollion on his triumphant expedition to Egypt in 1828, then died on a subsequent desert journey, leaving a mass of papers and notes behind him. L'Hôte's father asked Mariette to organize and publish the papers. Mariette was electrified by the fascinating world that opened up before him. Soon he was spending every moment of his spare time on hieroglyphs. Impulsively, he resigned his teaching position and moved to Paris, where he eventually found a minor job at the Louvre Museum cataloging manuscripts. Egyptologist Charles Lenormant of the museum was so impressed with Mariette's hard work that he organized a project for him to collect rare Coptic manuscripts from Christian monasteries in Egypt.

Mariette sailed for Egypt in 1850, but soon found that the monasteries were bitterly opposed to foreign collectors. Instead, his thoughts turned toward excavation. By late 1850 he was camped in the midst of the ancient cemeteries at Saqqara near Memphis, where he had located the head of a sphinx projecting from the sand. His wide reading in earlier years now paid off. He remembered that the Greek geographer Strabo had referred to a temple to the bull god Apis at Memphis dating to the 6th and 7th centuries BC. Strabo described an avenue of sphinxes that were constantly being buried by drifting sand. With almost no money and no official permit, Mariette recruited 30 workers and uncovered the avenue, two temples of the god Apis, and a huge cache of bronze statues of Osiris, the god of the dead, and other ancient Egyptian gods under one of the temple floors. In November 1852, he finally reached the tomb of Apis, sealed by a fine sandstone door. Huge granite sarcophagi of

> *"It behooves us to preserve Egypt's monuments with care. Five hundred years hence Egypt should still be able to show to the scholars who shall visit her the same monuments we are now describing."*
>
> —Auguste Mariette, *Voyage dans le Haute Egypte* (Travels in Upper Egypt, 1877)

sacrificial bulls lay inside, all looted in antiquity. He was lucky enough to find one undisturbed bull burial, complete with both the bull mummy and rich jewelry and gold, which caused a sensation when exhibited at the Louvre. The find brought Mariette considerable fame. He was promoted to Assistant Keeper at the Louvre on the strength of his discovery.

Auguste Mariette was a restless man who found great delight in archaeology. At Saqqara, he lived in a mud house surrounded by women, children, pet monkeys, and his laborers. He developed a powerful ambition to save Egypt's monuments from the epidemic of looting that besieged them. Among his admirers was Ferdinand de Lesseps, the French diplomat and entrepreneur responsible for building the Suez Canal. In 1857 de Lesseps persuaded the Pasha of Egypt to send for Mariette on the occasion of the visit of Prince Napoleon of France to the Nile. It was only when Mariette arrived that he discovered that he was supposed to dig for fine antiquities to be presented to the royal visitor. Mariette did not hesitate for a moment and started digging at Saqqara and Luxor with excellent results. The royal visit was canceled, so de Lesseps persuaded the Pasha to appoint Mariette to a new post as Director of Ancient Monuments for Egypt and curator of a new museum of antiquities to be built in Cairo.

The appointment was bitterly opposed by dealers and diplomats, who were prospering off illegal excavations. Mariette started a vigorous excavation campaign immediately, on the grounds that it was better that sites be excavated officially than by treasure hunters. He commandeered the services of entire villages when needed. At one point he was excavating at 37 different locations in Egypt in a frenzied race with looters for fine antiquities. Mariette needed spectacular finds to fill his museum and to satisfy the ruler. He used dynamite to blast into rock-cut tombs and cared little about recording the positions of artifacts or architectural details. His excavators cleared more than 300 tombs near the pyramids of Giza and at Saqqara alone. At Edfu in Upper Egypt, he moved an entire village built on the roof of the buried temple and exposed this magnificent shrine to full view for the first time in centuries. His men cleared the buried temple of Queen Hatshepsut across the Nile from Luxor, excavated much of the great temple of the sun god Amun at Karnak, also at Luxor, and carried off boatloads of statuary and small artifacts.

Mariette cared little about conservation and combated illegal digging by forbidding any unauthorized excavation and making it almost impossible to export any antiquities from the country. He worked under difficult conditions. The Pasha cared little about archaeology and had appointed Mariette to his post to appease the powerful de Lesseps and his wealthy backers. Mariette needed funds for his museum, which was housed in an abandoned mosque. The only way he could satisfy the Pasha

Auguste Mariette

BORN

February 11, 1821
Boulogne, France

DIED

January 18, 1881
Cairo, Egypt

EDUCATION

College of Boulogne, France

ACCOMPLISHMENTS

First professional Egyptologist in Egypt, did much to preserve ancient Egypt for posterity; discovered the temple of the bull god Apis and the Serapium temple, Saqqara; cleared and excavated numerous temples and tombs, including the temple of Queen Hatshepsut near Luxor; founded the Cairo Museum and built the core of its collections by excavation. Wrote *Voyage dans le Haute Egypte* (Travels in Upper Egypt, 1877).

Years of arduous excavation and constant efforts to save Egypt's past wore Auguste Mariette down and broke his health. However, by the time of his death, his Cairo Museum was well established and many artifacts had been saved for posterity.

was with a steady stream of fine artifacts. But even then he had to guard against the Pasha casually making gifts of them to distinguished visitors. This, of course, meant that everything was subordinated to frantic digging, which did incalculable damage to unique, undisturbed archaeological sites.

Early in 1859 Mariette learned that the gold-decorated sarcophagus of Queen Aahotep, mother of the Middle Kingdom pharaoh Ahmose the Liberator, who ruled about 1540 BC, had been found intact at Luxor. He also learned that the local governor had seized the coffin, removed the jewelry, and sent it to the Pasha as a gift. Mariette promptly set out in a steamer with an official order to stop all loaded vessels on the river. Tempers flared when the two steamers met. In a fury, Mariette fought first with his fists and then held the skipper at gunpoint until the precious gold and jewelry were handed over. The Pasha was so pleased with the finds and, one suspects, at the discomfiture of his official, that he ordered a new museum built to house the queen's burial furniture.

Mariette's long career also involved him in diplomacy. He accompanied the Pasha on an official visit to France, where the ruler received a tumultuous welcome in Boulogne, a gesture that earned Mariette a pension and the honorific title of Bey. In 1867, he spent a year in Paris setting up the Egyptian exhibit at the International Exhibition of that year. The Cairo museum was searched for its finest treasures. Queen Aahotep's jewelry was the sensation of France. None other than the Empress Eugénie admired the jewels. She graciously intimated to the Pasha that she would be pleased to receive the finds as a gift. It was a great moment for Egyptology when the Pasha hesitated. He told the empress that she would have

to receive Mariette's permission. Neither threats nor bribery could move Mariette, not even the displeasure of an empress or the Pasha. The jewelry returned safely to Egypt.

Archaeologist and part-time diplomat, Mariette was rarely idle. He wrestled with a growing influx of tourists to Egypt, many of them with souvenir hunting on their minds. He employed more than 2,800 laborers during his career in a frantic race to find artifacts for his museum before it was too late, setting up workshops at towns along the Nile to handle new finds, an innovation far ahead of his time. He was deeply involved in the glittering ceremonies that marked the opening of the Suez Canal, on November 17, 1869, when he had the quiet satisfaction of escorting the Empress Eugénie to Egypt's finest archaeological sites. The Pasha even commissioned him to write the libretto with an ancient Egyptian theme for Verdi's opera *Aïda*, which opened at the Cairo Opera House to celebrate the inauguration of the canal.

Mariette's last years were marked by tragedy. His wife and children died one by one, leaving him little to live for. A flood at the museum destroyed many of his notes and records. He became "aged rather than old like the colossi over which he watches," wrote a French nobleman in 1872. His health failed and he died peacefully in his house by his beloved museum in 1881. He was buried at the door of the museum after a state funeral that attracted tributes from around the world.

FURTHER READING

Fagan, Brian M. *The Rape of the Nile*. New York: Scribners, 1975.

Reeves, Nicholas. *Ancient Egypt: The Great Discoveries*. London: Thames and Hudson, 2000.

Charles Warren

EXCAVATOR OF BIBLICAL JERUSALEM

Captain Charles Warren (1840-1927), an army engineer, became an archaeologist by accident. He tunneled under Jerusalem and revealed traces of the Biblical city, becoming one of the founders of Biblical archaeology.

Charles Warren was an archaeologist who worked almost entirely underground. His work took him into the honeycomb of water channels and reservoirs that lay under the city of Jerusalem in his day. He suffered showers of stones thrown down on him by outraged Islamic worshippers, but found traces of the biblical city at a time when many people believed in the historical truth of the Scriptures.

Warren was born in England in 1840, the son of an army general. At an early age, Charles decided to follow his father into the army. He attended the Royal Academy at Woolwich, at the time a major military school for boys where the discipline was rigorous. The young Warren learned persistence and determination from his years at the academy, qualities that were to serve him well in later years. He was commissioned a lieutenant in the Royal Engineers in 1857 and spent seven years in Gibraltar, surveying for potential defense works and constructing artillery batteries. Gibraltar, then as now, was a strategic fortress at the mouth of the Mediterranean Sea. Warren's years with the garrison there gave him superb practical experience in tunneling and accurate surveying, essential qualities for anyone planning to excavate Jerusalem.

Not that Warren had any ambitions to become an archaeologist. He was posted to Jerusalem in 1864 to survey its topography and water supplies. Most of his work was belowground, where he explored a maze of cisterns and channels that lay beneath the modern city. His men made important archaeological finds during their surveys. Along the eastern wall, they uncovered a monumental Roman arch that once formed the entrance to biblical King Herod's palace. The temple, rebuilt on the ruins of an earlier temple by King Herod in the 1st century BC, had been demolished by the Romans in A.D. 70. Part of its wall survived and eventually became the Western, or Wailing Wall, one of Judaism's most sacred sites.

Warren's archaeological discoveries astounded and delighted his countrymen. In 1865, a public meeting in London launched the Palestine Exploration Fund, with Queen Victoria as its official patron. Its objective was to find traces of events and people mentioned in the Scriptures. Two years later the fund sent Warren and another detachment of Royal Engineers to Jerusalem with instructions to excavate under the Haram esh Sharif, a walled compound that housed some of Islam's most sacred shrines.

The adventurous 27-year-old Warren was an ideal choice for the job. In February 1867, he landed in the Turkish port of Jaffa, in what was then Palestine, accompanied by two

Lieutenant Charles Warren (left) poses with Joseph Barclay of the London Jews Missionary Society (center) and his chief enlisted man, Corporal Henry Phillips (right), in Jerusalem in August 1867. A traveler, F. A. Eaton, attracted to the Holy Land by adventure and hunting, lies in the foreground. A local guide can be seen in the background.

noncommissioned officers. His troubles began at once. The Turkish customs officials at the port confiscated his sextant, an instrument for finding one's location on the earth by taking readings of the sun and other heavenly bodies. They were convinced that it was a dangerous weapon. After recovering this vital piece of equipment, Warren set off inland. The weather was terrible, and he and his men had to travel to Jerusalem by mule along rough, wind-buffeted paths. He then spent months in Jerusalem waiting for an official excavation permit from the Sultan of Turkey in Constantinople.

Warren did not waste the time spent in waiting. He cultivated local officials and paid visits to local religious leaders and desert sheikhs, even spending time among some Bedouin goat herders notorious for their violence and thievery. Warren was soon well versed in the intricacies of local politics and religious rivalries, which was just as

well. The sultan's Muslim advisers were very nervous about Warren's plan. They denied him permission to dig, for they felt that any attempt to prove the historical truth of the Bible was subversive. His *firman* (permit) allowed him to work only outside the city walls, useless permission because the all-important archaeological layers lay under the temple mound.

Warren was in a difficult position. In Jerusalem he was dealing with corrupt and suspicious officials who were amenable to bribes. In London the Palestine Exploration Fund was pressing him for results. Warren asked for more money for bribes. The fund refused. So he took matters into his own hands, placed some judicious bribes with the money he had, and started to dig shafts downward, then toward the Haram from 150 feet (46 meters) outside the city walls. His men smashed through a blocked passageway alongside the Haram walls and so outraged worshipers in the mosque above that they showered the diggers with stones. The governor promptly forbade Warren's excavating on any official land, or closer than 40 feet (12 meters) from the Haram.

The young officer was not stymied for long. He leased private lots well away from the Haram, sunk vertical shafts to bedrock, and tunneled toward the shrines. He found that the 80-foot (24-meter) high walls of the Haram extended more than 100 feet (30 meters) below the surface. Warren became increasingly clever at bribery. On one occasion he seized his large green pet lizard and threw it on hot coals. A greedy official slavered over this fine delicacy. Licking his lips, he gave permission for work to proceed.

Warren and his corporals were expert tunnel diggers, but nothing prepared them for the hazardous task that lay ahead of them. Loose boulders

> "The strain on the nerves during this work was intense, and required of the men the greatest amount of fortitude and self-control; again and again they would entirely lose all power of restraining the involuntary movement of the muscles, so that their limbs refused to obey them."

> —Charles Warren, *Underground Jerusalem* (1876)

Charles Warren

BORN
February 17, 1840
London, England

DIED
January 21, 1927
London, England

EDUCATION
Woolwich Academy of the Royal Engineers (commissioned lieutenant, 1857)

ACCOMPLISHMENTS
First person to investigate the holy city of Jerusalem; made the first map of the walls of ancient Jerusalem and found important evidence of the Roman city. Wrote *Underground Jerusalem* (1876); *The Survey of Western Palestine* (1885).

and thick dust hampered progress. On one occasion their tools were buried by a sudden cave-in. They shored up the damage and continued. The tunnel now headed under the city walls and eventually reached a long buried wall, inscribed with the initials of the original builder. Warren sank 27 shafts and traced the northern and southern limits of the old city, following the walls of Jerusalem far underground. He and his colleague Sergeant Birtles made meticulous plans and drawings. They crawled through long-buried passages and down murky shafts as they mapped the topography of the biblical Jerusalem. Their discoveries included a shaft that once transported water to the ancient city, today known as Warren's Shaft. On another occasion they broke into a slippery, rock-cut passage leading to the center of the Temple Mount, 5 to 6 feet (1.5 meters) deep and filled with raw sewage. The diggers were hampered by constant money shortages, uncooperative officials, tunnel cave-ins, and the constant threat of malaria. Warren himself fell ill of malaria several times, and a corporal died of the disease.

When the sultan finally prohibited any further excavation, in 1870, Warren returned home to write *Underground Jerusalem* and *Tent Work in Palestine*, which described his work for a popular audience and were received with critical acclaim. His academic monograph, *The Survey of Western Palestine*, appeared in eight volumes in 1885 and is still useful today.

Charles Warren never returned to Jerusalem. He surveyed the borders of the territory of Griqualand West in South Africa from 1876 to 1882, settled tribal disputes in Bechuanaland, and commanded troops in the same general region. After a distinguished military career, he became Commissioner of Police at Scotland Yard in London, during the period of the Jack the Ripper murders. After Scotland Yard, he served as an administrator in Singapore for five years. In old age he became a controversial figure, much concerned with social reform. He once suggested that cities should let wolves run loose to keep children alert, and he engaged in intricate mathematical calculations that attempted, and failed, to explain the orbits of the planets. He died in 1927 at the age of 86.

Warren's Jerusalem discoveries provided the first framework for biblical archaeology. A century was to pass before anyone reinvestigated the city's ancient walls.

FURTHER READING

Kenyon, Kathleen. *Digging Up Jerusalem.* New York: Praeger, 1974.

Silberman, Neil A. *Digging for God and Country: Exploration, Archaeology, and the Secret Struggle for the Holy Land.* New York: Knopf, 1982.

Heinrich Schliemann

DISCOVERER OF TROY

Heinrich Schliemann rose from rags to riches, then indulged his fascination with the historical truth of the *Iliad* and its stories of the Trojan War. His obsession led him to excavate the ancient city of Troy and to make archaeological discoveries so spectacular that an international audience followed his work.

Born in 1822, the son of a Protestant minister in rural north Germany, Schliemann was strongly influenced by his father's interest in the classics, especially in the Greek writer Homer's *Iliad*, which told the story of the 10-year war between the Greeks under King Agamemnon and the city of Troy. The war ended in a Greek victory and Troy was totally destroyed. In later years Heinrich Schliemann embroidered his early life with elaborate fictions, but his

Heinrich Schliemann, dressed in Turkish costume, around 1858. Like other pioneer excavators and travelers in Greece and Turkey, Schliemann wore Turkish dress to blend in, and because it appealed to his romantic nature.

interest in Homer and Troy seems to have begun in boyhood.

Schliemann's family was so poor that his education finished at age 14, when he was apprenticed to a grocer. A chest infection threw him out of work in 1841, so he moved to Hamburg with the intention of emigrating to Venezuela. His ship was wrecked off Holland, but he survived to obtain a job as a shop clerk in Amsterdam. With the single-minded intensity that marked the rest of his life, Schliemann set out to educate himself. He learned to write properly, then mastered English and French in a year, helped by his exceptional memory. He quickly acquired four more European languages, displaying such a remarkable aptitude for foreign tongues that he got a job with the Schroeder brothers, Amsterdam merchants with major interests in the Russian indigo (dye) trade.

Schliemann hired a tutor to teach him Russian, which he learned so quickly and well that the Schroeders sent him to St. Petersburg as their local agent in 1846. He was so successful that he set up in business as an indigo merchant on his own, soon acquiring considerable wealth thanks to his aptitude for wheeling and dealing in many languages. In 1850 the ever-restless Schliemann set off for California. He set up a banking agency in Sacramento and made a fortune during the Gold Rush. Two years later he returned to St. Petersburg, married, and had three children, all the while making another fortune supplying war materials to the Russian army during the Crimean War. While making money, he never lost his interest in Homer. He learned classical and modern Greek. In 1863, at age 43, he abruptly retired from business to devote himself to Homer and a search for the archaeological site of Homeric Troy.

Schliemann took his time. He went on an extensive world tour, then studied archaeology in Paris before visiting Greece for the first time in 1868. At the time, most scholars thought that Homer's Troy was a mythical city. Schliemann was convinced the *Iliad* was the historical truth, so he set out to the plains at the mouth of the Dardanelles in northwestern Turkey, where Troy was said to lie. He came to a hill named Hissarlik 3 miles (4.8 kilometers) from the coast, where he met the American vice-consul Frank Calvert, who owned half a large city mound on the hill. Calvert had dug into the mound and declared it was Troy, but it was Schliemann who would take the credit for identifying the Homeric metropolis.

In 1871, Schliemann married his second wife, Sophia Engastromenos, a 17-year-old Greek girl, in what may been a marriage of convenience but evolved into an enduring relationship. In October of that year, the Schliemanns set 80 workers trenching into the Hissarlik mound. Six weeks later, a 33-foot (10-meter) trench revealed stone walls of a long-buried city. The following spring, between 100 and 150 men set to work under the supervision of engineers who had worked on the digging of Egypt's Suez Canal. Schliemann reached bedrock at 45 feet (14 meters), digging through layer after layer of human occupation with frenzied haste. He claimed the third city from the bottom was Homer's Troy, largely because the strata showed signs of burning.

At this stage, no one could call Schliemann an archaeologist. His methods were drastic and brutally direct. In mid-1873, the Schliemanns made their most controversial discovery: a collection of magnificent gold artifacts and ornaments in the deposits of the third city. According to the Schliemanns, they gave the workers the day off while they secretly gathered up the glittering finds of the "treasure" in Sophia's shawl. Scholars still argue over the Schliemann treasure: Was it a

Heinrich Schliemann

BORN
January 6, 1822
Neu Buckow, Germany

DIED
December 25, 1890
Naples, Italy

EDUCATION
Self-educated

ACCOMPLISHMENTS
Excavated and identified Homeric Troy, although not the first to do so; discovered the Shaft Graves at Mycenae, now known to be burials of Mycenaean Bronze Age chieftains; interested an enormous public audience in archaeology for the first time. Wrote *Ilios* (1873); *Troy and Its Remains* (1875); *Mycenae* (1878).

"I struck upon a large copper article of the most remarkable form, which attracted my attention all the more as I thought I saw gold behind it."

—Heinrich Schliemann, *Ilios* (1873)

hoard of gold artifacts buried in a time of peril long ago, or did the Schliemanns gather together isolated gold objects from many levels and "package" them to create a truly sensational find? Modern scholars are still doubtful about the treasure claim.

Heinrich Schliemann was a brilliant self-publicist. He wrote and lectured about his excavations so convincingly that no one questioned the facts. There is reason to believe that he even fabricated details of his early life. Controversy has dogged his finds since the 1870s. His golden treasure ended up in the Berlin Museum and vanished during World War II, only to reappear in Russia at the end of the Cold War, years after it was assumed to have been destroyed in an air raid.

Schliemann now turned his restless attention to another Homeric site— King Agamemnon's citadel at Mycenae in southern Greece. The excavations began with three teams of 63 men digging trenches around the entrance, the Lion Gate, and in an open area just inside the entrance. A circle of tombstones bearing engravings of charioteers came to light, then five graves containing 15 skeletons literally smothered in gold. Several of the skeletons wore gold death masks with clipped beards and mustaches. Fine headdresses, seals, and pottery lay with the burials. Schliemann was in his element, claiming in telegrams to the world's newspapers that he had found the tomb of Agamemnon himself. Two ruling monarchs and the Prime Minister of Britain were kept informed of the excavations. Today, we know that Schliemann discovered the glories of the Mycenaean civilization of Bronze Age Greece, which flourished in the late second millennium BC.

In 1878 Schliemann returned to Hissarlik. This time he took well-qualified archaeologists with him. German Wilhelm Dorpfeld was trained in the newest methods and worked with Schliemann at Hissarlik from 1888 to 1890. He was a highly trained observer, an expert on stratified city sites and small artifacts, who helped Schliemann identify the sixth, not the third, city as the Homeric settlement.

By this time, Heinrich Schliemann had become a respected archaeologist. But he remains today somewhat of an enigma, on the one hand a near-megalomaniac and ruthless myth maker, and on the other, by all accounts, a kindly and thoughtful man. Schliemann was planning a new large-scale excavation on the sixth city at Hissarlik when he died suddenly of a ear infection in Naples on Christmas Day, 1890. With his passing, the heroic age of archaeological discovery ended, as a new generation of trained archaeologists began work in Mediterranean lands.

FURTHER READING

Poole, L., and G. Poole. *One Passion: Two Lives: The Schliemanns of Troy.* New York: Random House, 1966.

Taylour, Lord William. *The Mycenaeans.* London: Thames and Hudson, 1990.

Traill, David A. *Schliemann of Troy: Treasure and Deceit.* New York: St. Martin's, 1995.

More Archaeologists to Remember

Bernardino Drovetti (1776–1852) achieved notoriety as French Consul General in Egypt from 1820 to 1829, when he aggressively collected ancient Egyptian antiquities. Unscrupulous and not afraid to use force, Drovetti accumulated huge collections of mummies, papyri, and statuaries, which he sold to European monarchs and museums. His greatest find was the so-called Turin Canon of Kings, one of the few papyri that records a list of ancient Egyptian kings. Drovetti's collections ended up in Berlin and Turin museums and the Louvre, but his methods were brutal and he did much damage to his finds. He was Giovanni Belzoni's major rival.

Jean François Champollion (1790–1832) gained scientific immortality for his decipherment of Egyptian hieroglyphs in 1822. A brilliant linguist, Champollion worked for years on the problem, using the signs for royalty and the trilingual Rosetta Stone, found in northern Egypt by one of Napoleon's officers in 1799. Years passed before his decipherment was fully accepted. He led a successful expedition to Egypt in 1828 and 1829, when he and his companions were able to read the temple inscriptions for the first time. Champollion was a meticulous observer with a broad interest in Egyptology. He died at an early age of a stroke.

Frederick Catherwood (1799–1854) was an Englishman who studied to be an architect and instead became an acclaimed artist. He traveled widely in Egypt and the Holy Land, but achieved international fame for his drawings and paintings of Maya sites and hieroglyphs executed when traveling in Central America with John Lloyd Stephens in the early 1840s. Some of his drawings rival photographs in their accurate portrayals of Maya inscriptions.

John Gardner Wilkinson (1797–1875) achieved fame as the author of *Manners and Customs of the Ancient Egyptians* (1835), the first popular book on ancient Egyptian civilization based on the decipherment of temple and tomb inscriptions and papyri. He was one of the most important Egyptologists of the 19th century. Wilkinson lived in Egypt from 1821 to 1833, spending most of his time copying inscriptions. He made several other survey trips to the Nile and completed the first systematic plan of ancient Thebes. His research on the chronology of Egyptian kings included an account of the Turin Canon.

Samuel Haven (1806–81) was a lawyer who became Secretary of the American Antiquarian Society in 1838, a post he held for the rest of his life. Haven published one of the classic works of American archaeology in 1856, *Archaeology of the United States*, which surveyed what was known

Amelia Edwards, a successful novelist, was one of the founders of the Egypt Exploration Society. Her visit to the Nile in 1873 alerted her to the destruction of ancient Egypt on every side. She spent the rest of her life fighting for Egypt's past and to protect those few temples showing "no sign of ruin or age."

about the first human settlement of the Americas. Haven dismissed much of the writing about the mound builders of North America as pure speculation. He believed the mysterious earthworks were constructed by Native Americans, an unusual conclusion at a time when most people believed foreign builders were responsible.

Karl Richard Lepsius (1810–84) was one of the most distinguished Egyptologists of the 19th century. He led the Prussian expedition to Egypt and Nubia in 1842 through 1845, the most elaborate such venture of the day. Lepsius acquired a huge collection of Egyptian antiquities and completed important surveys of major sites at the same time. He was also one of the scholars instrumental in the acceptance of Champollion's decipherment of hieroglyphs.

Ernst Curtius (1814–96), professor of classical philology and archaeology at Göttinger University acquired an international reputation for his excavations at Olympia from 1875 to 1881, the ancient site of the Olympic Games in Greece. The excavations were conducted scientifically, with an architect present. Curtius even built a site museum and paid careful attention to conservation of the ruins. His researches were a model for later classical excavations elsewhere in Greece.

Paul Emile Botta (1822–70) was appointed French vice-consul in the town of Mosul on the Tigris River in what is modern-day Iraq, in 1842. He excavated in the mounds of biblical Nineveh across the river, making few finds. But excavations at nearby Khorsabad between 1843 and 1845 yielded magnificent reliefs and the palace of an Assyrian monarch. The

discovery caused a sensation, with Botta claiming he had found ancient Nineveh. In fact, he had unearthed the palace of the Assyrian monarch Sargon, built in about 710 BC. With Austen Henry Layard, Botta was one of the discoverers of Assyrian civilization.

Ephraim Squier (1821–88) began his career as a journalist. In the mid-1840s he collaborated with physician Edwin Davis on an archaeological survey of the ancient mounds and earthworks of the Midwest. Their *Ancient Monuments of the Mississippi Valley*, published by the Smithsonian Institution in 1847, was the first systematic description of mound-builder sites. Many of the earthworks described by Squier and Davis have now vanished. Squier served as U.S. Commissioner to Peru from 1863 to 1865. He was one of the first outsiders to report on Inca architecture and archaeological sites.

Cyrus Thomas (1825–1910) was a man of diverse skills who worked for a while as a botanist before heading the Smithsonian Institution's mound-builder excavations from 1881 to 1910. The project found Thomas excavating and surveying Native American earthworks all over the central and eastern United States. His *Report on the Mound Explorations of the Bureau of Ethnology*, published in 1894, proved conclusively that the mounds were built by ancient Native Americans.

Hormuzd Rassam (1826–1910) was born in Mosul, in present-day northern Iraq, to a Christian family. He became Austen Henry Layard's assistant at the Assyrian city of Nimrud in 1845. After Layard's departure, Rassam worked independently at Nineveh, where he found magnificent wall reliefs of a royal lion hunt. He also excavated at Assur, the early capital of the Assyrians on the Tigris River. After a period as an interpreter in Aden and a mission to Ethiopia, he again excavated at Nineveh and also in southern Iraq, where he found many cuneiform tablets.

Amelia Edwards (1831–92) was an English novelist who visited Egypt and Syria in 1873 to 1877. Thereafter she published *A Thousand Miles up the Nile* (1877), an account not only of Egyptian sites but of the looting and destruction under way at many sites. Edwards devoted the rest of her life to lecturing and writing about Egypt. She was one of the founders of the Egypt Exploration Society, in 1882. Amelia Edwards left money in her will to found the first Professorship of Egyptology at the University of London. Flinders Petrie (see Part 3) held the post for more than 40 years.

Ernest de Sarzec (1836–1901) became French consul in Basra on the Persian Gulf in 1877. He learned from local antiquities dealers that large numbers of clay tablets were to be found in the dusty mounds of Telloh in the delta of the gulf. He dug large trenches into the mounds in 1877 and 1878, unearthing not only cuneiform tablets but statues of a ruler named Gudea, king of the city of Lagash. Sarzec discovered the Sumerian civilization, the earliest of all Mesopotamian civilizations. He continued to excavate at Telloh almost annually until 1900.

William H. Holmes (1846–1933) was an archaeologist and artist who based his studies of stone tools and prehistoric pottery on sound scientific principles, ushering in the work of later North American archaeologists. He was influential in showing that no Paleolithic (Old Stone Age) peoples settled in North America and that Native American settlement was relatively late, dating to about 4,000 years ago.

Hiram Bingham (1875–1956) was a historian who rediscovered the spectacular Inca city of Macchu Picchu high in the Andes, in July 1911. He was convinced that he had found the famed "last city of the Incas," the legendary Vilcabamba. A later trek into the jungle produced another Inca settlement, Espíritu Pampa. Bingham went on to become a U.S. senator and died in 1956 believing he had found the last city. Researches in the 1960s proved him wrong: Espíritu Pampa was the last Inca stronghold.

Ernest de Sarzec's excavations at Telloh in southern Iraq revealed the Sumerian civilization. This photograph, taken by de Sarzec himself, shows the mudbrick foundations of a Sumerian palace.

General Augustus Lane Fox Pitt-Rivers was a master excavator. This ditch at Worbarrow, England, shows his method of digging in shallow "spits," or artificial layers, which allowed him to record the position of every find, however insignificant.

3 The Birth of Scientific Archaeology

Scientific archaeology was born of the adventure and treasure hunting of 19th-century excavation. By the time novelist Amelia Edwards sailed up the Nile in 1873, new archaeological methods were slowly coming into use in the work of British and German archaeologists.

Prussian monarchs of Germany had long supported archaeology in the Near East, notably Egyptologist Richard Lepsius's expedition to the Nile in 1842 to 1845, which emphasized recording over artifact collection. Classical archaeologist Alexander Conze used much more rigorous excavations on the island of Samothrace in the Aegean in 1873 to 1875, with an architect on-site at all times. His student Ernst Curtius used the same scientific approach during his five years at Olympia between 1875 and 1880. His excavations emphasized stratigraphic (earth-layer) observations, the study of small objects, architecture, and conservation, and even included the building of a site museum. The German archaeologists ushered in an era of more scientific excavation in the eastern Mediterranean and classical lands.

Conze and Curtius were fathers of scientific excavation in the Mediterranean region. Simultaneously, English general Augustus Lane Fox Pitt-Rivers advocated highly scientific excavation in Britain at a time when most digs were little more than hurried searches for exciting finds. Pitt-Rivers was an advocate of total excavation of an entire site down to bedrock, of the recording of the position in time and space of every find, however insignificant, and of prompt, complete publication of information about every dig. Few archaeologists followed his example until another Englishman, Mortimer Wheeler, refined his excavation methods in the 1920s and revolutionized archaeological fieldwork in the process.

The Germans and Pitt-Rivers ushered in three quarters of a century of increasingly scientific archaeology, reflected not only in better excavation methods, but in a battery of new techniques, often from such disciplines as botany and biology. Fieldworkers moved away from a total fascination with large, attention-getting finds to more fine-grained approaches that concentrated as much on small, humble objects like pot fragments (potsherds) as they did on palaces and royal burials.

IN THIS PART

AUGUSTUS LANE FOX PITT-RIVERS

WILLIAM MATTHEW FLINDERS PETRIE

GERTRUDE BELL

HENRI BREUIL

HOWARD CARTER

ARTHUR JOHN EVANS

HARRIET BOYD HAWES

ALFRED VINCENT KIDDER

OSCAR MONTELIUS

SYLVANUS GRISWOLD MORLEY

AUREL STEIN

LEONARD WOOLLEY

VERE GORDON CHILDE

The British Egyptologist Flinders Petrie was a pioneer in pottery analysis and accurate surveying. He began his career when he made the first accurate survey of the pyramids of Giza, then moved on to large-scale excavations on pyramids, burials, and town sites throughout Egypt. Petrie insisted on the importance of the small object. He was the first to identify imported clay vessels from Crete and Greece in Egyptian sites, which allowed him to cross-date sites and cultures on the other side of the Mediterranean. When he excavated large cemeteries dating to before the time of the pharaohs, he developed a method of placing each grave in chronological order, using style changes in clay jars for the purpose.

Petrie's aims and concerns were admirable, but his methods often were far from modern standards, as were those of Arthur Evans, who excavated the Palace of Knossos on northern Crete in 1900. Evans had no formal training in excavation. Like Petrie, he was self-taught and used crude methods compared with those of his modern successors. He revealed the long-forgotten Minoan civilization by excavating room after room of the Palace of Minos, using dozens of workers to do so. Inevitably, much valuable information was lost, but one can argue that today's detailed knowledge of the Minoans results in large part from Evans's pioneering work.

Until 1900, archaeology was almost exclusively a male pursuit, a close-knit club of well-educated gentlemen, all of whom knew one another. Excavation was not considered suitable for ladies, who were, however, permitted to work on artifacts and art in the laboratory. Desert traveler Gertrude Bell was one of the first to break the male barrier. Self-taught and an expert traveler in Arab lands, Bell never excavated on her own account, but carried out pioneer archaeological surveys at a variety of sites in desert environments. After World War I she founded the Iraq Museum and devised antiquities laws to protect the country's cultural heritage from wholesale export and destruction. Gertrude Bell was a strong personality who had no patience for those with slow minds or set ways. Even powerful government servants were afraid to stand in her way. At the same time, she developed close ties with desert chieftains, who trusted her completely—a vital political asset in early Iraq.

Other women started work at about the same time. Notable among them was the American Harriet Hawes, who went out to work on mainland Greece with a classical archaeology scholarship, but was not allowed by her supervisors to go into the field. Arthur Evans encouraged her to excavate in Crete, where she found the Minoan town at Gournia. Like Bell, Hawes got on very well with her workers. But her researches were almost forgotten until the 1990s, when her daughter wrote her biography.

Flinders Petrie also encouraged women in the field, despite the notoriously tough conditions in his excavation camps. Gertrude Caton-Thompson was one of his later students (see Part 4). She was remarkable for her interest in stone artifacts and Stone Age sites rather than ancient Egyptian civilization. Petrie left her alone, for he believed that training was best gained from practical experience on one's own. The experiment was a success. Caton-Thompson went on to find some of the earliest farming settlements in the world west of the Nile, and unraveled the mysteries of ruins at Great Zimbabwe in southern Africa, in 1929. She became one of the most respected Stone Age archaeologists of her time.

The early years of the 20th century were still a time of spectacular discoveries. The year 1922 saw the finding of pharaoh Tutankhamun's tomb by Howard Carter and his sponsor, Lord Carnarvon. Sir Leonard Woolley excavated the biblical city of Ur in southern Iraq with its dramatic royal cemeteries. Woolley was one of the last excavators to work with small armies of laborers. It is said that he employed a

Euphrates River boatman to sing rowing songs to keep the work pace steady whenever his laborers were shifting large amounts of earth.

American archaeology also made remarkable advances during the early 20th century. Alfred Kidder excavated Pecos Pueblo in the North American southwest, and revolutionized the study of ancient Native Americans by working from the present back into the remote past. At the same time, the astronomer A. E. Douglass invented tree-ring dating, a method of determining the age of ancient pueblo beams by using the concentric tree-rings in them, which were compared with the rings in trees still growing in the same area. The result was an accurate time scale for the ancestral pueblo cultures of the Southwest and dates for Pueblo Bonito, the Cliff Palace at Mesa Verde, and other major pueblo sites.

In the eastern United States, the haphazard excavations of Cyrus Thomas and others gave way to more precise fieldwork, which culminated in a series of large-scale river valley archaeological surveys in the 1930s, carried out in advance of dam construction. Fieldworkers like Gordon Willey and James Ford developed sequences of ancient Native American cultures for enormous areas of eastern and midwestern North America, where little had been known before.

Knowledge of the Maya civilization expanded dramatically, in large part because of the work of Alfred Maudslay and Sylvanus Morley. Of the two, Maudslay was probably the more adept and accurate in his recording, but both of them copied and recorded a remarkable body of Maya inscriptions, which helped later generations of scholars decipher the intricate Maya script.

Archaeological research was begun in many far-flung parts of the world in the first half of the 20th century, notably in China and southern Africa, as well as Peru and other parts of South America. Sir Aurel Stein was one of the few scholars and travelers who explored the hitherto unknown archaeology of Central Asia. He also investigated parts of the ancient Silk Road that linked China with the West. Much archaeology was still concentrated on cultures in the early recorded history of the classical and Mediterranean lands, Europe, and North America. Only a handful of scholars took a broader view of the prehistoric world. One of them was the Danish scholar Oscar Montelius, who developed some of the first classifications of later European prehistoric societies and linked them to the Mediterranean world. Another was French prehistorian Henri Breuil, the world's first expert on prehistoric art and a master classifier of stone tools.

Oscar Montelius died in 1921 just as a young archaeologist named Vere Gordon Childe began his lifelong study of the European past. Childe was a gifted linguist and a remarkable summarizer of archaeological data, whose encyclopedic knowledge of artifacts and archaeological sites enabled him to write about ancient times on a grand scale. In a series of widely read books, Childe wrote the prehistory of Europe in flowing narratives. He used artifacts and human cultures instead of kings and statesmen as the characters. For example, the first farmers who spread into Europe from the southeast along the Danube River became the Danubians, an agricultural society found from the Balkans to the Netherlands. He painted a picture of a continent that received ideas from the Near East, including agriculture and urban civilization. These great revolutions in human experience were defining points in the past that helped shape Europe long before Julius Caesar conquered Gaul in 55 BC.

Gordon Childe's ideas helped move archaeology from a narrow focus on artifacts and time scales to a much broader perspective, one that looked at the prehistoric past on a truly global canvas. New generations of archaeologists expanded on and refined his pioneering ideas after World War II.

Augustus Lane Fox Pitt-Rivers

FOUNDER OF MODERN
ARCHAEOLOGICAL
EXCAVATION

General Augustus Henry Lane Fox Pitt-Rivers, a world authority on ancient firearms, pioneered scientific archaeological excavation at a time when most digs were little more than hurried treasure hunts. He was a harsh disciplinarian who applied to his excavations a kind of military rigor that was unique in the 19th century.

Born Augustus Henry Lane Fox on 1827, he was the second son of an aristocratic family of modest circumstances. His noble birth assured him a position in a military school at age 13, but not much is known of his schooling or early aspirations. He was commissioned into a highly regarded infantry regiment, the Grenadier Guards, in 1845. The appointment required considerable private money to maintain the lifestyle considered fitting for an officer and gentleman, and that was assured by the death of his elder brother in 1852. The young officer developed a passion for guns and muskets. In 1854 he wrote a handbook on firearms for the British army titled *Instruction of Musketry*, which remained a standard work for

Augustus Lane Fox Pitt-Rivers was a revolutionary archaeologist. Unlike many of his contemporaries who focused on retrieving beautiful treasures, Pitt-Rivers stressed the importance of total excavation, accurate recording of layers and features, and recovering all objects no matter how small.

many years. His professional specialty also became a hobby, for he started a collection of antique firearms that formed the basis for his lifetime interest in the evolution of weapons of all kinds.

The publication of Charles Darwin's *Origin of Species* in 1859 was a turning point in Fox's intellectual life. He claimed in later life that he had "known" natural selection intuitively before *Origin* appeared, but this seems unlikely. He was soon arguing that the same rules of evolution and natural selection applied to human-made artifacts such as weapons, a controversial viewpoint for a military man. In 1862, now Lieutenant Colonel Lane Fox was appointed Assistant Quartermaster General in Cork, Ireland, a post that involved considerable travel and gave the impetus for his first excursions into archaeology. Many of his duties involved surveying the surrounding countryside, where he observed that many ancient raths (earthen enclosures) marked on previous maps had vanished. He started documenting vanished sites threatened by imminent destruction and collected artifacts such as bronze brooches, clay vessels, and daggers during his surveys.

Lane Fox's first foray into excavation came when he was transferred back to London. He investigated a construction site close to London's Roman wall, where the workers had found cartloads of ancient bones. He visited the site daily for two months and documented the layers of gravel and the marshy soil called peat at the site. This was his first experience at observing complex occupation layers, a method that was to become a vital part of his later excavations. He deplored the enormous numbers of fossil bones that were carted away. He wrote: "The vestiges are in a daily process of destruction at our own doors who are ignorant of their meaning and of the importance that attaches to them." In 1867 he went on half pay from the army and

devoted himself full time to archaeology and ancient weapons. He excavated the Cissbury Hill Iron Age fort in Sussex in southeastern England that year. He acquired numerous flint arrowheads for his collections, but otherwise found the dig unsatisfying. At the time he had little experience of the complex layering of such sites, which meant that he confused different building stages and occupation levels.

After several years of minor excavations, where he improved his excavation skills, Fox returned in 1875 to Cissbury, where he approached the site and neighboring locations with meticulous care. He now dug "sections," trenches cut at right angles across earthworks down to solid chalk, and recorded the exact position of small artifacts and stratified layers. To Fox, archaeology had become not a treasure hunt but a search for historical information, using the layers of a site to reconstruct its history. During three years of excavations, he investigated Stone Age flint mines, more hill forts, and even part of a Norman castle, laying the foundations for his later, much larger scale work.

A series of family deaths made Fox the sole and unexpected heir of his uncle's immense fortune and the extensive Cranborne Chase estates in southern England. He inherited the estate in 1880, took the family name Pitt-Rivers, and became master of 27,700 acres (11,220 hectares) with an income of £27,000 a year, several million dollars in today's money. Pitt-Rivers retired from the army and devoted the rest of his life to digging sites on his extensive properties. He revolutionized archaeological excavation in the process. In 1882 the British government appointed him Inspector of Ancient Monuments, a post that kept him in touch with the leading archaeologists of the day.

The huge estate he had inherited was a rural landscape, a great tract of medieval hunting country that had

Augustus Lane Fox Pitt-Rivers

BORN

April 14, 1827
London, England

DIED

May 4, 1900
Salisbury, Wiltshire, England

EDUCATION

Private

ACCOMPLISHMENTS

Well-known collector of firearms, student of cultural evolution, archaeologist; surveyed archaeological sites in Ireland, excavated Cissbury Hill fort in southern England; after 1880, made innovative excavations at Cranborne Chase that revolutionized archaeological methods. Wrote *Instruction of Musketry* (1854); *Excavations in Cranborne Chase* (1887–98).

The photograph shows the early stages of the Worbarrow ditch excavations at Cranborne Chase in southern England. The ditches yielded many earthwork artifacts. Pitt-Rivers himself stands on the mound with his cousin, Lady Magheramorne.

never been plowed. Pitt-Rivers realized that he had a unique chance to investigate ancient burial mounds, earthworks, and Roman villas on his property. He started with Bronze Age barrows (burial mounds), then moved on to Winklebury Camp, an Iron Age fort. There he cross-sectioned ramparts just as he had done at Cissbury in 1875.

In 1884 he turned from earthworks to a Roman military camp at Woodcutts Common, several acres of low banks, humps, and hollows. Pitt-Rivers had his workmen clear off the top soil, then dig out the dark irregularities in the white chalk subsoil and trace the outlines of ditches, hearths, pits, and postholes. This was revolutionary archaeology in the 1880s. In 1893, he turned

his attention to Wor Barrow, a Stone Age earthwork used for communal burials. His predecessors had simply trenched into burial mounds and removed the human remains and grave furniture. Pitt-Rivers excavated the entire mound, including 16 skeletons, leaving a row of earthen pillars down the center, which recorded the layering. At one end of the mound he found a rectangular outline of trenches in the chalk, where the uprights of a large building protected six bodies. In a final exercise in archaeological science, and to gain knowledge to better interpret his excavations, he left the ditches that surrounded the mound open for four years, then excavated what had collected in them to see how chalk

> *"Tedious as it may appear to some, to dwell on the discovery of odds and ends that have, no doubt, been thrown away by their owners as rubbish yet it is by the study of such trivial details that archaeology is mainly dependent for determining the date of earthworks."*

—Augustus Lane Fox Pitt-Rivers, *Excavations in Cranborne Chase* (1892)

ditches broke down and filled with sediment after abandonment.

A tall, moody man with a quick temper, Pitt-Rivers was gifted with superb organizational skills. He compiled four privately printed volumes, *Excavations in Cranborne Chase*, heavily illustrated books describing every detail of his excavations. He ran his projects on disciplined, military lines, working with small teams of trained workers, and site supervisors who had two assistants, one a draftsman, the other a model maker. From the very beginning, Pitt-Rivers recorded the position of every find, including animal bones and seeds, however small. Throughout his excavations, he thought of his sites in three dimensions, a legacy from his surveying days, and a cornerstone of modern excavation methods. Each site was excavated completely down to bedrock, each layer recorded, human disturbances of the soil noted. Pitt-Rivers pioneered the use of photography to record his sites and insisted on prompt publication of the results. Unlike his contemporaries, he was interested in how earthworks were formed and weathered by the elements.

Pitt-Rivers had no patience for archaeologists who just searched for objects. He considered science

"organized common sense," a principle he followed throughout his excavations. It was not until the 1920s that other archaeologists like Mortimer Wheeler followed his example and refined his methods. His contemporaries considered him eccentric, but he was firm in his own ways, which included providing free Sunday concerts for visitors to the museum housing his collections. There, his collections of firearms, tribal artifacts, and archaeological finds were displayed in evolutionary sequences, from the simple to the more complex. Pitt-Rivers believed that archaeology should be part of everyone's education, so that the public could learn the links between past and present.

General Augustus Lane Fox Pitt-Rivers was years ahead of his time, but his methods are the cornerstone of all modern archaeological excavation.

FURTHER READING

Bowden, Mark. *The Life and Archaeological Work of Lieutenant-General Augustus Lane Fox Pitt-Rivers.* New York: Cambridge University Press, 1991.

Thompson, M. W. *General Pitt-Rivers.* Bradford-on-Avon, England: Moonraker, 1977.

William Matthew Flinders Petrie

TOMBS, TOWNS,
AND CEMETERIES
BY THE NILE

William Matthew Flinders Petrie was arguably the greatest Egyptologist of the 19th century. His excavation methods revolutionized the archaeology of ancient Egypt. He also developed the first method for dating farming cultures that flourished along the Nile River before the pharaohs, and carried out important excavations in Palestine. Petrie was more than slightly eccentric and lived in squalor in his excavation camps while carrying out inspiring excavations. One of his young students, Leonard Woolley, who went on to dig at the Hittite city of Carchemish and the biblical city of Ur, wrote in his memoirs of a camp where "tinned kidneys mingle with mummy corpses and amulets in the soup." But Petrie revolutionized the study of Egyptology.

Flinders Petrie was born in Charlton, England, in 1853. His father was a civil engineer and surveyor, his mother a passionate collector of coins and minerals. His formal education was largely private and sketchy at best, as his parents were casual people. But the young Petrie read widely and picked up an excellent practical knowledge of geometry and surveying from his father. By age 13 he was already reading books on ancient Egypt and the pyramids. As a teenager he spent hours browsing among coins and books in the British Museum. He also walked for miles over the English countryside making maps of ancient earthworks. "I used to spend five shillings and sixpence a week on food, and beds cost about double that," he wrote in his autobiography. "I learned the land and the people all over the south of England, usually sleeping in a cottage."

In 1872 he and his father surveyed the stone circles at Stonehenge, producing a plan that was not improved on for years. Eight years later, at the age of 27, Flinders Petrie sailed for Egypt with his surveying instruments and almost no money. He set up camp in an abandoned ancient Egyptian tomb near the pyramids of Giza, then spent many weeks setting up accurate survey points and studying the construction of these stupendous monuments. Petrie also had ample time to observe the rough excavation methods used by Auguste Mariette and others. He wrote in disgust years later in his *Pyramids and Tombs of Egypt*: "It is sickening to see the rate at which everything is being destroyed, and the little regard paid to preservation."

Petrie's meticulous survey soon attracted the attention of both archaeologists and cranks. General Augustus Lane Fox Pitt-Rivers visited his camp and thoroughly approved of his approach, which mirrored the general's own work in England. In the intervals of surveying, Petrie picked up potsherds and other small objects ignored by most excavators and realized they held valuable historical clues. As a result, he paid careful attention to even the smallest finds throughout his long career. He kept unwanted visitors away by working in the pyramids' hot chambers in his underwear.

The Pyramid Survey 1880–82, Petrie's first book, enhanced his reputation considerably within the narrow community of Egyptologists, despite his lack of a formal education. Inevitably, he turned from survey work to actual digging. Between 1883 and 1887, Petrie excavated for the London-based Egypt Exploration Fund, which proved a somewhat unsatisfactory relationship because of funding shortages and quarrels with his superiors. Nevertheless, he made important discoveries at sites in the Nile Delta such as the Greek-Egyptian cities of Tanis and Naukratis, once important trading centers. Here he refined his own excavation methods, concentrating not on spectacular finds but on small artifacts such as pot fragments and beads.

Rough and ready by today's standards, Petrie's digging, based on teams of diggers and earth carriers, was a vast improvement on earlier techniques. In his first seasons he recovered huge quantities of pottery and papyri, which were exhibited in London. Most of it came from a system of paying his many workers tips for each find, which grew to the point that he effectively bought the contents of the site. In time, he began to appreciate the importance of distinctive potsherds and other artifacts as a way of dating important structures. When each digging season ended, Petrie set to work at once to write up his excavation, setting an example of prompt publication that even today's archaeologists do not achieve.

In 1887 Petrie severed his connections with the Egypt Exploration Fund and set up as a freelance excavator, financing his excavations by selling

A young Flinders Petrie, with a pet dog, outside the rock-cut tomb at Giza in 1880, his home for two years. Petrie lived simply and with only the roughest accommodations, often commandeering abandoned tombs for his camp. He was at his best in the field and often worked in his underwear to deter curious tourists.

artifacts to museums. He now followed a life routine that varied little for the rest of his career. He would spend the winters in Egypt excavating, the summers lecturing, traveling, and writing. Year after year, he excavated pyramids and tombs, towns, and cemeteries. Several generations of archaeologists learned excavation under him, a demanding experience. They received little formal instruction, were sent out to work without close supervision for many hours in the hot sun, and spent hours each evening sorting and classifying pot fragments. There were few comforts. Petrie was notorious for the austere regime in his camp, where the food was appalling. But those who survived several seasons with him became tough, competent excavators.

The important discoveries continued. In 1888 he found a cemetery of Egyptian-born Romans of AD 100 to 250 at Hawara in the Fayum Depression west of the Nile. Their mummies bore vivid portraits of the deceased, painted in colored wax on wooden panels. His excavations at the workers' town of el-Kahun provided a fascinating portrait of the lives of ordinary folk under the Middle Kingdom pharaoh

These mummies, unearthed by unknown European excavators, await shipment to the West in Hawara, Egypt, 1911. Even in the early 20th century, it was relatively easy for foreign expeditions to export mummies and other finds from Egypt.

Senusret II's rule (1897–1878 BC). Another community, Ghurab, dated to the XVIII Dynasty (1570–1293 BC) and yielded potsherds of brightly painted Mycenaean pottery from distant Greece, found in a walled enclosure close to the town temple. Petrie was one of the first to realize that ancient Egyptian civilization did not flourish in isolation, but traded with much of the eastern Mediterranean world. The Ghurab site, well dated by its inscriptions and artifacts, contained highly distinctive painted Mycenaean pottery, imported from Greece during the site's heyday. Thus, argued Petrie, Mycenaean civilization on the other side of the Mediterranean, dated to the same period, around 1500 to 1200 B.C. This innovative method made it possible to use closely dated sites in Egypt to date distant prehistoric sites. Obviously, the same pot fragments at Ghurab when found in sites on the Greek mainland provided a date for an otherwise updateable occupation level far from the Nile. This cross-dating method of Petrie's is still widely used by archaeologists today. Arthur Evans employed cross-dating to date the Minoan civilization of Crete a quarter century later.

Petrie was now a leading Egyptologist. In his textbook *Methods and Aims in Archaeology*, he wrote that he considered himself a collector of "all the requisite information," a tester of hypotheses, and someone who wove "a history out of scattered evidence." A major test of his skills came at el-Amarna on the Middle Nile, the capital of the heretic pharaoh Akhenaten, who ruled briefly over Egypt from 1350 to 1334 BC. El-Amarna was the only Egyptian capital with no overlying layers of occupation, so Petrie was able to clear large areas of the town, including the pharaoh's palace with its magnificent painted frescoes and pavements. Petrie roofed over the palace ruins and opened the site to tourists, who trampled a local farmer's crops. The angry villager promptly destroyed the paintings. Fortunately, Petrie had copied them. One of Petrie's el-Amarna helpers was a young archaeologist and artist named Howard Carter, later to achieve world fame for his discovery of the pharaoh Tutankhamun's tomb.

In 1892 Flinders Petrie was appointed the first Professor of Egyptology at the University of London, a remarkable appointment for a man who never earned a university degree. Two years later Petrie made one of his most important discoveries with the excavation of a series of enormous desert cemeteries near the town of Naqada in Upper Egypt. He cleared more than 2,000 graves in 1894 alone, each containing a skeleton and decorated clay pots. Petrie studied them grave by grave, each as a separate unit, and found there were gradual changes in the shapes of vessels and their decoration over time. For example, what were once practical handles for lifting pots eventually degenerated into mere painted squiggles. So many graves were found that Petrie was able to arrange them in chronological stages of development, working back from a royal

William Matthew Flinders Petrie

"It is sickening to see the rate at which everything is being destroyed, and the little regard paid to preservation."

—William Matthew Flinders Petrie, *Pyramids and Tombs of Egypt* (1883)

grave that linked his stages with older, undated graves. This bold and revolutionary attempt to date cultures much earlier than Egyptian civilization was used for years and described in his *Methods and Aims in Archaeology.*

Petrie set a frantic pace of excavation and publication. He dug at least one major site a year and published the results within 12 months. The season of 1899 to 1900 saw him sorting out looted sites at Abydos, where he found the tombs of four of eight 1st Dynasty kings. He also uncovered an inscription of the pharaoh Merneptah (1212–1202 BC), which provided the first known reference to the Kingdom of Israel. Unfortunately, Petrie had a somewhat abrasive and forthright personality, which led him to quarrel with the Egyptian authorities and with many archaeologists over permits, excavation methods, and his interpretations of ancient Egyptian archaeology. His lack of formal education caused him to believe that he alone was right and to ignore the work of expert colleagues.

However, he introduced new excavation methods and trained a generation of Egyptologists who refined his approaches. He continued excavating in most years until 1926, when new and stringent antiquities laws came into force to control foreign excavations along the Nile. These came as a direct result of the discovery of Tutankhamun's tomb. They were enacted to prevent the export of most finds, and certainly the selling of them. Petrie had paid for his excavations by selling artifacts to overseas museums and could no longer work in Egypt. Now his major source of funding was removed. After 40 years of fieldwork, he abruptly transferred his attentions to Palestine.

Petrie had worked for the London-based Palestine Exploration Fund as early as 1890. The fund had previously supported work in Jerusalem, following up on the efforts of Charles Warren. Flinders Petrie chose the city mound of Tell el-Hesi in southern Israel, where flood waters from a nearby valley had cut through the deep layers of the mound. Instead of excavating enormous trenches, Petrie simply took samples of pottery from each layer with very little effort. He then laid these out in the laboratory and produced a chronology of pot styles for the region as well as for this Bronze and Iron Age site of the first and second millennia BC. He found many Egyptian objects of known age in the layers of Tell es-Hesi and used them to cross-date the site from Egyptian ones. Petrie's pottery classification has been much modified since 1890, but is still in use today. Upon his return to Palestine in 1926, he continued using this scheme as he carried out several major excavations until his death in 1942.

FURTHER READING

Drower, Margaret S. *Flinders Petrie: A Life in Archaeology.* London: Gollancz, 1985.

Petrie, W.M. Flinders. *Ancient Egypt and Ancient Israel.* 1931. Reprint, Golden, Colo.: Ares, 1995.

———. *The Arts and Crafts of Ancient Egypt.* 1910. Reprint, Collingdale, Pa.: DIANE Publishing, 1998.

BORN

June 3, 1853
Charlton, England

DIED

July 28, 1942
Jerusalem, Palestine

EDUCATION

No formal schooling

ACCOMPLISHMENTS

First professor of Egyptology at the University of London; introduced new excavation and survey methods to Egyptology; carried out the first accurate survey of the pyramids of Giza; made many important discoveries at Tanis, Naucratis, el-Amarna, Abydos, and many other sites. Developed sequence dating for pre-Dynastic Egypt, and cross-dating using imports of known age to date sites outside Egypt; his Palestinian excavations clarified Bronze Age and Iron Age chronology in the eastern Mediterranean. Wrote *Pyramids and Tombs of Egypt* (1883); *Diospolis Parva* (1901); *Methods and Aims in Archaeology* (1904); *The Arts and Crafts of Ancient Egypt* (1910); *Ancient Egypt and Ancient Israel* (1931).

Gertrude Bell

DESERTS, POLITICS, AND MUSEUMS

ertrude Bell once wrote in an undated essay: "The great twin rivers, gloriously named; the huge Babylonian plains, now desert, which were once a garden of the world, their story stretching back into the dark recesses of time—they shout romance." This no-nonsense desert traveler and archaeologist had a passion for desert lands and Mesopotamia, the cradle of the world's first civilization. She blazed trails across the Syrian desert when women rarely traveled alone, and became a respected archaeologist at a time when Near East excavators were few, and invariably men. She was also responsible for the founding of the Iraq Museum.

Bell was born into the family of a wealthy iron foundry owner in Yorkshire, England, in 1868. She studied at Oxford in 1886, at a time when few women undergraduates attended

Gertrude Bell observes an excavation at Ur. Visits by Bell were important occasions, as she supervised the division of finds between the new Iraq Museum and Leonard Woolley's sponsoring museum. All the archaeologists on the site witnessed the division.

the university. A brilliant student, in only two years she obtained a modern history degree while enjoying an active social life. She graduated with an outspoken manner and a passion for travel, which she indulged with a trip to Tehran, Persia, in 1892, which at the time was well off the beaten track for most travelers, especially women. She also became interested in mountain climbing and was soon recognized as one of the leading female climbers of her day.

Bell discovered archaeology during a seven-month stay in Jerusalem, when she traveled across the desert to Petra and visited the Greek ruins at Palmyra, Syria. A gifted linguist, she learned to speak fluent Arabic and spent the next few years studying archaeology in Paris and Rome. At the same time, she studied Byzantine churches in Turkey, publishing an expert study of the Byzantine Thousand and One Churches at Birbinkilise, which have now largely vanished. This work established her as a respected scholar.

In 1909 Bell set off with a small military escort across the Syrian Desert from Damascus to the Euphrates River, and then on to the territory of the Deleim Arabs, who were notorious for kidnapping or robbing travelers. Her destination was the walled Abbasid (Islamic) caliphs' palace at Ukhaidir, a huge castle dating to the 6th century AD set in a fortified enclosure that had never been described scientifically before. In real danger of attack from desert nomads anxious for booty, she spent four days surveying the palace surrounded by heavily armed guards. The Ukhaidir journey was a turning point for Bell's career. Her fluent Arabic enabled her to pick up subtle undercurrents of political revolt and the early stirrings of Arab nationalism. She also made the acquaintance of important desert chieftains, contacts that were to stand her in good stead in later years. Her most famous book,

From Amurath to Amurath, appeared to wide acclaim in 1911. Three years later she published a detailed report on the great palace.

By now, Bell enjoyed a high reputation with desert chieftains. Over innumerable cups of coffee she learned the subtle shifts of desert politics and acquired an intimate knowledge of local political conditions. In contrast, the male British government officials in the region regarded her as opinionated and outspoken—a political liability. Right up to the outbreak of World War I in 1914, Bell was constantly on the move. She penetrated deep into Saudi Arabia, to the remote desert city of Hail, where the suspicious ruler imprisoned her as a spy. Bell acquired her expert knowledge of Arabia and the desert at a time when what is now Iraq was assuming great importance because of its oil. By 1914 the Royal Navy depended more on oil than on coal to fuel its ships. A rising market for automobiles also increased Britain's dependency on Arabian petroleum deposits.

In 1915 Bell was appointed to the Arab Intelligence Bureau of the British army in Cairo, Egypt, the only woman among dozens of military officers. The army regarded her with suspicion, both on account of her gender and because of her fluent Arabic. But she soon became indispensable, flattering desert chiefs, interviewing them, making use of her unrivaled knowledge of desert lands to keep a finger on the political pulse. The authorities transferred her to Basra on the Persian Gulf in 1916, where she served as a political officer during the critical years when Iraq became a monarchy under King Feisal. Bell worked with British High Commissioner Sir Percy Cox, serving as his Oriental Secretary. She was in her element, working with powerful sheikhs, defusing quarrels before they boiled over, paving the way to create a unified state in Mesopotamia. But as the

Gertrude Bell

BORN
July 14, 1868
Washington, Durham, England

DIED
July 12, 1926
Baghdad, Iraq

EDUCATION
Lady Margaret Hall, Oxford University (B.A. 1888)

ACCOMPLISHMENTS
Expert desert traveler and archaeologist; studied the Thousand and One Churches at Birbinkilise, Turkey, and the Abbasid Palace at Ukhaidir; founded the Iraq Antiquities Service and Museum. Wrote *The Desert and the Sown* (1907); *The Thousand and One Churches* (with Sir William Ramsey; 1909); *From Amurath to Amurath* (1911); *Palace and Mosque at Ukhaidir* (1914).

Dressed in a long skirt and sun hood, Gertrude Bell measures a building at the 6th-century fortified Abbasid palace at Ukhaidir, 75 miles (120 kilometers) south of Baghdad in southern Iraq, in 1909. Bell's goal was to record the dimensions of the little-known stone and wood Islamic palace, which was rapidly decaying in the harsh desert climate.

structure of government became more formalized, the outspoken Gertrude Bell was tactfully shunted aside. Increasingly, she led a busy life outside government, filling her time with archaeology, dogs, photography, and people of every kind. Her intense sympathy for the Arabs made her somewhat suspect to starched and conventional British colonial officials. Eventually, her only administrative responsibility was archaeology. From this responsibility came the Iraq Museum.

When World War I ended in 1918, scholars from America and Europe were anxious to resume excavations in Mesopotamia. German archaeologists had been reconstructing ancient Babylon for more than a decade before the war. French archaeologists were anxious to excavate at least one ancient city in the heart of Mesopotamia. The British Museum and the University of Pennsylvania sought an excavation permit to conduct a major excavation at Ur, celebrated in the Old Testament as Abraham's city. They planned a dig to be headed by British excavator Leonard Woolley. Bell sat down to organize an Iraqi Department of Antiquities, with responsibility for granting excavation permits, and to establish a new Iraq Museum to house artifacts found in the digs made by foreigners. She was in a difficult position. Foreign expeditions wanted as many finds as possible. Iraqis felt strongly that at least half the artifacts from any excavation should stay in the country. She drafted a new antiquities law that steered a careful course between the two viewpoints. The first test of the new regulations came at Ur.

Leonard Woolley was an expert excavator, with a genius for working with large numbers of workers. He

> *"I have found myself longing for an hour out of a remote century, wherein I might look my fill upon the walls that have fallen and stamp the image of a dead world indelibly upon my mind."*
>
> —Gertrude Bell, *From Amurath to Amurath* (1911)

started work at Ur in 1922, excavating the ancient Sumerian and biblical city on an enormous scale under Bell's eagle eye. Woolley was a strong character who was not afraid to speak his mind. In Gertrude Bell he encountered a formidable opponent who looked out for Iraqi interests before anything else. Bell would disembark at the tiny Ur railroad station and spend hours at the excavations even on the hottest days. Woolley dreaded her visit at the end of each digging season, for he had to fight hard to keep his finds, with two powerful overseas museums looking over his shoulder. Fortunately, the two strong personalities respected each other. They would argue for hours, taking the precaution of enlisting the services of an impartial mediator if they could not agree. Even Woolley quietly admitted that he was satisfied with the division of finds, but never to Bell herself.

Foreign excavators lived in apprehension of her awesome powers. "Who decides if we disagree?" asked British archaeologist Stephen Langdon of Oxford University, working at the Sumerian city of Kish. "I replied that I did," wrote Bell in her diary. "But he needn't be afraid for he would find me eager to oblige." In recent years, Bell has been criticized severely by Iraqis for surrendering too much of their national heritage. But she worked in a world of strong imperial powers, which had little respect for new nations or their antiquities and would simply commandeer them if challenged.

Back in Baghdad, Bell moved the collections into a few shabby rooms near the royal palace, until the government gave the new Iraq Museum a permanent home. She spent long hours cataloging potsherds and arranging the collections. Highhanded, even arrogant, Gertrude Bell felt an obligation to the new country of Iraq and its cultural heritage that few locals or foreigners shared at the time.

Eventually, the debilitating summer heat of Baghdad undermined her health and mental well being, already weakened by chronic overwork. In 1926, the 58-year-old Bell committed suicide with an overdose of sleeping pills. Huge crowds from all segments of Baghdad society attended her funeral.

FURTHER READING

Wallach, Janet. *Desert Queen*. New York: Doubleday, 1996.

Winstone, H. V. F. *Gertrude Bell*. New York: Quartet, 1978.

Henri Breuil

ROCK ART PIONEER

ew people have the stamina or the dedication to lie on their backs, more than 100 feet (30 meters) underground for weeks and months on end, copying ancient rock paintings. Abbé Henri Breuil devoted years to Ice Age art, tracing, copying, and sketching at a time when color photography lay far in the future. His paintings of prehistoric bison at Altamira Cave in northern Spain defined ancient rock art for a generation.

Henri Breuil was born at Mortain in France's La Manche department, in 1877. Little is known of his childhood years, but he entered the Catholic seminary of Saint-Sulpice in 1895 to become a priest. There he came under the influence of Abbé Guibert, Professor of Natural Science, who introduced him not only to the study of prehistoric archaeology, but to the theory of evolution and natural selection. That was very progressive for a Catholic teacher of the day, because the church had little tolerance for unorthodox

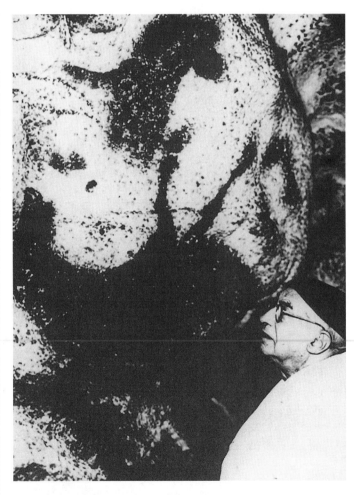

Abbé Breuil inspects rock paintings at Lascaux, France. The Lascaux paintings, executed by unknown late–Ice Age artists of 15,000 years ago, depict the animals that the people hunted.

thinking. At first Breuil was attracted to botany, but prehistory soon became his obsession. Guibert encouraged him to describe stone implements and bronze artifacts from private collections. After his first year at the seminary, Breuil participated in the excavation of a Stone Age (Neolithic) farming settlement at Champigny with the well-known archaeologist Louis Capitan. But a visit to the picturesque Dordogne region of southwestern France in that year changed his life.

The village of Les Eyzies is surrounded by huge limestone rock shelters, once occupied by late Ice Age reindeer hunters, known as the Cro-Magnons, after a rock shelter of that name near the local railroad station. At the time of Breuil's first visit, Stone Age archaeology was in its infancy. He met Edouard Piette, one of the few truly rigorous 19th-century scientists studying the people of the so-called Reindeer Age. In later life, Breuil called Piette his mentor, from whom he received hands-on instruction in artifact classification. But Piette was a local scholar, interested only in a tiny area around Les Eyzies and in the Pyrénées Mountains. Breuil had a much broader perspective, and both refined and expanded Piette's work to a much larger area encompassing the whole of western Europe.

Breuil was ordained as a priest in 1900, at a time when the Catholic church had rejected the existence of fossil humans on the grounds that they challenged the findings of the Old Testament. He came to prehistory from a theological background as part of a movement among scientifically inclined priests to reconcile prehistory and research into human evolution, with religious beliefs. One of his closest friends was a remarkable Jesuit, Father Teilhard de Chardin, who conceived of the evolution of life as having been "metaphysically oriented toward the appearance [evolutionary emergence]

of humans, in whom the reunion of spirit and matter was realized." In other words, science had much to tell us about early humanity, and could do so without challenging the belief that god created humankind. Breuil and Chardin worked together in France and later in China.

For 30 years after 1900, prehistoric archaeology in France was dominated by Breuil and his fellow priests such as the Abbé Bouyssonnie. Catholic priests were engaged in archaeology because of its intellectual and spiritual challenges. At the same time, they were scholars with stipends from the church, considerable spare time, also freedom to excavate, travel, and visit museums, at a time when archaeological jobs were rare. Henri Breuil may have been a Catholic priest, but he rarely allowed his ecclesiastical background to interfere with his archaeology. His researches into the Stone Age peoples of France and their remarkable cave art soon received wide attention.

Henri Breuil came to Les Eyzies at a time when archaeologists were grappling with ways to subdivide a long sequence of Stone Age hunter-gatherer societies in terms of their biological and cultural evolution. Edward Lartet was one of the first to dig the great Stone Age rock shelters of southwestern France. He proposed a subdivision of the rock shelter occupations into ages of the Mammoth, the Cave Bear, the Reindeer, and the wild ox or Aurochs, the latter period occurring after the Ice Age. Each age was named for the animal bones that were dominant in different stratified levels of his sites. Breuil and others (among them Gabrielle de Mortillet) focused on stone, bone, and antler artifacts, treating them as if they were human-made fossils which changed from one period of the late Ice Age to another.

In 1905 the young priest presented a scientific paper at the first Prehistoric Congress of France, a gathering of

Henri Breuil

BORN

February 28, 1877
Mortain, France

DIED

August 14, 1961
Paris, France

EDUCATION

Saint-Sulpice Seminary, Montreal (ordained 1900)

ACCOMPLISHMENTS

Carried out the first systematic surveys and interpretations of late Ice Age rock art in Europe, studied rock art in many other parts of the world, including southern Africa; developed the first elaborate, artifact-based classification of late Ice Age hunter-gatherer cultures, which remained the standard for generations. Wrote *La Préhistoire* (1937), *400 Centuries of Cave Art* (1952); *The Cave of Altamira at Santillana del Mar, Spain* (with Hugo Obermaier, 1935).

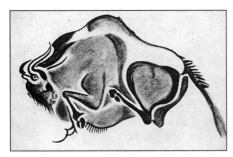

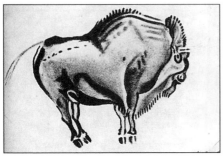

These two paintings of bison from Altamira, Spain, are classic examples of Breuil's exquisite copies of Ice Age rock art.

eminent archaeologists. There he summarized his studies of artifacts made by people of Piette's "Age of Reindeer." He criticized Mortillet and others for thinking of Stone Age prehistory as a series of universal stages that could be identified by different characteristic stone or antler artifacts made over enormous areas of the world. Rather, he said, the archaic Neanderthal people—whose characteristic stone spear points and hide scrapers were found at Le Moustier cave near Les Eyzies, and stratified below later occupations at other rock shelters—were succeeded by quite different Stone Age cultures, each with its own distinctive artifacts and other characteristics.

On the strength of this paper and his cave art researches, Breuil was appointed a professor at the University of Freiburg in 1905. Five years later he was appointed professor at the newly founded Institute of Human Paleontology in Paris, sponsored by Prince Albert of Monaco.

In a series of authoritative conference papers and articles, Breuil now laid out an elaborate subdivision of Stone Age cultures in southwestern France and northern Spain. Each culture, named after a major site: Aurignacian (Aurignac), Solutrean (Solutré), and Magdalenian (La Madeleine). Each had unfolding stages, and was marked by differences in artifact form. The Aurignacians used split-based bone points and fine scrapers, the Solutreans fabricated intricately worked leaf-shaped stone spear points, and the Magdalenians were masters of antler technology to make harpoons, needles, and other fine tools.

In a classic paper, "The Subdivisions of the Upper Paleolithic and Their Significance," published in 1912,

Breuil laid out this classification scheme. It has been the basis of all French Stone Age archaeology ever since. During the rest of his career he modified his scheme again and again, changing from one series of cultures to parallel tracks of human development, each reflected in different artifact forms. For example, he proposed that his Aurignacian culture had existed in southwestern France at the same time as another tradition, using finely made stone spear points, known as the Perigordian. The two traditions existed alongside one another until the Solutrean and Magdalenian cultures superseded them. The different Stone Age groups had either migrated into western Europe from the east or had developed one from another. Breuil's outline for Stone Age Europe forms the foundation for the far more elaborate researches of today.

Breuil was not a great archaeological thinker. Rather, he was a technician, a genius at detailed classification, a master of the minute features of individual artifacts. His background was in geology, in layers and fossils. But he was also a gifted artist who made rough copies in the field, then rendered them in pen and watercolors. He was the first scholar to undertake a systematic survey of late Ice Age art from northern Spain and southwestern France, the earliest known art tradition.

In 1864, Edouard Lartet was the first archaeologist to find beautifully engraved late Ice Age artifacts. Soon other finds were made, but when Spanish nobleman Marquis de Sautola found magnificent bison paintings on the walls of Altamira cave in northern Spain, they were dismissed as modern renderings. The young Breuil was one of those who discovered more painted caves near Les Eyzies and helped authenticate Altamira. He was the first archaeologist to visit the celebrated Font-de-Gaume and Les Combarelles caves, and to describe the magnificent bison of Niaux Cave near the Pyrénées.

Breuil devoted years to copying intricate friezes of paintings and engravings with an accuracy that stuns modern observers. He would lie for days on end on his back, holding paper against the painted wall, tracing paintings with light only from candles, flashlights, or a flickering acetylene lamp. Inevitably, as an artist with his own creative hand, Breuil introduced his own interpretations into his copies, but until improvements in the 1950s that made accurate color photography practical in such conditions, they were the definitive reproductions of later Ice Age art. What did the engravings and paintings mean? Breuil believed some were "art for art's sake." Using analogies from living peoples, he argued they were communal religious and magical expressions, many of them part of what he called "hunting magic."

During the course of his long career, Breuil became an international authority on rock art, studying paintings and engravings at sites as far afield as eastern Spain, the Sahara, Ethiopia, and southern Africa. On the strength of his research, he was appointed to the first professorship of prehistory at the Collège de France in 1929. He died in Paris in 1961, after an illustrious career that saw more than 800 publications.

All Breuil's work, whether on antler or stone artifacts, or on rock art, unfolded at a time of unparalleled discoveries and advances in Stone Age archaeology. The abbé was above all a classifier, a copier, and an organizer rather than a thinker. But his pioneer work on cave art and stone artifacts was an attempt to understand prehistoric cultures in more human terms than had been the case with his Victorian predecessors. He thought of Stone Age people not as brutes and savages, but as thinking human beings. Henri Breuil's remarkable achievements serve as an inspiration for today's more specialized archaeologists, who use his work as a foundation for much more sophisticated interpretations of the past.

FURTHER READING

Daniel, Glyn. *A Short History of Archaeology*. London: Thames and Hudson, 1981.

Howard Carter

THE TOMB OF TUTANKHAMUN

Howard Carter, for years an unknown archaeologist and artist toiling in the heat of Egypt, became an international celebrity overnight simply because he found an undisturbed pharaoh's tomb. But what a royal tomb: the last undisturbed sepulcher of an ancient Egyptian king, lavishly adorned in gold, the young occupant virtually unknown until the dramatic discovery of his burial place on November 6, 1922. Small wonder that the names Howard Carter and Tutankhamun became permanently linked.

Howard Carter was an unlikely adventurer, the son of a talented animal painter. He was born in London in 1874. Considered to be a weakling, he was brought up by two aunts in rural eastern England. From his earliest years he was happiest alone, recording beetles and birds with brush and pen. The young Carter inherited his father's artistic skills and talent for precise observation, but received only

Howard Carter just inside the opening of Tutankhamun's burial chamber. To ensure that there were no doubts as to the undisturbed state of the pharaoh's burial place, Carter opened the chamber in the presence of senior government officials and other archaeologists. His assistant, Alexander Callendar, is at right.

a modest education. At age 15 he left school and set out to earn a living as an artist under the patronage of a local landowner, William Tyssen-Amherst, a wealthy collector of Egyptian artifacts. Tyssen-Amherst's Egyptian collection was as good as that in many public museums, and included many mummies and documents written on sheets and scrolls of papyrus. The most famous, still called the Amherst papyrus, gives an account of tomb-robbing methods used by ancient Egyptian thieves, who often worked with the assistance of corrupt officials.

In 1891 the 17-year-old Carter accepted full-time employment with Amherst, cataloging and illustrating the collections. Soon Carter's painstaking work led to copying tasks at the British Museum in London, where he met the leading Egyptologists of the day. Later that year he went to Egypt to record the tomb paintings of royal governors at Beni Hasan in Middle Egypt under a well-known Egyptologist, Percy Newberry. Carter brought a new standard of copying to the murals, especially those with birds, executing them with a brilliant command of color and attention to detail. He loved the work. "There can be fewer brighter days," he wrote in his diary after an arduous survey of rock-cut nobles' tombs at Al Bersha, downstream of Beni Hasan.

The following year, he worked at the pharaoh Akhenaten's capital at el-Amarna (reigned about 1350 BC) under Flinders Petrie, like himself a self-educated Egyptologist. Akhenaten was the most controversial of all Egyptians, for he challenged the worship of the god Amun, a personification of the sun, and replaced it with a cult that revered the bright disk of the sun itself. He moved his capital away from Amun's temples at Thebes downstream from el-Amarna. His new city was occupied for only 17 years.

Within a few weeks the young archaeologist was excavating the king's

"Each [visitor] had a dazed, bewildered look in his eyes, and each in turn, as he came out, threw up his hands before him, an unconscious gesture of impotence to describe in words the wonders he had seen."

—Howard Carter, *The Tomb of Tut.ankh.Amen* (1923)

great temple and parts of the town on his own. Petrie instilled the principles of disciplined archaeological excavation in Carter and gave him a burning desire to become an excavator. "To me the calling had an extraordinary attraction," he wrote in his journal in 1892.

By this time the quality of Carter's work ensured him continual employment on a variety of copying assignments, culminating in six years copying the wall sculptures, paintings, and historical inscriptions of the mortuary temple of Queen Hatshepsut at Deir al-Bahari near Luxor under the direction of Egyptologist Edouard Naville. Carter was in his element, reviving the art of 4,000 years ago with accuracy and respect. "In those six years, although full of hard work, I learnt more of Egyptian Art, its serene simplicity, than in any other place or time," he wrote in his diary years later. Unlike many copyists, Carter preserved the spirit of the originals. Some authorities rank Carter's wildlife copies alongside the finest of John James Audubon's American bird drawings.

During these years Carter had become a strong, contemplative man who was quite happy with his own company for months on end. In his spare time he wandered though the rocky hills and valleys west of the Nile. His notebooks reveal an increasing obsession with ancient tombs and with the work of Giovanni Belzoni and other pioneers. In 1899 he accepted an important post in the Egyptian

Carter and an Egyptian assistant carefully separate Tutankhamun's mummy from the walls of the coffin. The ancient priests poured so much ceremonial oil over the inner coffins that they often adhered to one another.

Antiquities Service as Inspector of Monuments for Upper Egypt, based in Luxor. This powerful position gave Carter new authority to enforce antiquities law and oversee excavations. He was already familiar with the vast ancient Egyptian cemeteries that lay in the desert west of the Nile, opposite Luxor. They were the domain of the ancient dead. Carter learned the narrow paths that crisscrossed the valleys and cliffs, and every corner of the Valley of Kings, where Egypt's most powerful pharaohs were buried more than 3,000 years earlier. He supervised excavations for American millionaire Theodore Davis, locating the plundered tomb of the pharaoh Tuthmosis IV, who died in 1386 BC, in the Valley of Kings.

In 1905 Carter resigned abruptly and made his living as a freelance artist at Luxor for two years before obtaining employment with another wealthy patron, the Earl of Carnarvon. An aristocrat and sportsman, Carnarvon came to Egypt to recuperate after a

car accident in Germany. He developed a passion for archaeological excavation, which he indulged each winter with Carter's assistance. "He only cared for the best, and nothing but the best would satisfy him," wrote Wallis Budge, a high British Museum official. "His taste was faultless." Carter and Carnarvon made few spectacular finds, working outside the Valley of Kings, where crews employed by Theodore Davis still labored. The first season yielded nothing more than a "large mummified cat in its case." Far from being discouraged, Carnarvon plunged himself into archaeology even more enthusiastically.

Meanwhile, Theodore Davis did find a scatter of artifacts bearing the royal seal of an obscure pharaoh named Tutankhamun. Eventually he became discouraged by the lack of finds and relinquished his excavation permit there. As a result, a 10-year permit for the Valley of Kings passed into Carnarvon's hands in 1914. But World War I intervened and excavations did not begin until three years later.

Carter now began a systematic search for the tomb of one of ancient Egypt's least-known pharaohs: the boy king Tutankhamun, who died in about 1323 BC. He was convinced that the sepulcher of this obscure king lay in the valley. For six years, Carter cleared rubble from the floor of the Valley of Kings and found nothing. By 1922 Carnarvon had spent the equivalent of several million modern-day dollars without any major results. Reluctantly, he agreed to a final season, focused on a small area near the tomb of Rameses VI, where Carter had started work in five years before. Just three days after starting work on November 1, 1922, Carter's workers uncovered a flight of rock-cut stairs leading to a sealed doorway. For three weeks Carter waited until Carnarvon arrived from England. Then, on November 26, the two men stood in front of the sealed doorway that bore the seal of the pharaoh Tutankhamun. Carter made a small hole in the plaster and shone a flickering candle into the opening. Impatiently, Carnarvon asked him what lay within. "Yes, wonderful things," Carter replied, as gold glinted in the faint light. Howard Carter had discovered the undisturbed tomb of Tutankhamun, the only unlooted king's sepulcher ever found in Egypt and one of the greatest archaeological discoveries of all time.

The find caused a worldwide sensation. The press and hundreds of curious visitors descended on the Valley of Kings, threatening to overwhelm the delicate work of recording the tomb. Both Carter and Carnarvon were under severe stress, for the experience of finding the tomb and the unprecedented media attention overwhelmed them. They had a series of blazing arguments that ended with them barely on speaking terms. Shortly afterward, Carnarvon was bitten by a mosquito, then nicked open the bite with his razor while shaving. The bite turned septic. He was only reconciled with his partner a few days before his death on April 5, 1923, his already delicate health undermined by blood poisoning. Inevitably, the press wrote of a deadly "curse of the pharaohs" that had struck Carnarvon down. The fact that many of Tutankhamun's excavators lived into their 80s is conveniently forgotten.

Carter worked on alone. He spent 10 arduous years clearing Tutankhamun's tomb, usually with grossly inadequate funding, but did not live to publish his extraordinary findings. The American Egyptologist Henry Breasted described in a letter one of the many dramatic moments, when he and Carter opened

the innermost shrines and observed the pharaoh's stone sarcophagus within. "I felt for the first time the majesty of the pharaoh's presence," he wrote. Nearby, the ostrich feather plumes carried by the king's servants lay on the floor, crumbled to brown dust. Without sufficient money, Carter struggled to perform miracles of conservation and artifact preservation along the way. For example, he used plaster and liquid wax instead of more expensive and more suitable materials to stabilize fragile wooden thrones. The tremendous stress of the meticulous work and of dealing with difficult government officials, the press, and a persistent public wore him down. Carter passed his last years between England and Egypt, until he died in London in 1939, a week shy of his 65th birthday.

Carter's Tutankhamun excavations unfolded as Leonard Woolley was making impressive finds at Ur in southern Iraq. Woolley returned home to a knighthood and honorary degrees from major universities. The difficult and sometimes moody Carter received but one official honor: an honorary degree from Yale University. Throughout his life and at the height of his fame, Howard Carter was always an outsider.

FURTHER READING

Carter, Howard, and Arthur Mace. *The Tomb of Tut.ankh.Amen Discovered by the Late Lord Carnarvon and Howard Carter.* 3 vols. London: Cassell, 1923–33.

Reeves, Nicholas. *The Complete Tutankhamun.* London: Thames and Hudson, 1990.

Treasures of Tutankhamun. New York: Metropolitan Museum of Art, 1976.

Winstone, W. V. F. *Howard Carter and the Discovery of the Tomb of Tutankhamun.* London: Constable, 1991.

Howard Carter

BORN

March 9, 1874
London, England

DIED

March 2, 1939
London, England

EDUCATION

Parish school in Suffolk, England, and private

ACCOMPLISHMENTS

Drew and painted highly accurate naturalistic copies of ancient Egyptian tomb paintings; Excavated with several wealthy patrons, notably Lord Edward Carnarvon; discovered the tomb of Tutankhamun in 1922.

Arthur John Evans

MINOAN CIVILIZATION

O n June 26, 1926, English archaeologist Arthur John Evans lay in bed in his villa close to the great Palace of Minos at Knossos in Crete. Suddenly, the building creaked and heaved as a strong earthquake rocked northern Crete. Nearby church bells rang. Women and children screamed as dwellings collapsed. A dull sound rose from the earth, like the muffled roar of a bull. Evans was electrified. The noise of the earthquake reminded him of the great bull god of ancient Crete, whose great horns tossed the earth, the great Minotaur—half human, half beast—whom the ancient Minoans had sought to appease with constant sacrifice. Evans was convinced he had lived through a reenactment of the death of Minoan civilization.

Arthur Evans was born into a family of wealthy English paper manufacturers. His father, John Evans, was a well-known art connoisseur, amateur geologist, and antiquarian (see Part 2), so young Arthur was brought up in a family

Sir Arthur Evans appraises a find. Evans was blessed with sharp eyesight, which enabled him to assess the significance of even the smallest artifacts. He was the leading expert on Mediterranean pottery and jewelry of his day.

with a strong appreciation for art objects of all kinds, and also for archaeology and the past.

Evans was educated privately, then went to Oxford University in 1870. Of small stature, with keen eyesight and an insatiable curiosity, he complained that Oxford life was dull, and spent his summers trekking over Europe, often far off the beaten track. After graduating from Oxford in 1873, he traveled through the Balkans, where he developed a passion for political intrigue and was arrested by the Austrian police on suspicion of being a spy. The *Manchester Guardian* newspaper sent Evans back to the Balkans as a special correspondent in 1875 to report on the unrest caused by Austrian rule over the region. Evans threw himself into an atmosphere of constant plotting and rebellion with such enthusiasm that the Austrians jailed him for six weeks on the grounds that his articles were subversive. He was then expelled from the country forever. Evans was lucky to escape a long prison sentence. In the intervals between rebellions he had collected artifacts of all kinds, using his almost microscopic eyesight to examine even the tiniest objects. As a result, Evans began to appreciate small finds in ways his contemporaries did not.

In 1884 Evans was appointed Keeper of the Ashmolean Museum in Oxford, a post he held for 25 years. The Ashmolean was a curious dumping ground for antiquities and natural history specimens accumulated by collectors and university professors over more than three centuries. The collections were in chaos, the displays haphazard. With characteristic energy, Evans stirred up the neglected and moribund institution, lobbying for a new building, and spending much of his time in Mediterranean lands adding to his collections. His Assistant Keeper answered all queries by saying: "The Keeper, Sir, is somewhere in Bohemia." These years of collecting and travel brought Arthur

Evans in contact with many archaeologists, among them Heinrich Schliemann of Troy and Mycenae fame (see Part 2).

Unlike Schliemann, who thought of Mycenae as the palace of Homer's hero King Agamemnon, Evans considered it to be the remains of a Bronze Age civilization, a major trading center which received exotic pottery, metals, and engraved gemstones and seals from other parts of the Greek mainland and the Aegean islands. Evans had an advantage over archaeologists. His unusual nearsightedness allowed him to examine even the smallest details of artifacts. He visited antique dealers in Athens, bombarding them with questions about the minute engraved seals they sold by the dozen. He soon learned they came from the island of Crete.

Like a terrier, Evans followed the scent and decided to excavate on Crete. He dug on the island for the first time in 1894, on a hillside named Knossos, where he found Mycenaean pottery. For two years he negotiated with the local landowners before purchasing the site in 1896. By this time he had traveled throughout the island and found traces of at least two undeciphered ancient writing systems—minute signs written on clay tablets. He named the two kinds of writing Linear A and Linear B, without any idea of which was the earlier. The scripts were the first bits of evidence of a lost culture. Later discoveries would show that it was a great and flourishing civilization that maintained close ties with the Greek mainland. Four more years passed before Evans started work at Knossos. The delay was because the islanders were fighting their hated Turkish masters. Characteristically, Evans wrote dispatches about the Cretan cause for the *Manchester Guardian* and distributed relief supplies as he collected antiquities.

The Knossos excavations began in March 1900 and continued intermittently

ARCHAEOLOGISTS

Arthur John Evans

BORN

July 8, 1851
Nash Mills, Hertfordshire, England

DIED

July 1, 1941
Oxford, England

EDUCATION

Oxford University (B.A. 1873)

ACCOMPLISHMENTS

Excavated the Palace of Minos at Knossos, Crete, and discovered the Minoan civilization. Wrote *The Palace of Minos* (1921–35), a systematic description of his palace excavations.

The wooden supports of Knossos's Grand Staircase had rotted by the time Arthur Evans had uncovered them, so he used reinforced concrete and cement to rebuild it in 1905.

for 30 years. On the very first day the diggers uncovered building foundations; on the second, a house with faded wall decorations. Evans realized immediately that his new palace was neither Greek nor Roman, but the home of ancient Cretan kings. He recovered clay tablets covered with the mysterious scripts he had noted before, some with Linear A, others with Linear B. There were also jewels. He promptly named this hitherto unknown civilization "Minoan," after the legendary King Minos of Crete, who was said to have lived at Knossos thousands of years ago. Within a few months Evans had uncovered more than 2 acres (0.8 hectare) of the palace, including a throne room complete

with stone throne and wall benches, living quarters, storage chambers, and a magnificent wall painting of a male cupbearer. Evans sent for Swiss artist Emile Guillieron, who helped him reconstruct the palace paintings: young people in formal processions, a young boy gathering saffron, mythical griffins and other beasts, and reliefs of charging bulls. Unlike some of his faster working predecessors, Evans filled notebook after notebook with meticulous notes of layers and small finds, with architectural details of individual rooms.

The Palace of Minos at Knossos was an extraordinary structure built around a central courtyard, entered from the north through a pillared hall.

> *"Less than a generation back the origin of Greek civilization, and with it the sources of all great culture that has ever been, were wrapped in an impenetrable mist."*
>
> —Arthur John Evans, "The Palace of Minos" *Monthly Review* (March 1901)

Rows of storage rooms opened into a narrow passageway to the west of the courtyard, with the capacity to store at least 75,000 gallons (284,000 liters) of olive oil alone. Two staircases of imposing design led to what Evans believed were the royal living quarters below. In 1908 Evans inherited a large fortune from a relative, much of which he spent on an ambitious architectural reconstruction of portions of the palace. By judicious rebuilding and reconstruction, he tried to show both Cretans and tourists an impression of Minoan civilization. He replaced wooden columns with concrete pillars painted to conform with Minoan decor. Any reconstruction of an archaeological site is controversial, but on the whole Evans succeeded in giving a fair impression of parts of the palace, even if his reconstructed wall friezes owe a considerable amount to his fertile imagination.

All later research on the Minoan civilization and its chronology begins with Arthur Evans's excavations. From 1900 to 1935 Evans commuted between Knossos and Oxford, studying the thousands of potsherds and other small finds from the palace. He had no radiocarbon dating methods or other modern chronological techniques to date the palace. Fortunately, the Minoans had traded with many other lands, including Egypt, where accurately dated artifacts abounded. By using Egyptian cross-references, Evans produced the first chronological framework for Minoan civilization, beginning with simple village farmers before 3000 BC. By that date "Early Minoans" were trading with other Aegean islands and Cyprus. Between 2200 and 1250 BC, the Middle and Late Minoan periods saw Cretan civilization at its height. The island was densely settled. Minoan ships traded as far afield as Egypt and Syria. The palace itself was rebuilt many times over its long life, partly because of earthquake damage, then abandoned before Minoan civilization collapsed in about 1200 BC. Today's chronologies place the end of the Minoans up to two centuries earlier, but the general outlines of Evans's framework are still in place.

Arthur Evans devoted the rest of his life to Knossos and the Minoans. He published his great four-volume report, *The Palace of Minos at Knossos*, over 14 years between 1921 and 1935, a colossal task by any standards. He painted a picture of a colorful, peaceful civilization with gifted artists, where bulls and a goddess of fertility played a central role in human life. But despite decades of effort, Evans failed to decipher the mysterious Cretan script, which had been the original objective in 1900. King George V knighted him for his work in 1931. Sir Arthur Evans died at the age of 90 in 1941. Eleven years later, another Englishman, Michael Ventris, unlocked some of the secrets of the script, which is still only partially deciphered to this day.

Few archaeologists discover lost civilizations, but Arthur John Evans was one of those few. His pioneering researches on Minoan civilization have, for the most part, stood the test of time. Radiocarbon dates and more refined excavation methods have changed many details, as archaeologists excavate further at Knossos and other lesser Minoan palaces. However, these changes in no way diminish the great achievements of an archaeologist born in the 19th century who excavated a lost civilization with methods belonging to the 20th.

FURTHER READING

Evans, Joan. *Time and Chance*. London: Longmans, 1942.

MacGillivray, John Alexander. *Minotaur: Sir Arthur Evans and the Archaeology of the Minoan Myth*. New York: Hill and Wang, 2000.

Harriet Boyd Hawes

EXCAVATOR OF
GOURNIA, CRETE

"You would think us mad, running from one fallen rock to another, discussing the number of columns, the use of this threshold or that conduit," wrote Harriet Boyd Hawes in a letter from Epidauros, Greece, in 1896. But this was her most profound enthusiasm, at a time when few women ever became archaeologists or went into the field. She was a woman of deep passions—for archaeology and the ancient Minoan civilization, for social justice and an end to war. She blazed a trail for women in archaeology both with her excavations on Crete and in the classroom.

Hawes was born in Boston, Massachusetts, to a family in the firefighting equipment business. At an early age she had an easy familiarity with the technology of hoses and firefighting foam. Her mother died when she was 10 months old. Hawes grew up in a family of four brothers, an experience that taught her to stand up for herself at an early age. She entered Smith College in 1881, where she developed a passion for the plight of workers and for humanitarian causes. At Smith she met Amelia Edwards, a British novelist turned Egyptologist, who came to lecture at the college and kindled her interest in ancient civilizations. After graduating in 1885, Hawes worked for some years as a teacher in private schools, eventually saving enough money to travel to Europe in 1895.

Europe was a revelation. Hawes fell in love with classical Greece and returned in 1896 to study at the British School of Archaeology in Athens. A fortunate encounter with the sister of actress Sarah Bernhardt on a train gave her access to high society in Athens and to the Greek royal court. (Greece at the time was still a monarchy.) Already independent-minded, she caused a stir by riding around the capital on a bicycle. In the intervals between social activities, Hawes studied ancient and modern Greek and toured the major archaeological sites. At the same time she followed the tumultuous politics of southeastern Europe, then as now a whirlwind of competing factions.

When war broke out between Greece and Turkey in 1897, Hawes volunteered for Red Cross duty in central Greece. She encountered the horrors of war firsthand, tending the wounded and coming under fire on several occasions while evacuating dying soldiers from the battlefield. Eventually she became accustomed to hardship and the terrible conditions of the field hospitals, where men lay so close together it was hard to dress their wounds. When the fighting ended, she stayed on to nurse victims of a typhoid epidemic among the troops. The Greeks never forgot the debt they owed Harriet Hawes.

Harriet Hawes and her mule party carry supplies on the road near Canea, Crete. She is on her way to her excavations at Gournia. Gournia was a remote place, and she had to import all her equipment, surveying instruments, food, and medicine on the backs of mules.

Back in the United States, Hawes won an 1898 Yale University Research Fellowship to study inscriptions at ancient Eleusis near Athens. However, she wanted to excavate, an archaeological activity which the American School of Classical Studies in Athens considered "men's work." By chance, she met a Cretan refugee who had fled from civil war on the island. He urged her to visit his homeland, where almost no one was digging. She contacted British archaeologist David Hogarth, who was already excavating on the island, and Arthur Evans, who was about to start work at the Palace of Minos at Knossos. They encouraged her plans, as did none other than Sophia Schliemann, Heinrich's widow, who lived in Athens. This formidable personality arranged for Hawes to meet other prominent archaeologists who were passing through the city. Among them was German excavator Wilhelm Dorpfeld, who had taken over the excavations at Troy after Schliemann's death.

Hawes arrived on Crete at a time when there were only 12 miles (19

kilometers) of paved roads. Archaeologists had to travel on muleback, and Hawes was no exception. She explored a stretch of the north coast around Mirabella Bay, following Evans's and Hogarth's advice to talk to the local people. Soon word of her explorations spread. Farmers brought her potsherds, bronze tools, and other artifacts plowed up from their fields. Then one peasant took her to Gournia Bay, where she found the foundations of stone walls and hundreds of painted potsherds. More artifacts came from the nearby hillside, and there were traces of small houses and a narrow stone-paved alleyway. The next day she returned with a crew of workers. Soon she had 100 men and 10 girls at work uncovering a small Minoan town, with potsherds and other finds identical to those being found by Arthur Evans at the Palace of Knossos to the west.

The Gournia excavations were an extraordinary achievement by any standards, the more so because they were carried out with very little money, by a woman living almost alone. Hawes lived in a rat-infested hovel near the

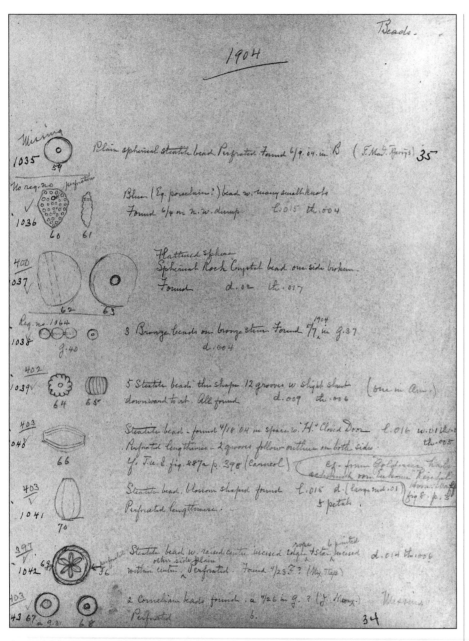

A partial inventory of Hawes's finds from Gournia, Crete. Her notes describe individual artifacts such as beads and clay vessels. She has assigned each artifact a number and provided a brief description, including its exact position in the dig.

nearly 3 acres (1.2 hectares) of the town and 75 dwellings, some with seven or eight rooms. The months of her excavation were some of the happiest times of her life. She was like a queen among the local villagers, dispensing medicines and even setting up a small lending library for her workers. At Gournia she met her future husband, Charles Henry Hawes, a quiet traveler with a taste for anthropology, who had arrived out of curiosity to see the site.

The Gournia excavations were a triumph. In 1902 Hawes became the first woman to lecture before the Archaeological Institute of America. Her work was praised for its value by fellow archaeologists, and in addition because she had dug the town virtually without expert colleagues, assisted only by a team of Cretan villagers. She published a book on Gournia in 1909, paying for its publication from her own pocket and with subscriptions contributed by potential readers living as far afield as Australia. She insisted on accurate drawings and beautiful color plates to illustrate artifacts that were unknown outside Greece. The Gournia monograph is still of value today.

Had World War I not intervened, Harriet Hawes would certainly have returned to Crete, and perhaps to Gournia. By this time she and her husband had the responsibilities of parenthood added to their professional duties. But she was appalled by the human suffering caused by the war. As the German army advanced on Serbia, she used most of her family's savings to purchase a ton of food and clothing. Then she set off for the island of Corfu off eastern Greece in February 1916, representing an organization called the American Distribution Service.

shore, while her crew camped under brush shelters. Everyone started work at 6 a.m. and finished 12 hours later, with a two-hour break in the middle of the day. Over three years of arduous, intermittent excavation, Hawes uncovered a compact, unfortified town with narrow paved alleyways and small stone houses. Steps led to a small courtyard and what may have been a tiny palace. During the excavations, Hawes exposed

Harriet Boyd Hawes

"Our men . . . worked vigorously, uncovering the home of a highland chieftain of Homer's time, exploring his 13 rooms and discovering his household utensils and his stone gaming-table, the oldest circular one yet found in Greek lands."

—from Harriet Hawes's diary (May 1900)

BORN

October 11, 1871
Boston, Massachusetts

DIED

March 31, 1945
Boston, Massachusetts

EDUCATION

Smith College, (B.A. 1885)

ACCOMPLISHMENTS

First woman to excavate on Crete; discovered and investigated Gournia, a Minoan town; taught archaeology at Wellesley College for many years; led humanitarian work in Greece and on Western Front in World War I. Wrote *Gournia, Vasiliki and Other Prehistoric Sites on the Isthmus of Ierapetra, Greece* (1908).

Thousands of starving Serbian soldiers had fled to Corfu. The Greek authorities quartered the sick and dying under primitive tents on a small island nearby. Hawes effectively took charge of the island, delivering supplies, cooking meals, and eventually building a temporary barracks. She achieved near miracles under terrible conditions, paying closest attention to the dying, who were accommodated in a special tent. The Corfu experience had a powerful effect on her. When she returned to the United States, she refused to lecture about archaeology, only about her wartime experiences. Archaeology, she said, was unimportant in times of war. She ended World War I as a nurse volunteer in American Red Cross Military Hospital Number 5 near Paris. Calling herself the "Old Lady Aide," she insisted on working the night shift.

In 1918, Henry Hawes became the financial officer of Boston's Museum of Fine Arts. Harriet Hawes threw herself into teaching the history of ancient art at nearby Wellesley College, a course she taught for 16 years. She returned to Crete just once—in 1926 with her daughter Mary. This time she was a respected and beloved celebrity. Arthur Evans himself gave her a tour of the Knossos excavations. She traveled to Gournia on a mule to a rapturous welcome from the local people and found the site unchanged. Back home, she continued to teach, but became increasingly preoccupied with socialism and union politics rather than archaeology. Always an activist, she insisted on traveling in Czechoslovakia as the Nazis were entering the country. She spent World War II in Massachusetts, nursing her ailing husband and growing vegetables for the war effort. She died soon after her husband, on March 31, 1945.

By 1939, this pioneer archaeologist had been almost forgotten. Several important books and articles on Minoan archaeology actually gave credit for the Gournia excavations to a male archaeologist, Rodney Seager, who had acted briefly as one of her assistants, then gone on to excavate other well-known Minoan sites. Were he alive today, Seager would have been the first to give her credit. The Gournia report shows that Harriet Boyd Hawes was the equal of any archaeologist of her day. Only in recent years has her important contribution to archaeology been recognized with the publication of her biography in 1992, and because of an increased interest in the careers of early women archaeologists.

FURTHER READING

Allsebrook, Mary. *Born to Rebel: The Life of Harriet Boyd Hawes*. Oxford: Oxbow, 1992.

Alfred Vincent Kidder

A PIONEER OF SOUTHWESTERN ARCHAEOLOGY

Alfred Vincent Kidder was a pioneer of North American archaeology. His excavations at Pecos Pueblo in the Southwest between 1915 and 1922 revolutionized our understanding of the ancient Pueblo Indian societies of the region. Kidder was born at Marquette, Michigan, in 1885. When he was seven years old, his family moved to Cambridge, Massachusetts, where his well-read father, a retired businessman, befriended many of the leading scientists of the day. The young Kidder met archaeologist Raphael Pumpelly, who was excavating cities in Central Asia, Alexander Agassiz, one of the pioneers of Ice Age geology, and the Harvard archaeologist Frederick Ward Putnam, an expert on the ancient mound-builder cultures of eastern North America. He attended the best private schools, grew up in an atmosphere of intellectual curiosity and scholarship, and acquired a lifelong interest in natural history as a result. At age 15 he published an article on birds.

In 1904 Kidder entered Harvard with the intention of becoming a physician. But his dislike of chemistry and mathematics turned his thoughts in other directions. During his junior year, in 1907, he applied for a summer field survey in the Southwest under the direction of archaeologist Edgar Hewitt. The survey was nominally a field school, but Hewitt

Alfred Kidder takes a break by resting outside a Pueblo dwelling in Pecos, New Mexico. Kidder's excavation technique of examining stratified layers of debris transformed our understanding of the Pueblo Indian culture.

merely showed Kidder and his companions the area they were to work on and left them to it. He reappeared every six or seven weeks on horseback to check on their progress, assuming correctly that the undergraduates would develop their own methods. Kidder and his now close friend Sylvanus Morley, later to become an eminent Maya archaeologist, mapped sites in Colorado and New Mexico. The summer changed Kidder's life. He returned to Harvard, where he took up archaeology seriously. He graduated in 1908, then spent another field season with Hewitt, this time in Utah.

In 1908 Alfred Kidder entered graduate school at Harvard University to work on a doctorate in anthropology. He received training in field methods from the Egyptologist George Reisner. Art historian George Chase gave him a sound grounding in the analysis of ceramic (clay) vessels of all kinds. It was no coincidence that Kidder's doctoral dissertation was on the style and decorative motifs of Pueblo pottery. Harvard was a remarkable experience for Kidder; the rich curriculum included an opportunity to take courses from anthropologist Franz Boas, who was a visitor for a term. Boas was a fanatic for minor details and the cultural traits of Native American civilizations. He gave Kidder a sense of the importance of detailed analysis of any human society, something Kidder took to heart.

While studying for his doctorate, Kidder excavated in Newfoundland and again in the Southwest. He also traveled in the Near East, where he had a chance to visit excavations by George Reisner and others on the Nile. There he absorbed excavation methods unknown in the United States, such as the systematic excavation of human burials and careful observation of sequences of human occupation through time. Such techniques were still in their infancy. He also realized just how important the humble pot fragments and other tiny

artifacts were for the study of the past. These lessons served him well in the Southwest. He received his doctorate in 1914, just before the outbreak of World War I.

In 1915 Kidder embarked on the most important work of his career. He started excavating into the deep, stratified layers of Pecos Pueblo, New Mexico, a settlement close to a Spanish mission, and known to have been occupied far back into ancient times. Investigating and recording the layers, or strata, in such a location is critically important to archaeology, for it provides the only way of studying changes in human societies through time. Stratigraphic observation, as the method is called, starts with the proven assumption that the earliest occupation was at the bottom. This was largely a new approach in the area. Up until then, most Southwestern excavation had been little concerned with recording different periods of occupation, but more with clearing ruins and recovering fragile artifacts such as baskets and beautifully decorated Pueblo pots.

In 1914, archaeologist Nels Nelson had dug into San Cristobal Pueblo, New Mexico, in 1-foot (3 meter) depths in various layers, from which he recovered different pottery types. But it was left to Kidder to explain what these differences meant. Were they reliable indi-cators of changing Pueblo culture, or merely shifts in pot-making fashions? The answer could only come from more investigation.

Kidder excavated into the deep layers of Pecos on a massive scale. During the early seasons he refined Nelson's San Cristobal approach by abandoning arbitrary levels and making detailed sketches of the way the refuse discarded by the inhabitants had accumulated. He traced the natural strata of the middens—buried heaps of discarded bones, broken utensils, and the like—and carefully recorded the pot fragments found in them. Kidder

Alfred Vincent Kidder

BORN
October 29, 1885
Marquette, Michigan

DIED
June 11, 1963
Cambridge, Massachusetts

EDUCATION
Harvard University (A.B. 1908; Ph.D. 1914)

ACCOMPLISHMENTS
Developed first stratigraphic cultural sequence for southwestern United States, using a multidisciplinary approach there for the first time; as Director of Carnegie Institution's Division of Historical Research, introduced multidisciplinary approach to and supervised Maya research. Wrote *An Introduction to the Study of Southwestern Archaeology* (1924), a classic on the subject.

"The Southwest owes to outside sources little more than the germs of its culture. Its development from these germs has been a local and almost wholly an independent one."

—Alfred Vincent Kidder, *An Introduction to the Study of Southwestern Archaeology* (1924)

followed the example of Reisner's work in Egypt and used pegs and strings to mark off each specific areas. Horizontal and vertical measurements made from the strings recorded the location of every element in three dimensions. This made it possible to map the precise rise and fall of even the smallest ash layers. His potsherd catalogs were also modeled on those used by Reisner along the Nile to develop a meticulous analysis of the profound changes in pottery forms and, above all, surface decoration over many centuries. For example, Kidder found that the first occupants of the pueblo made a distinctive black-on-white style of pottery. He also recovered hundreds of human skeletons.

While waiting for induction into the army in 1917, Kidder visited modern-day Hopi and other pueblos in the Southwest and acquired a knowledge both of Southwestern ethnography and of modern Pueblo culture. In all his subsequent researches he melded anthropology and archaeology, the study of both the living culture and the ancient, into definitive summaries of ancient Pueblo society.

After Kidder's military service, Excavations at Pecos resumed in 1920 and produced the discovery of still more human burials. Kidder called on the expert services of biological anthropologist Ernest Albert Hooton. He insisted that Hooton visit the excavations so he could study the human remains as they emerged in the trenches and witness the actual field conditions of their discovery. This was one of the first cases where a skeletal expert worked in the field alongside a North American archaeologist. Soon Kidder had data on the sex and age of the skeletons, as well as some interesting information on life expectancy and ancient pathology. Hooton showed, for example, that most of the Pecos people died in their 20s.

By 1922 Kidder had turned his attention to the architecture and expansion of the pueblo, and excavated some of the earliest occupation levels. After that, he virtually ceased excavation there to turn his attention to analyzing his many finds, and to surveying and digging other sites in the neighborhood of Pecos. He extended his approach of combined archaeology and anthropology to include studies of modern-day agriculture, human remains, even public health.

By 1927 his stratigraphic excavations and pottery studies from Pecos had produced a great amount of evidence and data. He was confident enough of his understanding and interpretation of this information to develop a detailed sequence of ancient Pueblo and pre-Pueblo cultures for the Southwest. Kidder's sequence began with Basket Maker cultures, at least 2,000 years old, which eventually evolved into the Pueblo societies of later periods. At the same time, he founded an annual Pecos Conference, where he and his colleagues gathered to report on their latest researches and to discuss problems of common concern. The Pecos Conference is still an annual event today.

The Pecos excavations established Kidder as a superlative fieldworker. The dig trained a generation of students who later used Kidder's methods in the field on their own digs throughout the Southwest. These accomplishments established Kidder as one of the founders of modern North American archaeology. But that was not all.

The second half of Kidder's archaeological career took him to Central America. In 1929 he became director of the Carnegie Institution's Division of Historical Research. The Carnegie served as a national research institute. Its main interests were in the physical sciences, but it poured considerable sums into archaeology and the social sciences in the 1930s and 1940s. Although Kidder spent most of his time on administration, he supervised field projects, most of which followed his multidisciplinary approach perfected at Pecos. He called a meeting of all archaeologists supported by Carnegie at the Maya city of Chichén Itzá in 1930, to share new ideas about Maya archaeology. Kidder felt that too many archaeologists just dug in their "own little patches" without taking any account of what other scientists like botanists or historians were doing. He persuaded aviator Charles Lindbergh to join forces with him in an aerial survey of the Yucatán Peninsula, which resulted in the discovery of many new locations. He employed his friend Sylvanus Morley to continue his groundbreaking work on Maya inscriptions. Anthropologist Robert Redfield studied modern Maya communities with Carnegie support.

Kidder retired in 1950, but he still exercised great influence on Maya archaeology. By 1953 he was insisting that environmental research was all-important. He posed fundamental questions: How had the Maya modified their rainforest environment? What effects had environmental change had on the development of their civilization? But now the Carnegie Institution was placing more and more emphasis on the physical sciences as a result of World War II. Funds for archaeology shrank sharply. Kidder retired from the institution in 1950. The Division of Historical Research was abolished in 1958. Meanwhile, Kidder retired to Cambridge, Massachusetts, where his home became a gathering place for both fellow archaeologists and students until his death in 1963.

Alfred Kidder established many of the basic principles of North American archaeology. The artifact classification

systems he developed at Pecos arranged potsherds by such categories as method of manufacture, decoration, and form, in much the same kind of taxonomy that Carl Linnaeus used for plants. As both fieldworker and archaeological administrator, Kidder had few peers in the 20th century.

FURTHER READING

Givens, Douglas R. *Alfred Vincent Kidder and the Development of Americanist Archaeology.* Albuquerque: University of New Mexico Press, 1992.

Woodbury, Richard B. *Alfred V. Kidder.* New York: Columbia University Press, 1973.

This illustration from Kidder's Pecos report shows painted Pueblo vessels. He was able to determine the sequence of the pottery after years of excavation, and he demonstrated a change from vessels with black designs painted on white backgrounds to pots with painted glazes on their surfaces.

Oscar Montelius

MASTER ARTIFACT CLASSIFIER

Oscar Montelius was a world authority on the prehistoric artifacts of Europe. He used changes in such artifacts as Bronze Age brooches and swords to trace chronological links from one side of the continent to the other.

F ew archaeologists become Royal Antiquaries, but Oscar Montelius did. He was appointed to that post in the court of Sweden in honor of his life's work, which had made him one of the most influential European archaeologists of the late 19th and early 20th centuries. He was not an excavator, but a kind of classifying detective who developed an impressive amount of new information from studying the most prosaic of prehistoric artifacts—the bronze brooch, dagger, pin, and sword, for example.

Montelius was born in Stockholm, Sweden, and developed an interest in ancient history during childhood. After obtaining a doctorate in archaeology at the University of Uppsala in 1867, he went on a series of study tours across Europe, examining stone, bronze, and iron artifacts from dozens of archaeological sites. Montelius was deeply influenced by the evolutionary teachings of Charles Darwin. He also built on the careful excavations of his intellectual predecessor, Danish archaeologist J. J. A. Worsaae, who had proved the chronological validity of the Stone, Bronze, and Iron ages. Montelius soon became an expert on prehistoric artifacts of every kind, especially bronze brooches, bowls, and swords. In 1873 he published a pioneering study of these artifacts from northern and central Sweden, using evolving series of artifacts to distinguish between an early and a late Bronze Age in the region.

Montelius published this research as numerous new excavations throughout Europe produced hundreds of new artifacts. Although attached to the State Historical Museum, he spent much of each year traveling away from Stockholm, visiting museums and newly excavated sites, combing all parts of Europe for new material. He produced a series of brilliant and highly detailed technical reports, culminating in his *Brooches from the Bronze Age* (1881), an artifact study that drew on finds not only from Scandinavia, but also from much richer collections from Greece and Italy.

Montelius followed this important work with *On the Dating of the Bronze Age, particularly in relation to Scandinavia* (1885). This closely argued archaeological masterpiece refused to take nationalistic perspectives, which were characteristic of European archaeology at the time. Instead, he focused on the artifacts themselves, in an innovative use of artifact classification that was to dominate European archaeology for more than half a century. "I have given individual consideration to each of the main series of weapons, tools, ornaments, and pottery, together with their ornamentation, so as to determine the course of their evolution, and to find out in what order the types . . . succeed one another," he wrote at the end of his career in 1903.

"Almost all the finds of past centuries have disappeared without a trace . . . We can readily imagine the importance of these facts if we imagine that an antiquarian some thousand or two thousand years hence should attempt to represent our own manner of life, and yet had scarcely any other material for the purpose beyond the verdigrised and rusty remains of our metal works."

—Oscar Montelius, *The Civilisation of Sweden in Heathen Times* (1888)

Oscar Montelius

BORN
September 9, 1843
Stockholm, Sweden

DIED
November 4, 1921
Stockholm, Sweden

EDUCATION
University of Uppsala (Ph.D. 1865)

ACCOMPLISHMENTS
Developed the first comprehensive artifact classifications for prehistoric Europe, which linked Scandinavia with the Mediterranean world and work is the foundation of all later research into European prehistory. Wrote *Brooches from the Bronze Age* (1881); *On the Dating of the Bronze Age, particularly in relation to Scandinavia* (1885); *The Civilisation of Sweden in Heathen Times* (English translation 1888).

Oscar Montelius was a genius at a kind of typology—artifact classification—that involved tracing minute details of Bronze Age artifacts from one end of Europe to the other. He focused on the shapes of sword blades, for example: narrow ones being used to stab, while the wider ones were slashing weapons. In jewelry, even the smallest details of brooches used to adorn clothing had significance in Montelius's eyes, for he assumed that changes in fashion and design came slowly and over time. He was careful to base his Bronze Age research on artifacts found with undisturbed burials. His classifications depended on accurate dating, finds that had never been disturbed by later activity, and careful observation of stratigraphic layers in archaeological sites. Bronze Age burials were ideal for his purpose, because they were plentiful and contained a wide range of distinctive artifacts. Montelius's classifications traced the development of artifacts from strictly practical prototypes like simple pins, then showed how hitherto strictly functional features like the hasp of a pin became more elaborate and decorative until, centuries later, a once simple Bronze Age pin had become a highly elaborate ornament worn by important chieftains.

Montelius not only assumed the simple and functional was the earliest, he set out to document it with reference to other artifacts found in the same graves. For example, Bronze Age axes and adzes first appeared as artifacts with low flanges that held the handle. Soon, the makers elaborated them with deeper flanges and set them at an angle to better secure the wooden handle. Montelius followed the evolution of a spiral design used to hold the two prongs of the shaft set between them to prevent splitting as it fused with the axe, then showed how it was modified into a purely ornamental feature as the Bronze Age axe developed a socket to hold the handle. He drew on modern comparisons to make fundamental points. A brilliant teacher, Montelius demonstrated how his system worked by showing how railroad coaches developed from basically stagecoaches set on flanged wheels into a much more efficient design, which, however, still retained an outside entrance to each compartment, as would a series of stagecoaches fastened end to end.

By 1881 Montelius had subdivided the European Bronze Age into six periods, cross-dating the later ones by using artifacts of known historical age in Egypt and southwestern Asia as the

This illustration of a dolmen-style megalithic tomb in Denmark appeared in Oscar Montelius's *Civilizations of Sweden*. A dolmen is an ancient tomb with upright stones that support a heavy capstone. The structure was originally covered with earth to form a burial mound.

basis for a provisional chronology. He showed how bronze first appeared in Egypt by the third millennium BC and in Greece with the Mycenaeans of the second millennium, with iron only appearing there in about 1000 BC. Since Bronze Age artifacts found north and south of the Alps resembled each other closely, Montelius was able to show that the Bronze Age began in central Europe in the mid-second millennium BC and ended in northern Europe in the 5th century BC.

The importance of *Brooches from the Bronze Age* cannot be overestimated. At one step, Oscar Montelius placed European prehistory on a new, scientific footing, even if his evolutionary conclusions were controversial to some of his colleagues, who did not believe that it was possible to trace minute design changes through time. From the Bronze Age he turned his attention to the Stone Age (four periods) and Iron Age (eight periods), using the same approach. His classifications are still a fundamental part of the structure of modern European archaeology more than a century later.

A scholar of exceptional perception and intelligence, Montelius developed his Bronze Age classifications while serving as a widely traveling member of the State Historical Museum. He made a point of cultivating close relationships with staff members of lesser museums in Denmark. His calm disposition and diplomatic manners made him friends throughout Europe and Scandinavia. Montelius favored order and peaceful cooperation. His abilities were recognized by his appointment to the honorific post of Royal Antiquary in 1907 at the age of 64.

Montelius was always surrounded by a lively group of students and enjoyed good working relationships with several important colleagues, among them his Danish counterpart Sophus Müller, an archaeologist and prominent official of the National Museum who spent his entire career working on the rich collections in that institution. Like Montelius, Müller was an artifact expert. The two men would stand in a museum laboratory for hours arguing amiably about the fine details of the Bronze Age brooch, and rarely agree with one another. But in the end Müller accepted Montelius's classification of the Bronze Age and added many details to his scheme.

Artifact classification is not the most glamorous part of archaeology, but it remains the foundation of the science. Oscar Montelius's brilliant classifications of prehistoric European artifacts placed both Scandinavian archaeology and the prehistory of Europe on a scientific footing for the first time. All subsequent research into ancient Europe still depends on his pioneering work.

FURTHER READING

Astrom, Paul, ed. *Oscar Montelius, 150 Years*. Stockholm: Almquist and Wiksell, 1995.

Klindt-Jensen, Ole. *A History of Scandinavian Archaeology*. London: Thames and Hudson, 1975.

Sylvanus Griswold Morley

EXAMINER OF ANCIENT MAYA

Sylvanus Morley was one of the first archaeologists to make systematic copies of Maya glyphs (picture-writing symbols) and to interpret them. He was also untiring in his efforts to bring the achievements of Maya civilization to a wide public audience.

Sylvanus Griswold Morley, known to his many friends as "Van," was born in Chester, Pennsylvania, in 1883. His father, Benjamin, was an engineer who became vice president of the Pennsylvania Military Academy. His mother taught languages at the same institution until 1894, when the family moved west to Romley, Colorado, where Benjamin Morley became a partner in a successful gold mine.

The young Morley became interested in archaeology at the age of 15 as a result of reading popular books about ancient Mexico. Before he graduated from high school, Morley had already decided he wanted to become an archaeologist. He corresponded with Frederick Ward Putnam, the director of the Peabody Museum of Archaeology and Ethnology at Harvard University. Putnam recommended that he read H. H. Bancroft's *The Native Races*, the most up-to-date summary of American archaeology at the time. His father saw no future in archaeology and enrolled his son in the Pennsylvania Military Academy in 1903, intending that he become a civil engineer. Dutifully, Sylvanus completed his degree and graduated in 1904, just after his father's death. His engineering training taught him field survey methods, which were to prove invaluable in later life.

With his father no longer looking over his shoulder, Morley now enrolled at Harvard to study anthropology, his studies paid for by a wealthy aunt. At first, Egyptology attracted him, but his mentor, Frederick Putnam, turned Morley's attention to Central America. He paid his first visit to the Yucatán Peninsula in 1904 and was captivated. Another Harvard archaeologist, Alfred Marsten Tozzer, narrowed his focus to the Maya. This resulted in a chance to study linguistics in the Yucatán under the auspices of the Archaeological Institute of America. His travels brought him to the Maya city at Chichén Itzá, where archaeologist Edward Thompson was dredging the Sacred Cenote, a deep pool, in a search for sacrificial offerings. Morley spent some time watching Thompson at work in the murky depths of the Cenote and pored over his collections of pottery and sacrificial objects, such as figurines, from the pool. The experience changed his life. He soon abandoned pure linguistics as a scholarly subject and became an archaeologist with a particular interest in the still-undeciphered Maya system of symbol-writing.

Sylvanus Morley explores Maya country in 1915, accompanied by two local guides. Fieldwork in the Maya rainforest was never easy, and Morley hated it much of the time. He once said: "Anyone who says he likes the bush is either a . . . fool or a . . . liar."

Back at Harvard, Morley took Maya archaeology courses from Tozzer. He began to delve into the fascinating mysteries of Maya writing, which was to become his specialty. Morley also worked with Alfred Kidder in the Southwest as part of New Mexico archaeologist Edgar Hewitt's "field school," forging a lifelong friendship and learning field methods at the same time. His expertise as a surveyor and his cheerful manner made a long summer's work in effectively unmapped country a good deal easier.

Morley had no profound interest in the Southwest, but he continued to work for Hewitt at the School of American Archaeology until 1915. He owed much to Hewitt's rugged common sense and tough approach to fieldwork, which shrugged off hardships and believed in leaving students alone in the field to learn for themselves.

Sylvanus Morley was appointed to a research position in Maya archaeology at the Carnegie Institution of Washington D.C. in 1915, largely on the basis of his enthusiastic proposal for field research. This was the job of his dreams, one that allowed him to spend 10 years surveying some of the most inaccessible parts of the Maya homeland. He traveled by mule and on foot under the most trying conditions. Flies and ticks besieged him everywhere. Morley hated the discomfort of fieldwork, but he persisted because he was determined to acquire the basic data on Maya symbols to permit decipherment of their ancient writing. "Anyone who says he likes the bush is either a . . . fool or a . . . liar," he would remark when anyone extolled the romance of fieldwork.

The 1916 expedition was a typical Morley field trip. Plagued with recurring bouts of malaria, he took a doctor with him as he traveled from New Orleans to Guatemala, visiting such major sites as the ancient Maya city of

Copán. The only people who knew the forest well were the native *chicleros*, men who tapped chicozapote trees to collect the raw material for chewing gum. Morley offered them a reward of $25 in gold for every unknown ruin with inscriptions reported to him. A rich bounty of sites resulted, among them the large city of Uaxactún, a day's walk north of the great Maya metropolis at Tikal. Returning from Uaxactún, Morley's party was mistaken for a party of revolutionaries and ambushed by government soldiers. The doctor and Morley's guide were killed. Morley himself would have been killed had he not dismounted a few moments earlier to recover his glasses, which had been ripped off by a liana vine. The survivors hid in the bush for hours until the troops moved on.

During the later years of World War I, Morley worked for U.S. Naval Intelligence under the disguise of a traveling scientist in Central America, until being posted to the Naval Coast Defense Reserve in Washington D.C. When the war ended, he resumed Carnegie Institution field seasons, mostly in the Petén region of the southern Yucatán. The Carnegie post was ideal for him, for it involved no teaching responsibilities and supplied abundant funds and plenty of help from graphic artists and other technicians. He copied inscriptions from site after site, publishing a steady stream of important reports on the still undeciphered Maya writing. *The Inscriptions of Copán* appeared in 1925—643 pages, with 33 photographs and 91 drawings. This was one of the first systematic records of the Maya symbols ever made, and an important basis for future research. The people of Copán made him an honorary citizen of the town for his work, and he received a honorary

doctorate from his alma mater, the Pennsylvania Military Academy. Publication in 1937 and 1938 of his five-volume work *The Inscriptions of Petén*, with its 2,065 pages, 187 plates, and 39 maps, added to his already illustrious reputation. The Guatemalan government honored him with the Order of the Quetzal.

By this time, Morley was increasingly obsessed with understanding the Maya calendar and writing system, and with the importance of telling the public about the great achievements of Maya civilization. The Maya calendar was based on secular and religious sequences of days that interlocked in a kind of giant gear wheel, the sequences repeating themselves every 52 years. This cyclical calendar was combined with a "Long Count," a linear sequence of years that extended far into the remote past.

Morley's ultimate ambition was to study the Maya of Chichén Itzá in the northern Yucatán, but he never achieved his wish. As director of all Carnegie archaeological work in the region, he was in charge of excavations at Chichén Itzá, but had no interest in administering the fieldwork or dealing with budgets. Instead of excavating to establish the history of the city, he devoted most resources to reconstructing temples and other structures for tourists. Morley himself spent a great deal of time seeking out inscriptions from as many Maya sites as possible. His friend Alfred Kidder took over the directorship he had held for many years. Morley was quietly shunted to one side. His narrowly focused research was considered old-fashioned in an era when Kidder and others were looking at the Maya from much broader perspectives rather than focusing only on inscriptions.

Sylvanus Griswold Morley

BORN

June 7, 1883
Chester, Pennsylvania

DIED

September 2, 1948
Santa Fe, New Mexico

EDUCATION

Pennsylvania Military Academy
(graduated 1904)
Harvard College (A.B. 1908)

ACHIEVEMENTS

Developed the first comprehensive surveys of Maya sites in the Yucatán Peninsula; carried out fundamental research on the Maya calendar; was a major spokesperson about ancient Maya achievements. Wrote *The Inscriptions of Copán* (1925); *The Inscriptions of Petén* (1937–38); *The Ancient Maya* (1946).

> *"We may safely acclaim the ancient Maya, without fear of successful contradiction, as the most brilliant aboriginal people on the planet."*
>
> —Sylvanus Griswold Morley, *The Ancient Maya* (1946)

Sylvanus Morley continued to work on Maya glyphs until his retirement from the Carnegie's Division of Historical Research in 1947. He then returned to the Southwest. After a year as director of the Museum of New Mexico in Santa Fe, he died in 1948.

Morley was a gregarious, charming man who spent a lifetime as the ancient Maya's spokesman to the outside world. Unfortunately, he had an obsession with the Maya calendar, so his copies of inscriptions and his writings are concerned almost entirely with dates. He wrestled with details of the celebrated Maya Long Count linear calendar and cyclical time scale in inscriptions to the exclusion of virtually every other kind of archaeological information. One can hardly blame him, for his work reflected the abiding interests of Maya specialists at the time, who believed the Maya were peaceful priests, obsessed with astronomy and the measurement of time using the heavenly bodies. He and his contemporaries never produced a comprehensive publication of Maya inscriptions that would be of value today. They ventured no further than the calendars. Nor were Morley's copies good enough for serious scholarship. They were nothing beside the brilliant photographs taken by his immediate predecessor Alfred Maudslay with an immense glass-plate camera in the 1880s.

Morley's greatness came from his unending enthusiasm and his passion for Maya civilization. He introduced numerous young scholars to the excitements of Central American research and helped make the ancient Maya a household word. Today, Maya archaeology is highly specialized and the glyphs have been deciphered, in one of the great scientific achievements of the 20th century. But today's great and continuing advances in our knowledge of the Maya would not be possible without the devoted, often solitary work of Sylvanus Morley.

FURTHER READING

Brunhouse, Robert L. *Sylvanus G. Morley and the World of the Ancient Maya.* Norman: University of Oklahoma Press, 1971.

Coe, Michael. *Breaking the Maya Code.* London: Thames and Hudson, 1992.

Aurel Stein

CENTRAL ASIAN TRAVELER

Aurel Stein used his education in Asian languages to travel through little-known parts of Asia and do extensive research. In his research, Stein often used methods that today would be considered looting or piracy, but he managed to preserve hundreds of priceless artifacts of ancient Asian culture.

xplorer, Asian traveler, and archaeologist, Aurel Stein was one of the last great archaeological adventurers. His journeys through remote parts of Central Asia provided the outside world with its first scientific glimpse of the Silk Road that once linked ancient China with the West.

Aurel Stein was born into a Jewish family in Budapest, Hungary, in 1862. Nathan and Anna Hirschler Stein faced intense persecution, so they baptized their son a Protestant to make it possible for him to attend a prestigious school. When he was 10, they sent him to the highly regarded Kreuzschule in Dresden, Germany. Young Aurel soon showed considerable intellectual talents, but also went through Hungarian military training, which gave him valuable surveying skills and an eye for landscape, essential qualifications for an archaeologist. He received his doctorate in linguistics from the University of Tubingen, Germany, in 1883, then carried out two years of

When Aurel Stein found the temples and facades of the Cave of the Thousand Buddhas in 1907, they were crumbling and succumbing to the ravages of time.

already acquired a reputation as a traveler. In 1900 and 1901, he had explored remote country on the Chinese and Indian borders, where he made a study of the still little-known Khotan Empire, an early center for the spread of Buddhism from India to China. Khotan fell to the Arabs in the 8th century AD and grew rich on Silk Road caravan trade between China and the West. Stein's primary objective was to examine the trade in artifacts and sacred books that were being sold to European collectors at the time. He was among the first Europeans to venture into Khotan country, so his collections and first two books, *Chronicle of Kings of Kashmir* (1900) and *Ancient Khotan* (1907), aroused considerable interest.

Aurel Stein traveled deep into Central Asia on a second long journey from 1906 to 1913, probably his best known expedition, into the least accessible parts of China. It was on this trip that he visited the Caves of a Thousand Buddhas, carved into sandstone at Dunhuang, in extreme western China. "I noticed at once that fresco paintings covered the walls of all the grottoes . . . The 'Caves of the Thousand Buddhas' were indeed tenanted not by Buddhist recluses, however holy, but by images of the Enlightened One himself," he wrote in *The Ruins of Desert Cathay* (1912). Almost all the shrines contained a huge seated Buddha, with divine attendants.

Chinese monks had founded the earliest shrine in these caves in AD 366, forming important communities in the region, which was an important crossroads for the Silk Road. The 492 caves here contain elaborate Buddhist artworks of every kind. Stein had heard rumors of a cache of ancient manuscripts. He made discreet inquiries and

post-doctoral research in Asian languages and archaeology at Oxford University in England.

Stein's strong language qualifications and surveying expertise ensured him a civil service career with the Indian Educational Service, beginning in 1887. He became Principal of the Oriental College in Lahore, India, but transferred to the Indian Archaeological Survey in 1910. By this time he had

was able to see a scroll—a "beautifully preserved roll of paper, about a foot high and perhaps 15 yards long"—covered with undecipherable characters. Stein bought this priceless manuscript for a small piece of silver. Some weeks later he witnessed a great festival at the shrine attended by thousands of pilgrims. He learned that a monk had discovered a hidden deposit of ancient manuscripts about two years earlier while restoring one of the shrines. A walled-off chamber contained "a solid mass of manuscript bundles rising to a high of nearly 10 feet," undisturbed for almost a thousand years.

In a neighboring room, Stein unrolled manuscripts and paintings on silk and linen, many of them designed to be hung in shrines. The manuscripts, which were Chinese versions of Buddhist texts, had been compiled in the third and fourth centuries AD. With infinite care, Stein examined the entire collection and bought seven cases of priceless manuscripts and more than 300 paintings for four horseshoes of silver. He discreetly packed them and carried them away on his camels and ponies. They now are in the British Museum. While his methods are condemned as unethical robbery today, it is an open question whether the manuscripts would have survived for posterity had Stein not passed them into expert hands.

By the time he returned to India, Stein had acquired an international reputation for his archaeological discoveries and manuscript finds. The Indian Archaeological Service continued funding of his journeys, which the Indian government saw both as a way of acquiring vital geographical and political information, and of collecting priceless artifacts for the national collections.

In 1913 to 1916, Stein left on a third expedition, outside India. This time he faced keen competition from French, German, and Russian archaeologists, who were attracted to Central Asia by his previous remarkable discoveries. He penetrated deep into Mongolia and traced unknown parts of the Silk Road, acquiring artifacts at every turn. Word of his activities had spread to local officials, who were now more suspicious and harder to deal with. Nevertheless, Stein returned with many unique manuscripts and magnificent jade ornaments and fine pottery. Never an excavator, he preferred to purchase articles for as low a price as possible, or to collect them from deserted archaeological sites.

During the 1920s, Stein became interested in the Harappan civilization, centered on the Indus River in what is now Pakistan, which dated to about 2000 BC. He followed excavations at the sites of the ancient cities of Harappa and Mohenjo-daro with great interest, realizing that these ancient trading centers might have links to Mesopotamia and the Mediterranean world far to the west. He set out on numerous small-scale expeditions into the wilds of Persia and Iraq, searching for these links, following a punishing routine, despite being in his 60s. He wrote: "I am hard at work daily from 7:00 a.m. to 6:00 p.m., pushing on as well as my poor pen, and my inveterate claim at critical soundness, permit the account of . . . my expedition."

During the remainder of his career, Stein undertook many difficult tours of central Asian lands, partly on intelligence missions and also on archaeological ones. In 1932 he found the site of Gendrosia in Persia, a stop on Alexander the Great's expedition to India in 332 BC. As late as the 1940s, when he

Aurel Stein

BORN
November 26, 1862
Budapest, Hungary

DIED
October 25, 1943
Kabul, Afganistan

EDUCATION
University of Tubingen (Ph.D. 1883), Oxford University (post-doctoral study)

ACCOMPLISHMENTS
One of the first Western experts on the archaeology and ancient societies of Central Asia and the Silk Road, his books are important sources on still little-known parts of Central Asia. Wrote *Sand-buried Ruins of Khotan* (1903); The *Ruins of Desert Cathay* (1912); *Innermost Asia: Detailed Report of Explorations in Central Asia, Ken-su, and Eastern Iran* (1928).

> *"The recollection of this fascinating site will ever suggest the bracing air and the unsullied peace and purity of the wintry desert."*
>
> —Aurel Stein, *Sand-buried Ruins of Khotan* (1903)

was in his 70s, Stein was mapping the inaccessible eastern frontiers of the Roman Empire in modern-day Iran, where he found Babylonian artifacts that linked the region to early Mesopotamian civilization.

Aurel Stein spent much of his later years writing three classic works about his archaeological travels. *On Central Asian Tracks* (1933), *Archaeological Reconnaissances in Southeast Iran* (1937), and *On Old Routes of Western Iran* (1940) offer insights into the difficulties of his remote travels, as well as describing key archaeological discoveries which linked largely forgotten ancient civilizations that had once traded with one another. Almost single-handed, and in the face of intense rivalries from archaeologists of other nations, Stein amassed huge collections and priceless information about an archaeological wilderness where East had met West. He was knighted for his services to scholarship and the British Museum.

By today's standards Stein's looting activities and associations with treasure hunters and tomb robbers are ethically indefensible and his reputation is discredited, especially in China. His great contribution was to link the ancient East and West. His contemporary, Sir Leonard Woolley, who himself dug the biblical city of Ur in Iraq under tough conditions, remarked once that Stein performed "the most daring and adventurous raid on the ancient world that any archaeologist has attempted." There is much truth in this remark. Stein's methods were questionable, but he opened the eyes of the scholarly world to a huge cultural and archaeological blank on the world map.

Tough, oblivious to harsh conditions on the road, and obsessed with travel and archaeology, Aurel Stein remained active until the end of his long life. He died of a stomach condition in Kabul on October 25, 1943, at the height of World War II. Today, many of his achievements are forgotten, his findings superseded. But the rough-and-ready Aurel Stein, with his archaeologist's instinct for landscape and past history, opened up a new archaeological frontier.

FURTHER READING

Mirsky, Jeanette. *Sir Aurel Stein: Archaeological Explorer*. Chicago: University of Chicago Press, 1977.

Stefoff, Rebecca. *Accidental Explorers*. New York: Oxford University Press, 1992.

Leonard Woolley

EXCAVATOR OF BIBLICAL UR

A t first glance, Leonard Woolley did not stand out from the crowd. An anonymous archaeological contemporary wrote: "He was a man of slight stature and no commanding appearance. But presence, yes!—and even a blind man would have known what manner of man he was." This charisma enabled Woolley to excavate the biblical city of Ur in southern Iraq with only a handful of European assistants supervising several hundred Arab workers. In the process, he found one of the most spectacular royal cemeteries known to archaeology, and claimed he had discovered evidence for Noah's flood in Genesis.

Charles Leonard Woolley was born in London in 1880. The son of a parson, he became an archaeologist by accident. He entered New College, Oxford, in 1901 with the vague notion of becoming a clergyman or a schoolmaster. One spring day in 1904 he was summoned by the warden

Leonard Woolley and his workers dig out stone tablets at the biblical city of Ur. This 12-year excavation took climaxed with the uncovering of the Royal Cementary, a sensational find rivaled only by those of King Tutankhamun's tomb.

> *"The whole thing [firing rifle volleys when important discoveries were made] may seem childish, but in fact it is such things that make the work go well, and when digging at Jerablus [Carchemish] ceases to be a great game and becomes as in Egypt, a mere business, it will be a bad thing."*
>
> —Leonard Woolley, *Dead Cities and Living Men* (1954)

(president) of the college, who inquired as to his career plans. Woolley mentioned that he thought of becoming a schoolmaster. "Quite so," replied the warden. "I have decided that you shall be an archaeologist," in a memorable quote recorded in Woolley's memoirs. One did not argue with the warden, so Woolley became an archaeologist and never regretted it.

In 1905 he was appointed assistant keeper of the Ashmolean Museum at Oxford, under the directorship of Sir Arthur Evans, who had just discovered the Palace of Minos at Knossos on Crete. Evans was never in Oxford himself, and soon had Woolley out in the field. After a brief experience digging on a badly run excavation on Hadrian's Wall in northern England, Woolley spent five years in the Sudan, working with the Eckley B. Coxe Expedition. Between 1907 and 1911 Woolley worked on sites of the mysterious Meroitic civilization, a Sudanese state that flourished at about the time of Christ.

For the most part he dug unspectacular cemeteries, which taught him about excavating burial sites and their contents—clearing them in place, photographing them, then lifting the bones and artifacts with the body. This experience stood him in good stead later in his career. The unexciting discoveries were more than compensated for by the fascinating people he met on the digs. Some were trained Egyptian workers who had worked on many excavations. Others were less skilled Sudanis, from whom he learned the art of handling laborers from other cultures. At the time, the Nile Valley was a magnificent training ground for a young archaeologist.

As the expedition drew to a close, Woolley was offered a new opportunity as director of the British Museum excavations at the ancient city of Carchemish on the Euphrates River. Carchemish had guarded a strategic river crossing during the time of the Hittites, about 1500 BC, was sacked by the Assyrians in 717 BC, and later was an important Roman outpost. The museum had dug there sporadically since 1878, but Woolley directed the major effort, assisted by a young archaeologist named T. E. Lawrence, later to achieve fame as Lawrence of Arabia.

The Carchemish excavations lasted until the outbreak of war in 1914. Woolley and Lawrence got along well and lived in a high style in a specially constructed mud-brick house. From the beginning, Woolley took a firm hand with local officials and with his workers, who adored him. When a local official refused to issue an excavation permit, Woolley drew a revolver and held it against the official's head until he signed. He could get away with it, for British power and prestige in the area was at its height.

The work at Carchemish began with the removal of much of the old Roman city. Woolley was able to dispose of the stone to German engineers who were building a railroad line to Baghdad nearby. At the same time, he and Lawrence quietly spied on German activities for the Foreign Office. Once the lower, Hittite, levels of the site were exposed, Woolley divided his workers into teams of pickmen, supported by shovelers and basketmen, a method he used at all his excavations over the next 50 years. There was nothing new in this approach; it had been established practice since Austen Henry Layard's excavations at Nineveh a century earlier.

But Woolley introduced one new wrinkle: Important finds were rewarded with a cash payment and a volley of rifle fire. It was a silly practice to the outside observer, perhaps, but Woolley knew that his men prized this noisy symbol of success. He worked closely with his assistant Sheikh Hamoudi, a man who admitted to two passions in his life: archaeology and violence.

Carchemish was the final stage in Woolley's apprenticeship, which was strenuous; he could never relax because of the volatile nature of the local tribes, who were constantly fighting. The archaeologists carried firearms for protection. Woolley found that the best strategy was to behave like the surrounding desert chieftains, so that he was treated as one of their equals. As a result, he was trusted on all sides, and uncovered a magnificent Hittite city at the same time.

Woolley served as an intelligence office during World War I and spent two years as a Turkish prisoner of war. He returned briefly to Carchemish when peace returned, but was soon appointed director of an ambitious joint British Museum and University of Pennsylvania Expedition to excavate the biblical city of Ur. By this time he enjoyed a formidable reputation for getting things done. For 12 seasons, from 1922 to 1934, Woolley uncovered the Sumerian city of Ur with a ferocious energy that exhausted those around him.

He was an exacting taskmaster who ran the excavations with the smallest of European staffs, relying heavily on Sheikh Hamoudi and his three sons to handle the laborers. The excavations began every day at dawn and, for the European staff, rarely ended before midnight. Among those who worked at Ur was a young archaeologist named Max Mallowan, who married a visitor he met at the dig, the

detective story writer Agatha Christie. She drew on her Ur experiences to write *Murder in Mesopotamia*. Woolley would work until two or three in the morning, then be at the excavation at dawn. He was the ideal archaeologist for the job, capable of unraveling layers of long-abandoned buildings from jumbles of mud brick with uncanny skill. He could dissect a temple or recover the remains of a fragile wooden harp in the ground with equal skill. He also had a genius for knowing when to wait. One of his 1922 trial trenches uncovered gold objects, perhaps from a royal cemetery. Woolley waited four years to gain the experience to excavate it fully. He wrote: "Our object was to get history, not to fill museum cases with miscellaneous curiosities."

To Woolley, Ur was not a dead city, but a crowded settlement with busy streets. His huge excavations uncovered entire urban precincts. He would rejoice in taking visitors from house to mud-brick house, identifying their owners from cuneiform tablets found inside. The excavations revealed the architecture of the great ziggurat, a stepped-wall pyramid temple at Ur, and probed the depths of the city mound to the earliest settlement of all: a tiny hamlet of reed huts. He even claimed to have found traces of the biblical flood—a thick layer of sterile clay covering a tiny farming village at the base of the ancient city. The claim in fact originated with Woolley's wife Kathleen, a somewhat eccentric artist, whom he married in 1927. The find caused a great sensation at the time, but is in fact evidence of a much later flood.

The climax of the Ur excavations came in the late 1920s when Woolley finally exposed the Royal Cemetery, with its spectacular burial pits. The

Charles Leonard Woolley

BORN
April 17, 1880
Hackney, London

DIED
February 20, 1960
London, England

EDUCATION
New College, Oxford University
(B.A. 1904)

ACCOMPLISHMENTS
Excavated the Hittite city of Carchemish in Syria and biblical Ur in southern Iraq, injecting new scientific rigor into Near Eastern archaeology; introduced archaeology to an enormous general audience. Wrote *Excavations at Ur* (1927–51; one-volume ed. 1954); *Dead Cities and Living Men* (1954).

This dramatic photograph of the great Flood Pit at Ur demonstrates the pit's enormous depth; Wooley's workers indicate its scale. The base of the pit dates to about 2900 to 2800 BC.

scale of the excavation is astonishing. Woolley cleared more than 2,000 commoners' burials, and 16 royal graves, using teams of specially trained workers. A series of "death pits" chronicled elaborate funeral ceremonies where dozens of courtiers dressed in their finest regalia took poison, then lay down in the great pit to die with their master or mistress. Unfortunately, Woolley's notes are inadequate for modern archaeologists to establish whether his vivid reconstructions were in fact accurate. But his achievement at the time was undeniable, as it is today. King George V of England knighted him for his services to archaeology in 1935.

Woolley's lucid and dramatic accounts of the royal burials and "The Flood" made him one of the most widely read archaeologists of the day. "At one end, on the remains of a wooden bier, lay the body of the queen, a gold cup near her hand; the upper part of the body was entirely hidden by a mass of beads of gold, silver, and lapis lazuli . . . long strings of which, hanging from a collar, had formed a cloak reaching to the waist," he wrote in a popular book, *Ur of the Chaldees*, published in 1929. The spectacular finds rivaled those of Tutankhamun's tomb.

Woolley closed the Ur excavations in 1934, in the belief that a period of study and analysis was needed before more digging took place. He himself wrote most of the massive 10-volume report on the excavation, which took a half-century to complete. After World War II he conducted excavations in Syria and elsewhere, but nothing on the scale of his Ur campaigns, which rank as one of the classic excavations of history. Woolley never held an academic post, but relied on modest private funds and earnings from his writings for a salary. He died in London in 1960.

Few archaeologists have ever matched Leonard Woolley's pace of work and flair for brilliant scientific discovery. His methods were rough and ready by modern standards, but his achievement was prodigious and laid the foundations for modern knowledge of the Sumerians, the world's earliest civilization.

FURTHER READING

Fagan, Brian M. *Return to Babylon*. Boston: Little, Brown, 1979.

Winstone, H. V. F. *Woolley of Ur*. London: Secker and Warburg, 1990.

Vere Gordon Childe

THE BEGINNINGS OF EUROPEAN SOCIETY

Vere Gordon Childe was the most widely read archaeologist of the 20th century. His popular books on prehistoric Europe and the ancient Near East influenced popular thinking about archaeology for a half-century. His theories about the origins of agriculture and ancient civilization argued that these major milestones resulted from great revolutions in human society.

Gordon Childe was born in 1892, the son of a conservative Church of England minister in Sydney, Australia. He soon rebelled against his staid upbringing. While an undergraduate at Sydney University he became a militant liberal, with strong views on worker's rights. He held liberal, even communist, beliefs for the rest of his life. Childe studied Greek, Latin, and philosophy, and graduated in 1913. After two years studying classical archaeology at Oxford University, he returned to Australia and became actively involved in Labour Party politics, an experience that alienated him permanently from political life. He returned to England to resume his studies of European archaeology, supporting himself by translating foreign archaeological books into English.

Throughout the 1920s Childe traveled widely in Europe, visiting archaeological sites and studying museum collections, especially in eastern and southeast Europe, where few British scholars ventured at the time. Unlike most of his archaeological contemporaries, Childe was a brilliant linguist, so he was able to converse easily with archaeologists all over Europe, even in obscure museums in the Balkans. He also had a powerful visual memory, which enabled him to note and remember similarities among artifacts in widely separated locations. For example, he traced the distinctive round-based clay vessels made by the earliest farmers on the Danube River Valley in southeastern Europe right across Germany and the Rhine Valley to the Netherlands and the shores of the North Sea far to the northwest. Years of arduous traveling and library research trained Gordon Childe to become a master of the broad sweep of European history, one of the few scholars with an ability to summarize obscure archaeological data from widely separated lands into a coherent story.

Three books established Gordon Childe as one of the leading archaeologists of his day. The first was *The Dawn of European Civilization*, published in 1925. He wrote the book as a form of narrative history, using artifacts and ancient societies as his subjects instead of kings, statesmen, and common people. *The Dawn* uses what Childe called "archaeological cultures," similar assemblages of artifacts and other culture traits, to trace the movements of ancient peoples across

Excavations at Maes How by Gordon Childe in 1954. Childe is the figure in the black suit in the middle ground. His trench cut a cross-section across the mound, on a scale which would not be permitted on a protected site like Maes How today. Colin Renfrew reexcavated the site in 1973 to obtain radiocarbon dates, a dating method unavilable in 1954.

Europe. He believed that the great changes in the European past resulted from the movements of people and the spread of new ideas such as farming and metalworking, many of them originating in southwest Asia, then spreading into temperate Europe.

The Aryans (1926) looked at some of these population movements in terms of ethnic and linguistic groups like the celebrated Indo-Europeans, a popular but controversial approach to ancient migrations of the day. His third book, *The Danube in Prehistory* (1929), was one of the greatest of Childe's writings. It presented a detailed study of a vital region from where so many pivotal ideas for ancient Europe developed, among them metallurgy and agriculture. Childe was an advocate of culture history—the use of artifacts and chronologies to define long series of changing prehistoric cultures through time, which could be compared with others from neighboring areas. He turned European prehistory into an intricate jigsaw puzzle of artifacts, human cultures, and archaeological sites, building on the earlier work of Oscar Montelius and others. His work still forms the basis of what we know about ancient Europe today.

In 1927 Gordon Childe was appointed the first Abercromby Professor of Prehistoric Archaeology at Edinburgh University. He was not a good teacher and had few students, so he spent most of his time traveling and writing articles and books. Between 1928 and 1955 he also carried out excavations at more than 15 sites in Scotland and northern Ireland. His most important excavation was that of Skara Brae, a Stone Age village on the Orkney Islands north of the mainland, where he found internal furnishings still intact. He interpreted the furnishings by the simple expedient of comparing them to 19th-century rural dwellings in the Scottish highlands. As a result, he was able to show which parts of the dwellings were used to

Vere Gordon Childe

"Archaeology's revelations . . . dispose no abstract evolution but the interaction of multiple concrete groups and the blending of contributions from far-sundered regions."

—Vere Gordon Childe, *New Light on the Most Ancient East* (1934)

BORN
April 14, 1892
North Sydney, Australia

DIED
October 19, 1957
Blue Mountains, Australia

EDUCATION
University of Sydney, Australia (B.A. 1915), Oxford University (M. Phil. 1917)

ACCOMPLISHMENTS
Wrote pioneering summaries of European prehistory based on sites, cultures, and artifacts; tied ancient European societies to important developments such as agriculture, metallurgy, and urban civilization in southwestern Asia; influenced generations of archaeologists and historians with his ideas of culture change. Wrote: *The Dawn of European Civilization* (1925); *The Aryans* (1926); *The Most Ancient East* (1928); *The Danube in Prehistory* (1929); *New Light on the Most Ancient East* (1934); *What Happened in History* (1942); *Social Evolution* (1951); *Piecing Together the Past* (1956); *The Prehistory of European Society* (1956).

house humans and which cattle, and distinguish the hearth areas where women prepared food. This was one of the first attempts to distinguish between men's and women's activities in prehistoric houses.

Meanwhile, Childe continued to write about wider issues of archaeology. His interests shifted from artifacts to broad economic developments in the past, especially agriculture and the origins of urban civilization. For these developments, he looked to southwestern Asia. In a book titled *The Most Ancient East* (1928), he argued that extensive droughts at the end of the Ice Age caused human societies in the region to settle in oases, where they came in close contact with both wild goats and sheep, and wild grasses. Within a short period of time they began farming and herding animals, innovations that had a profound effect on human history. He called this cultural development the Agricultural Revolution.

In *The Bronze Age* (1930), Childe turned his attention to the origins of metallurgy. He argued that metalworking required the services of full-time specialists, people who, like miners and prospectors, functioned independently of any village community or tribe. Thus, Stone Age communities became dependent on outsiders, developed long-distance trade routes, and lost their ancient self-sufficiency.

These metallurgical arguments soon proved wrong, but his *New Light on the Most Ancient East* (1934) developed his revolution hypothesis even further. Childe argued that the Agricultural Revolution soon led to an Urban Revolution, to the emergence of state-organized societies. Each revolution produced more-productive technologies, greater food surpluses, and massive population increases. He believed they had as much impact on human history as the Industrial Revolution of the 18th and 19th centuries AD. From southwestern Asia, these innovations and technologies spread far and wide to Europe, Africa, and eastern Asia. "From the east came light," he proclaimed; a generation of archaeologists and historians believed him.

In 1935 Childe visited the Soviet Union, where he toured museums and was exposed to communist doctrines. He began writing about human cultural evolution, about the ways in which increasing scientific knowledge gave humans greater control over the natural environment. Later, he argued that social, political, and economic institutions played important roles in such changes, and flirted with notions of class struggles and other features of Marxist dogma, but without much success.

In 1946 Childe left Edinburgh to become a professor of European Archaeology at the Institute of Archaeology,

In his field notes from his excavations at Rinyo, Orkney, in 1938, Gordon Childe records the discovery of an ancient clay oven.

of his great syntheses of ancient Europe. The last of these was *The Prehistory of European Society* (1956), in which he stated that the nature of society was a powerful factor in determining ancient kinship patterns, political systems, and other forms of social relations.

By this time, Childe was thoroughly depressed about the limitations of archaeology, a discipline based on artifacts and material remains of the past. He felt there was no chance of studying religious beliefs or other intangibles of the past from such finds. His depression became more intense after his retirement. Childe was very much a loner; he never married and became increasingly lonely in later life. Three months after his retirement, he returned to Australia and committed suicide by jumping off a cliff in the Blue Mountains.

Childe was the most widely read archaeologist of his day. His major books were translated into numerous languages. His ideas on the Agricultural and Urban revolutions influenced generations of archaeologists and historians. Childe never visited the United States, where his ideas were often misunderstood, especially in an era of militant anti-Marxism. He himself believed that the prehistoric cultures of southwestern Asia and Europe represented the mainstream of the human past. For all his outmoded ideas, the great syntheses and scholarship of Vere Gordon Childe continue to exercise a powerful influence on today's archaeologists.

FURTHER READING

Harris, David R. ed. *The Archaeology of V. Gordon Childe*. Chicago: University of Chicago Press, 1994.

Trigger, Bruce G. *Gordon Childe: Revolutions in Prehistory*. New York: Cambridge University Press, 1980.

London University. He remained there until he retired in 1956. Giving up excavation, he threw himself into writing more theoretical works, among them *Piecing Together the Past,* a model of clear explanation of the basic principles of archaeological method that is still of use today. He began to write about the ways in which environmental differences produced different Stone Age farming cultures in Europe and southwestern Asia, but concentrated mostly on his unrivaled knowledge of artifacts. These were the real substance

More Archaeologists to Remember

Sophus Müller (1846–1934) was a Danish archaeologist who spent his entire career in the National Museum of Denmark, Copenhagen. Like Oscar Montelius, Müller was an expert at artifact classification. He did much to link Scandinavian prehistoric cultures with those of western and central Europe. He developed his own classification of the European Bronze Age, but later adopted Montelius's rival scheme. Müller was also a powerful influence on scholars studying the Stone Age settlement of Scandinavia.

Alfred P. Maudslay (1850–1931) was a Cambridge University–educated archaeologist whose imagination was inspired by the Maya discoveries of John Lloyd Stephens. He traveled repeatedly to Guatemala between 1881 and 1894, recording and photographing inscriptions and buildings with

Alfred Maudslay shot this photograph of a western court and tower ruins in Palengue. Maudsley's photographs, drawings, and sculptures were so scientifically accurate that his work became the standard for later archaeologists.

an accuracy was rarely exceeded until today's electronic age. His eight-volume *Biologia Centrali Americana*, four volumes of which focus on archaeology, is a classic of Maya archaeology and laid the foundations for the decipherment of Mayan script three-quarters of a century later.

Robert Koldeway (1855–1925), a German scholar, was the first archaeologist to master the technique of excavating sun-dried brick in Mesopotamia. He excavated extensively in southern Iraq, notably, in 1899 through 1912, in the ruins of Nebuchadnezzar's Babylon, (which had defeated generations of diggers. Koldeway trained teams of skilled local diggers, who used picks to identify the subtle differences between mud brick and the surrounding soil. Thanks to these diggers, Koldeway traced Babylon's walls and also reconstructed the magnificent, frieze-covered Ishtar Gate.

Max Uhle (1856–1944) was a pioneer of Peruvian archaeology. German-born and -trained, Uhle worked in Peru for more than 30 years, excavating the great Inca shrine at Pachacamac south of Lima on the Pacific coast and digging numerous coastal cemeteries. He is also famous for stratigraphic excavations in a shell midden at Emeryville in California's San Francisco Bay area, which showed significant changes in artifacts over more than 1,000 years.

Gustaf Kossina (1858–1931) was a Central European archaeologist with an expertise in archaeology and ancient languages. He achieved notoriety for his preoccupations with finding the homelands of Germans and speakers of Indo-European languages. His nationalistic views were embraced by the Nazi government in the 1930s, but were discredited elsewhere.

Marcellin Boule (1861–1942), a French paleontologist and archaeologist, made the issues of human evolution central to Stone Age archaeology. His famous study of a Neanderthal skeleton from the La Chapelle-aux-Saints rock shelter in southwestern France propagated a now discredited view that the Neanderthals were shambling, clumsy brutes.

George A. Reisner (1867–1942) was an American Egyptologist who spent his career at Harvard University. He made many important discoveries in Egypt and especially in Nubia (now the Sudan). His excavations were much more thorough than those of Flinders Petrie and other contemporaries. Reisner's greatest discovery was the tomb of the Old Kingdom Queen Hetepheres (reigned about 2600 BC) at Giza in Egypt. She was the mother of the pharaoh Khufu, builder of the Great Pyramid of Giza. Reisner also unearthed cemeteries and numerous tombs in Nubia, including royal burial mounds at the ancient capital of Kerma.

Percy Newberry (1869–1949) was an English Egyptologist who became a professor of Egyptology at the University of Liverpool in 1919, then Professor of Ancient Art and History at Cairo University, from 1929 to 1932. He was famous for his researches in the tombs of provincial governors at Beni Hasan in Middle Egypt, also for a survey of the ancient Egyptian tombs opposite Luxor, the so-called Theban necropolis.

Alfred Kroeber (1876–1960), one of the great pioneers of American anthropology, made important contributions to archaeology. He was the first to use artifact-ordering methods on pottery from the American Southwest. His methods were adopted by

Alfred Kidder for use at Pecos and by many others.

Teilhard de Chardin (1881–1955), paleontologist and expert on human evolution, spent his life trying to reconcile his Catholic faith with the findings of science. He carried out important work on Stone Age sites in China and Mongolia and worked closely with his friend Henri Breuil. His major work, *The Phenomenon of Man*, written in 1938 to 1940 but published after his death, argued that humanity is in a continuous process of evolution toward a perfect spiritual state.

Manuel Gamio (1883–1960), a Mexican archaeologist, was one of the first to carry out a stratigraphic excavation in the Americas. From 1917 to 1922 he carried out a multidisciplinary survey of the city of Teotihuacán and its hinterland northeast of Mexico City that is still of great importance. His later career was devoted to anthropology and the rights of indigenous peoples.

Herbert E. Winlock (1884–1950) was a prominent Egyptologist who worked for the Metropolitan Museum of Art, New York, for his entire career. Winlock was famous for his excavations, which included the discovery of the remains of pharaoh Tutankhamun's funerary feast in the Valley of Kings. He made numerous spectacular discoveries, among them models of the household of Middle Kingdom Chancellor Mereketre and the bodies of a regiment of Middle Kingdom soldiers who had perished during a siege. He also worked at the temple of New Kingdom Queen Hatshepsut at Luxor and was well known as a writer about Egyptian archaeology.

Albert E. Van Giffen (1884–1973) was a Dutch archaeologist whose

Manuel Gamio's excavations at Teotihuacán, Mexico in the 1920s were of immense importance because they were the first scientific investigation of the great city. Today, the Pyramid of the Sun draws thousands of visitors to its sacred steps.

excavations in prehistoric burial mounds in the 1920s and 1930s pioneered the recovery of vanished wooden structures from sandy soils by identifying the discoloration they caused in the subsoil. He was also a pioneer in the excavation of stratified occupation mounds in swampy areas, which he preserved from peat diggers by purchasing them outright.

James A. Ford (1911–68) carried out archaeological research in many parts of North America, including Alaska, but is best known for his work in the Southeast. Ford was an expert on prehistoric pottery who spent much of his career working on river valley survey projects. His chronologies for the ancient Southeast were extremely influential for several generations, but are now outdated.

Sir Mortimer Wheeler used a grid method of horizontal excavation at Maiden Castle in England. This technique allows a researcher to uncover large areas where buildings may be found. The use of a grid allowed him to establish whether widely separated dwellings were of the same age, by tracing stratified layers from one cross wall to another.

4 Great Fieldworkers

The great archaeologists of the post–World War I period achieved much of their most important work between the 1930s and the 1960s. They witnessed not only remarkable changes in archaeology itself, but also staggering advances in both archaeological methods and dramatic new discoveries. All of them, without exception, were superb fieldworkers. They developed new ways of excavating and used every innovative scientific method at their disposal. The result was the first truly global archaeology.

Some of the greatest advances came in scientific methods and archaeological excavation. The British archaeologist Mortimer Wheeler and his first wife Tessa revolutionized excavation in Britain and much of Europe in the 1920s and 1930s with their refinements of the Victorian methods of excavator General Augustus Lane Fox Pitt-Rivers. They worked on late prehistoric Iron Age sites and on Roman towns, fortifications, and ceremonial structures, training an entire generation of young archaeologists who transplanted their work to often remote corners of the world. Others contributed to the remarkable transformation of excavation during the mid-20th century, among them another British archaeologist, Stuart Piggott, and the German scholar Gerhard Bersu, who pioneered the excavation of ground plans of prehistoric houses and entire villages.

The 30 years of the mid-20th century saw a dramatic expansion in new scientific methods applied to archaeology. These included pollen analysis, a method for studying changes in ancient vegetation from minute fossil pollens found in waterlogged swamps. Pollen studies allowed European archaeologists of the 1930s to study the ways ancient societies responded to rapid climactic change after the Ice Age as great ice sheets retreated from Scandinavia. Pollen analysis and other climatic studies brought a new interest in changing environments and human adaptations to them, an approach pioneered by Grahame Clark. A Cambridge University archaeologist, Clark devoted much of his early career to the study of Stone Age cultures against an environmental backdrop. His most notable excavation, from 1949 to 1951, was that of the Star Carr hunting camp in northeastern England, where he was able to reconstruct the natural environment surrounding the long-forgotten camp.

Gordon Willey, an American archaeologist, learned his fieldwork on the great river basin surveys of the 1930s, where teams of archaeologists worked in

IN THIS PART

GERTRUDE CATON-THOMPSON

DOROTHY GARROD

KATHLEEN KENYON

MORTIMER WHEELER

LOUIS AND MARY LEAKEY

GRAHAME CLARK

JOHN DESMOND CLARK

GORDON R. WILLEY

advance of huge dam projects in the United States, recording thousands of sites. He later became an expert on Maya civilization, and also worked in the Virú Valley in coastal Peru. Here he pioneered research into the changing patterns of human settlement within the confines of a single river valley, using aerial photographs and field surveys for the purpose.

Landscape and settlement archaeology was nothing new, for European archaeologists like O. G. S. Crawford had been walking the countryside mapping archaeological sites and using aerial photographs for a generation. But Willey's approach was more systematic, combining excavation and survey to produce a map of changing settlement within a single narrow area. The Virú Valley project made settlement archaeology popular in the Americas, and regional surveys of such areas as the Valley of Mexico and the Four Corners area of the American Southwest resulted from it.

By far the most revolutionary advance in scientific archaeology during these years was the development of radiocarbon dating by University of Chicago physicists Willard Libby and J. R. Arnold in 1949. For the first time, archaeologists had a seemingly reliable way to date organic materials from archaeological sites dating to the past 40,000 years. Grahame Clark was one of the first archaeologists to recognize the potential of radiocarbon dating. He realized one could now date archaeological sites all around the world, and compare the dates of such developments as the beginnings of agriculture in widely separated parts of the world. In 1961 he published *World Prehistory*, a summary of the human past from its beginnings to the rise of civilization, based on radiocarbon chronologies. For the first time, a truly global prehistory could be written from dated archaeological sites.

World Prehistory would not have been possible without a new generation of archaeological discoveries from outside the narrow confines of Europe, the eastern Mediterranean, and North America. Women played an important part in these advances. Dorothy Garrod and Gertrude Caton-Thompson both worked far from the comfortable world of their homeland. Garrod wrote the first summary of late Ice Age cultures in Britain, then worked on Neanderthal settlement on Gibraltar before carrying out excavations at Mt. Carmel on the eastern Mediterranean coast that made her famous. There she found important evidence for the early origins of modern humans. Meanwhile, Caton-Thompson trained herself in Stone Age archaeology in Egypt, resolved the dating of the Great Zimbabwe ruins in East Africa, then devoted the rest of her career to notable Stone Age excavations in the Nile Valley region.

Kathleen Kenyon trained under Mortimer Wheeler and retained a lifelong interest in Roman sites and pottery styles. But she is best known for her excavations into the depths of ancient Jericho, where she found some of the earliest farming settlements in the world in the 1950s. With her one excavation, she extended the history of agriculture by at least 4,000 years.

Impressive advances in our knowledge of early human evolution came between 1930 and the 1960s, thanks in large part to the researches of Louis and Mary Leakey in East Africa. Louis Leakey was a missionary's son who trained in archaeology at Cambridge. While still in his 20s he discovered an entire sequence of ancient Stone Age cultures in Kenya, working on a financial shoestring. Mary Leakey was a gifted artist with an interest in archaeology who met Louis at Cambridge and became his second wife. Together and separately, they worked at many early Stone Age sites, among them the 300,000-year-old hunting site at Olorgsesaillie in the heart of Kenya's Rift Valley. Together they pioneered the excavation of ancient living sites and hunting camps, leaving the artifacts and associated stone tools in place where they originally lay.

At irregular intervals between 1931 and 1959, the Leakeys worked at Olduvai Gorge on northern Tanzania's Serengeti Plains, recovering thousands of finely made stone tools and numerous broken bones of fossil animals killed by early humans. In 1959 Mary unearthed one of the great archaeological finds of the 20th century—the well-preserved skull of a robust ape-human, *Zinjanthropus boisei*, "East African human of Boise" named for a benefactor, Mr. Boise. With this single find, and the development of the potassium-argon dating method—a way of dating ancient lavas by measuring radioactive decay rates in the rock—the prehistory of humanity was expanded to over 2 million years ago.

The 1930s to 1960s were years when the Belgian, British, and French empires covered much of the world. Archaeology flourished in colonial territories around the globe, especially in Africa in the work of Louis and Mary Leakey and a handful of other dedicated fieldworkers. Notable among them was J. Desmond Clark, who trained under Grahame Clark and Mortimer Wheeler before going to Northern Rhodesia (now Zambia) as a museum officer in 1938. Clark worked with minimal funding, but with extraordinary effect. He studied the Stone Age cultures of the Upper Zambezi Valley, excavated strategic rock shelters, and collected and surveyed dozens of sites in Somalia and Ethiopia during his war service. During the 1950s he excavated the 250,000-year-old Kalambo Falls prehistoric site on the Zambia-Tanzania border, one of the most important early Stone Age settlements in tropical Africa.

All of these men and women exercised a profound influence on dozens of young archaeologists, who began their studies of the past in the 1950s and 1960s. They learned from the single-minded enthusiasm and hard work of a small number of men and women who had a passion for the past that was truly infectious. Working almost alone, with almost no money, and often under extremely uncomfortable, even dangerous, conditions, they paved the way for the remarkable archaeological discoveries of today.

In 1949, University of Chicago physicists Willard Libby, shown here, and J.R. Arnold developed radiocarbon dating. This innovative process allowed archaeologists to accurately pinpoint the age of excavation sites and recovered artifacts.

Gertrude Caton-Thompson

GREAT ZIMBABWE AND THE STONE AGE

She arrived at the Great Zimbabwe ruins in Central Africa riding on an ox cart, her car unable to cross rivers flooded by heavy rain. She was a tough, no-nonsense archaeologist who went out to work in tropical Africa in 1929 never having been there before. She was also the first woman archaeologist to work there. Her name was Gertrude Caton-Thompson. By sheer strength of character and a down-to-earth approach to her work, she showed that Zimbabwe was the work not of some white civilization, as many believed, but of indigenous African peoples, the ancestors of the modern inhabitants. This was a controversial conclusion in 1929, but the forthright and hard-headed Caton-Thompson cared little for public opinion.

Gertrude Caton-Thompson was born in London in 1888, the daughter of a well-known lawyer who died when she was five years old. Until the outbreak of war in 1914, she enjoyed a comfortable life as a member of a wealthy English family, visiting Egypt and the Holy Land with her mother in 1907. They toured the pyramids and ancient Jericho, experiences that kindled an interest in the past in an impressionable

In 1939, Gertrude Caton-Thompson had just returned from important excavations on Stone Age sites in Egypt's Kharga Oasis. Eight years earlier, Caton-Thompson had published the results of her Zimbabwe excavations, which brought her an international reputation.

young woman. She was to make lasting contributions to the field.

Caton-Thompson did not study archaeology seriously until 1919, after gaining valuable administrative experience during World War I requisitioning merchant ships for convoy duty. She studied Egyptology and Mediterranean archaeology at the University of London, graduating in 1920. The practical work in some of her courses was unusual. Gertrude learned her surveying in a small urban park "where trees and seats were the only fixed objects; the seats in particular were mainly identifiable by their inhabitants, mostly old ladies in hats who moved away before their position was safely established." Unlike her fellow students, who preferred later, more complex civilizations, Caton-Thompson became interested in Stone Age archaeology and early prehistory. She soon developed an expertise with stone artifacts that was to stand her in good stead later in her career.

In 1921 Caton-Thompson went out to work with the great Egyptologist Flinders Petrie at Abydos in Upper Egypt, searching for Stone Age sites in the desert while Petrie cleared Old Kingdom tombs. She soon found more than two thousand 100,000-year-old stone tools, while learning a great deal of Egyptology back in camp from Petrie's after-dinner discourses by lamplight. In Luxor she met archaeologist Howard Carter, who was working in the Valley of Kings and complaining that he was finding nothing. A year later he discovered the tomb of the pharaoh Tutankhamun.

Caton-Thompson's Egyptian experience established her as a serious archaeologist. She now excavated a cave on the island of Malta, then returned to Egypt in 1924 on an expedition of her own. Flinders Petrie had long declared that the dry Fayum Depression west of the Nile River had once been a vast lake, formed when the river burst into the depression in the 5th century BC. But Caton-Thompson had some geological training and realized there had been more than one lake in the depression. She and geologist Elinor Gardner spent two long field seasons reconstructing the history of the Fayum lake, which had teemed with fish and wild fowl on several occasions since the end of the Ice Age about 10,000 years ago.

Caton-Thompson searched for archaeological sites along the ancient lake shores. She electrified the archaeological world by finding a humble farming settlement of crude brush shelters and basket-lined storage pits that contained carbonized barley and wheat seeds, estimated to date to at least 4000 BC. The Fayum site was the earliest known farming site in the world, discovered at a time when archaeologists were beginning to search seriously for evidence of the earliest farmers in the world. This remarkable discovery not only marked Caton-Thompson as an up-and-coming archaeologist, but remained the earliest farming settlement on earth until new finds in the 1950s at Jericho in Jordan and in Iran, and the new radiocarbon dating technique, pushed back the beginnings of agriculture to about 8000 BC. (The latest dates are nearer 10,000 BC.)

In 1928 Caton-Thompson received an important research assignment from the British Association for the Advancement of Science. She was to excavate the famous Great Zimbabwe ruins in southern Africa and report on them to a meeting of the Association to be held in South Africa in the following year. Great Zimbabwe was a controversial site, north of the Limpopo River in what is now the country of Zimbabwe. An elaborate complex of large stone structures occupied a small valley overshadowed by a low hill covered with artificial enclosures.

European settlers had puzzled over the freestanding Great Enclosure and

Gertrude Caton-Thompson

BORN
February 1, 1888
London, England

DIED
April 18, 1985
Broadway, England

EDUCATION
University of London (B.A. 1920)

ACCOMPLISHMENTS
Became a leading 20th-century Stone Age archaeologist; studied Stone Age cultures in the Nile Valley, discovered early agricultural settlements of the Desert Fayum;. also famous for excavations of ruins at Great Zimbabwe, southern Africa, which established their construction by native Africans. Wrote memoirs and *The Zimbabwe Culture: Ruins and Reactions* (1931).

rock-covered hill ruin in 1890. A series of archaeologists had then examined the ruins at the request of the colonial authorities. The more imaginative of them declared Zimbabwe to be a long-lost palace of the biblical Queen of Sheba, built by the Phoenicians of the ancient Mediterranean world. They declared that Africans could never have built such sophisticated buildings. In contrast, archaeologist Randall MacIver, also under British Association patronage, had concluded in 1905 that they were built by the ancestors of the modern-day African inhabitants only a few hundred years earlier. The local white settlers were so angry with MacIver that no further excavations took place for 20 years.

Caton-Thompson entered this controversy eagerly, despite never having traveled in tropical Africa or excavated a site south of the Sahara Desert. The ruins had been battered by earlier excavators, who had shoveled away rich archaeological deposits, leaving little intact. Any new excavator was confronted with a jigsaw puzzle of small patches of occupation deposits scattered over the site, a task that challenged all of Caton-Thompson's skills. She approached Great Zimbabwe with meticulous care, digging carefully placed trenches to establish the sequence of occupation in various parts of the site. For example, she dug down to bedrock through a series of abandoned occupations at the western end of the low hill known as the Acropolis, which overlooks the enclosures in the valley beneath. Here she was able to reconstruct the sequence of events at Zimbabwe, starting with a small farming settlement, then a spectacular expansion of the site and the building of freestanding stone walls and enclosures.

Unlike her predecessors, she paid careful attention to the tiny glass beads and other imported artifacts from the site, which had been carried there by traders from the distant Indian Ocean. Her largest excavation backed up against a stone wall, allowing her to tie a changing sequence of African pottery styles to the architecture of the site. Experts on Chinese pottery and ancient glass confirmed that Mac-Iver had dated Zimbabwe correctly to the centuries immediately before Portuguese explorers arrived off the southeast African coast in AD 1497. Judging from these imports, Great Zimbabwe was far later than the Phoenician chronology proposed by those who assumed on racial grounds that Africans could never have built such structures.

It took considerable courage for Caton-Thompson to announce her conclusions at a time when the local white settlers, and many archaeologists, believed Africans were too "primitive" to build such a stupendous site. Her address to the British Association in Johannesburg was a model of straightforward, unsensationalized reporting. She expressed her amazement that any thinking person would consider Great Zimbabwe anything but African. Her conclusions were greeted with anger by settler interests, who disputed her findings. They refused to believe that Africans, whom they believed were inferior, were capable of building such elaborate structures. Meanwhile, Caton-Thompson's scientific reputation was never higher, especially after she conducted a delegation of experts around her excavations at the site itself.

Caton-Thompson now returned to Egypt, where she excavated an important series of Stone Age sites in the Kharga Oasis, west of the Nile River. Her long report on Kharga records Stone Age settlement over a period of more than 300,000 years and is still the definitive account of the area. She went back to tropical Africa only once,

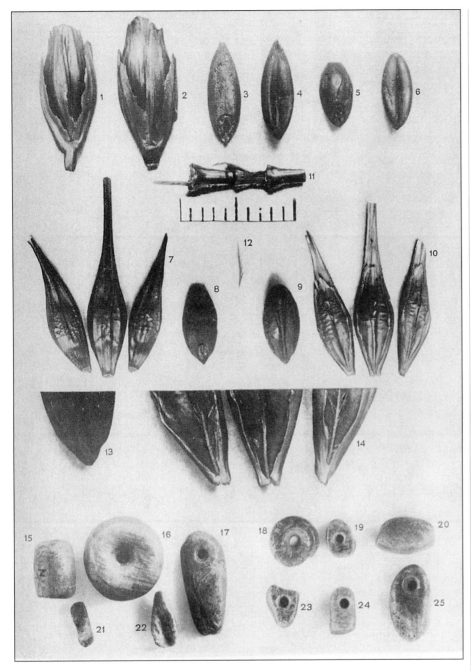

Caton-Thompson found these wheat and barley seeds in an early farming settlement in the Fayum, Egypt. The Fayum sites were her greatest archaeological discovery because they dated farming in the Nile Valley to before the times of ancient Egypt.

for an archaeological conference in 1955, where she was able to revisit the scene of her greatest archaeological triumph. However, she retained a strong interest in African archaeology until her death at the age of 97 in 1985.

Gertrude Caton-Thompson set new standards in Stone Age archaeology at a time when almost no women worked on early prehistoric sites. Strong-minded, and a get-on-with-the-job researcher, she was one of the last field archaeologists who became an expert in more than one field of the subject, a world authority on both the Stone Age and the still little-known recent history of tropical Africa.

FURTHER READING

Caton-Thompson, Gertrude. *Mixed Memoirs*. Gateshead, England: Paradigm, 1983.

Dorothy Garrod

EXCAVATOR OF THE MOUNT CARMEL CAVES

Dorothy Garrod made history not only as the first prehistoric archaeologist to become a professor of archaeology at Cambridge University, but also as the first woman to be appointed to a professorship at the university. A quiet, unassuming person, she preferred to work far from the limelight, with only a few helpers. During the early 1930s Garrod acquired an international reputation by excavating the Mount Carmel caves in what was then Palestine, working with a handful of companions. Her excavations threw new light on the origins of modern humans: *Homo sapiens sapiens*, "the wise person."

Dorothy Anne Elizabeth Garrod was born in London in 1892. Her father was a physician and she enjoyed a happy childhood, during which she acquired a lifelong interest in reading and books. She entered Newnham College, Cambridge, in 1913 and graduated three years later with an undistinguished degree. One can hardly blame her, for all three of her brothers were killed in the early years of World

Tough and single-minded, Dorothy Garrod worked with small budgets and only a few companions, relying on the local people and her fluent Arabic to find promising caves in the Near East.

War I. After a short spell in the Ministry of Munitions, she went to France with the Catholic Women's League to care for the wounded. The job was very stressful. Garrod was forced to withdraw for convalescence to Malta, where her father was director of war hospitals. The island's prehistoric tombs, built of massive boulders more than 6,000 years ago, fascinated her. She spent days traveling from tomb to tomb by car and mule, searching for pot fragments and trying to decipher the architecture of these ancient sepulchers. By the time she left Malta, Dorothy Garrod had acquired a passionate interest in archaeology.

After the war, her father was appointed professor of medicine at Oxford. She now enrolled in anthropology courses under the direction of the distinguished social anthropologist R. R. Marret of Exeter College. For some years Marret had been excavating a cave occupied by Neanderthal people on the island of Jersey in the English Channel. He instilled Garrod with a passion for Neanderthal research, in particular with an interest in the ways in which these ancient humans were different from modern people in their technological achievements and mental capacities.

After she earned a degree with distinction in 1920, Marret sent her to study under the French prehistoric archaeologist Abbé Henri Breuil in Paris. Garrod not only dug at several major Stone Age rock shelters in southwestern France, but also acquired a detailed knowledge of Stone Age artifacts of all kinds, which was to stand her in good stead in future years. Garrod spoke fluent French and worked closely with Breuil throughout her life. She was strongly influenced by his conviction, expressed in print in 1912, that prehistoric Europe was but a peninsula of Africa and Asia.

Garrod returned to Oxford and, with Breuil's strong encouragement,

"Today prehistory has suffered the fate of so many of the component parts of the orderly universe of the 19th century. New knowledge has given a twist to the kaleidoscope and new pieces are still falling about before our bewildered eyes."

—Dorothy Garrod, "The Upper Palaeolithic in the Light of Recent Discovery" (1938)

embarked on a meticulous study of all the late Ice Age sites and artifacts known in Britain. This research involved extensive traveling to visit archaeological locations, long hours in museum collections examining artifacts, and months in libraries reading everything that had been written on the subject. The resulting book, *The Upper Palaeolithic Age in Britain* (1926), received wide attention for its accuracy and shrewd judgements.

Breuil now recognized that it was time for Garrod to excavate on her own. He suggested that she investigate the Devil's Tower in Gibraltar at the extreme southern tip of Spain. She dug into the site for five months in 1925 and duly recovered Neanderthal remains together with stone artifacts and many animal bones. Her fossil bone finds were so fascinating that she was able to attract a team of distinguished specialists to collaborate on her report, which attracted wide attention when it appeared in 1928.

While Garrod was working in Gibraltar, another English archaeologist, Francis Turville-Petre, had found a young Neanderthal adult skeleton in the Zettupeh Cave by the Sea of Galilee. The find attracted the attention of the American School of Prehistoric Research, which had been founded in 1921 to encourage American archaeologists to work in Europe.

Encouraged by her mentor, the prehistorian Abbé Henri Breuil, Dorothy Garrod did her first solo excavation among the rocks of Gibraltar, where she found the skull remains of a Neanderthal child.

In 1926 the school's interests shifted, largely as a result of the Zettupeh discovery. This was the easternmost known Neanderthal find at the time. The school engaged Garrod to look for finds even farther to the east. She visited the Kirkuk region in northeastern Iraq in 1927, where in a cave she found characteristic Neanderthal artifacts such as crude stone spear points and scraping tools used for cleaning animal skins. A year later she returned to excavate two more caves in the same area. The Hazar Merd and Zarzi caves yielded Neanderthal occupation neatly sandwiched below later Stone Age levels.

Fresh from these excavations, Garrod traveled to the eastern Mediterranean coast, where she found promising caves at Mount Carmel in what is now Israel. These, she realized, were sites that would yield a sequence of

changing Stone Age cultures potentially as rich as those in southwestern France investigated by Henri Breuil. Between 1929 and 1934 she excavated the Mount Carmel caves with the assistance of American biological anthropologist Theodore McCown, an expert on human remains. Garrod and McCown excavated three caves, one of which contained a virtual cemetery of Neanderthal skeletons. The excavations at Mugharet el-Wad, et-Tabun, and es-Skhul rank among the most important archaeological investigations of the 20th century.

Garrod worked near-miracles with a small team of colleagues and local workers. She uncovered deep layers of human occupation that extended far back into the Ice Age—at least 75,000 years ago. The finds were very different from those in western European caves, where tools made on fine blades followed simpler, Neanderthal artifacts. Everything was more complicated at Mount Carmel. Instead of a simple progression from crude spear points and scraping tools to fine-blade artifacts in later layers, some Neanderthal levels also contained fine blades and scrapers.

These artifacts were virtually identical to those made by Cro-Magnons in Europe many thousands of years later. Most archaeologists had assumed that modern people and their fine stone technology had first evolved in Europe, then spread elsewhere. The Mount Carmel discoveries turned everything on its head. Now the earliest blade technology, thought to be the work of modern humans, appeared in southwestern Asia, as if *Homo sapiens sapiens* had first evolved there, then spread into Europe.

The European Neanderthals were short, primitive looking people with receding foreheads, prominent snouts, flat noses, and massive bone brow ridges over their eye sockets. When Garrod excavated the es-Skhul cave at Mount Carmel, she found a Neanderthal cemetery where the skeletons showed a remarkable mix of thick Neanderthal bones and compact limbs combined with such traits as high foreheads and reduced eyebrow ridges that are more typical of modern humans. The Mount Carmel Neanderthals were anatomically more advanced than their European contemporaries.

In 1936 Dorothy Garrod gave an address to the British Association for the Advancement of Science in which she proclaimed that the distinctive culture of the Cro-Magnons had originated not in Europe, but in southwestern Asia. From there, modern humans had spread north and westward, she stated. At the time, her report caused a stir, especially among those who believed that modern humans had originated in western Europe. Garrod was one of the first prehistoric archaeologists to look at human prehistory from a global perspective, to argue that the story of early humanity could not be understood from Europe alone.

The publication of the first volume of *The Stone Age of Mount Carmel* in 1937 established Garrod as a prehistorian of the first rank. Two years later she was elected Disney Professor of Archaeology at Cambridge, the first fieldworker to hold the post. Unfortunately, her tenure was broken by World War II, when she served in the Royal Air Force aerial photography interpretation unit. After the war, she devoted much energy to expanding degree programs in prehistoric archaeology at Cambridge, insisting that a course on world prehistory be introduced into

what had previously been a somewhat narrow curriculum. But her heart was not in the administrative and committee work expected of a university professor. Nor was she comfortable in a predominantly male academic environment. She took early retirement in 1952 and moved to France, where she resumed fieldwork on Stone Age caves.

Her retirement years saw more excavations, this time in France at the late Ice Age Angles-sur-Anglin rock shelter, where she found a 16,000-year-old bas-relief of animals and women. The depiction of women in was rare in Cro-Magnon sculpture. She also returned to the Near East, where she undertook a series of digs in an attempt to clarify the relationships between Neanderthal and modern human occupations of some 50,000 years ago. These were on a smaller scale than the Mount Carmel excavations, but nevertheless did much to describe the prehistoric cultures of a vital region in human prehistory. She died at her home in France in 1968.

Dorothy Garrod was a shy, retiring person who was at her best in the field. She was one of a small group of women, including Gertrude Caton-Thompson and Kathleen Kenyon, who led the way for the many female archaeologists of the next generation. She herself would have denied she did anything special, but her Mount Carmel discoveries turned archaeology from a provincial undertaking into the study of a truly global human prehistory.

FURTHER READING

Clark, Grahame. *Prehistory at Cambridge and Beyond.* New York: Cambridge University Press, 1989.

Dorothy Garrod

BORN

May 5, 1892
London, England

DIED

December 18, 1968
Villebois-Lavalette, Charente, France

EDUCATION

Newnham College, Cambridge (B.A. 1916); Exeter College, Oxford (M.A. 1920)

ACCOMPLISHMENTS

Made the first study of late Ice Age peoples in Britain; discovered Neanderthal fossils and artifacts at Devil's Tower, Gibraltar; excavated the Mount Carmel caves in Palestine; the first prehistorian and first woman to be appointed Disney Professor of Archaeology at Cambridge University; one of the earliest archaeologists to develop ideas of world prehistory. Wrote *The Upper Palaeolithic Age in Britain* (1926); *The Stone Age of Mount Carmel* (with Dorothea M. A. Bate, 1937).

Kathleen Kenyon

EXCAVATOR
OF JERICHO

Kathleen Mary Kenyon was passionate about archaeology and dogs. Everywhere she went, she was accompanied by her fox terriers, who terrified her workers. In her archaeological work, she found one of the earliest farming settlements in the world at the base of the great city mound at Jericho in Jordan, dating to more than 8,000 years ago. Many of her excavations threw important light on the historical narratives in the Old Testament.

Kenyon was born in London in 1906. She was the elder of the two daughters of Sir Frederick Kenyon, a distinguished biblical scholar and Director of the British Museum. His researches included both textual criticism and biblical archaeology. Young Kathleen grew up in a family where archaeology and the Holy Land were constant topics of

In 1959, Kathleen Kenyon stands in the 10th millennium BC shrine, Natufian, in Jericho. Through her work, Kenyon discovered a firm transition from the hunter/gatherer stage of human development to the settled pastoralist period.

conversation. Her interest in archaeology began long before she went to Somerville College, Oxford, in 1926. Three years later, she graduated with honors in archaeology. Archaeologist Gertrude Caton-Thompson promptly offered her the job of photographer on the British Association for Advancement of Science's expedition to Great Zimbabwe in southern Africa. Kenyon not only took photographs but also supervised some of the excavations. The Zimbabwe digs were of great importance because they proved that these stupendous stone ruins were built not by colonizing Europeans, but by indigenous Africans before AD 1500.

The Zimbabwe expedition gave Kenyon excellent credentials as a fieldworker. She next spent four years, from 1930 to 1935, as a member of the excavation on the Roman town at Verulamium, just north of London. The project was directed by Mortimer Wheeler and his wife Tessa, both expert fieldworkers and specialists in digging Roman sites. From the Wheelers, Kenyon acquired rigorous excavation skills that were to stand her in good stead in her later career in southwestern Asia. In particular, she learned Mortimer Wheeler's specialty: careful excavation and recording of thin strata of human occupation lying one above the other like layers of a cake, each with its distinctive pottery, which helped date the layer. The Wheelers gave her the task of excavating Verulamium's Roman theater, the only one of its kind in Britain.

Verulamium was not her only excavation. She spent much time during the winters between 1931 to 1934 on excavations sponsored by the Palestine Exploration Fund at the ancient city of Samaria. Here she gained invaluable experience investigating mud-brick architecture and the complex local pottery styles from the Neolithic to Greek times. She analyzed the complex sequence of different occupations in a degree of detail unimaginable during earlier Harvard University excavations in 1908–10.

Kenyon's association with Mortimer Wheeler continued after 1935, when he moved to London University's newly founded Institute of Archaeology. She served as its administrative secretary, and as acting director from 1942 to 1946, while also working for the British Red Cross in World War II. During her years at the institute she studied the huge pottery collections excavated in Palestine by the Egyptologist Flinders Petrie. Pottery became her primary interest in her later career, for she believed it was an excellent way of dating the layers buried beneath modern cities. Her excavations on the Jewry Wall area of the city of Leicester from 1936 to 1939 produced a remarkable chronicle of little-known Roman pottery styles that is still widely used. By studying the minute changes in decoration and pottery form, Kenyon produced a detailed catalog of how these styles changed through time. She was also able to date many of the styles, thereby providing a time scale for hitherto undated Roman pottery designs.

From 1948 to 1961 Kathleen Kenyon served as a lecturer in Near Eastern Archaeology at London University, a post that did not prevent her from excavating further Roman sites in Britain. She also collaborated with archaeologist John Ward-Perkins on the excavation of the Roman town of Sabratha in Libya in 1948 and 1949 and again in 1951, one of the first British overseas excavations after the war. Sabratha was founded by Phoenician merchants in the 5th century BC, then became an important Roman settlement in the 2nd century AD, before being extensively damaged by an earthquake in AD 365. Kenyon's primary interest was the pottery, recovered from both public buildings like the forum and from houses in the town. Just as at Leicester, she worked out a complicated

This plan of Jerusalem, in a Byzantine Christian mosaic in a church floor in the small town of Madaba, Jordan dates to the 6th or 7th century. It is said to be one of the best maps of the biblical lands and is still in the floor of the church.

sequence of changing pottery styles through the centuries, designed as a yardstick for studying and dating Roman sites over a large area. Unfortunately, she never had time to publish her studies in full.

By 1951 she had turned her attention entirely to the Near East, working closely with the British School of Archaeology in Jerusalem on a large-scale excavation into the biblical city of Jericho. From 1952 to 1958 an international team of archaeologists and students worked under her direction, digging into the lowermost levels of the great city mound.

Both German and British expeditions had worked at Jericho, but neither had used excavation methods as meticulous as those Kenyon brought to the site. She introduced very accurate site recording, careful pottery cataloging, and precise surveys of buried buildings. Initially, her primary goal was to identify the biblical Jericho, whose walls had been felled by Joshua's trumpets during the 13th century BC— a dramatic Old Testament account

that appealed to wealthy donors. The previous British excavator, John Garstang, had discovered substantial city walls, which he claimed were the very fortifications blown down by trumpets. But Kenyon proved conclusively that they were Bronze Age fortifications, much earlier than Joshua's walls. Biblical scholars were disconcerted by these findings, which caused much controversy between archaeologists and those who believed that the Old Testament was the historical truth and an accurate account of what had happened in the past. Joshua's siege took place much later, during the Iron Age occupation of the city. No trace of collapsed walls in that period came from Kenyon's excavations.

Meanwhile, Kenyon continued to dig ever deeper into the lowest levels of the city mound. To her surprise, she found stratified Stone Age towns, or at least large villages, below the Bronze Age levels, with distinctive architecture and one with a substantial stone defense wall, complete with watchtower. The earliest Jericho was a tiny

> *"Jericho can make the proud claim to be the earliest known town on earth."*
>
> —Kathleen Kenyon, *Digging Up Jericho* (1957)

farming village located by a natural spring; it was 4,000 years older than Gertrude Caton-Thompson's Fayum villages in Egypt. Kenyon's meticulous excavations caused a worldwide sensation, both because they provided very early dates for agriculture in the Jordan Valley, around 8000 BC, and because they dated settled agricultural towns at least 4,000 years earlier than hitherto suspected.

Kenyon continued to work on publications about the Jericho excavations for the rest of her life. Meanwhile, she again collaborated with the British School in Jerusalem, this time on excavations in East Jerusalem, at that time inside Jordan. This area of the historic city had close associations with the Old Testament and was undergoing rapid development. Between 1961 and 1967 she worked at a variety of Jerusalem sites, producing a steady stream of articles, reports, and two books on the excavations, which did much to clarify the intricate history of the city.

The year the Jerusalem project began, she was appointed Principal of St. Hugh's College, Oxford, a prestigious post that kept her much occupied with administrative duties and committees of every kind. But she managed to publish a series of books, among them the influential *Beginning in Archaeology* (1952), aimed at encouraging students to enter the field, and *Archaeology in the Holy Land* (1960), a textbook on

Palestinian archaeology for beginners. She stressed the deep roots of history in the Near East, writing: "In Palestine and other places in the Near East, archaeology has pushed back our knowledge of places and people to thousands of years before written history."

Just before she retired from St. Hugh's in 1971, Kathleen Kenyon was appointed a Dame Commander of the Order of the British Empire by Queen Elizabeth II for her services to archaeology. She continued to be active as a public lecturer and on committees of learned societies until her death at the age of 72.

This remarkable archaeologist brought the study of biblical archaeology to a wide popular audience and revolutionized our understanding of the world's earliest agriculture. She also trained a generation of now eminent archaeologists, as well as Jordanian scholars and excavation workers. Kenyon's research was very detailed, much of it focused on the use of pottery to interpret sequences of occupation levels with highly technical methods. At Jericho, she focused on digging vertically down to the bottom of the city mound rather than uncovering broad areas of different communities. Had she worked on a broader canvas, much more could have been learned there. To date, no one has taken over where her Jericho excavations left off. But with her popular writings she introduced thousands of people to the enduring fascination of biblical archaeology. Her work will continue to be debated for generations.

FURTHER READING

Moorey, P. S., and P. Parr, eds. *Archaeology in the Levant: Essays for Kathleen Kenyon.* Warminster, England: Aris and Phillips, 1978.

Kathleen Kenyon

BORN
January 5, 1906
London, England

DIED
August 24, 1978
London, England

EDUCATION
Somerville College, Oxford
(B.A. 1929)

ACCOMPLISHMENTS
Expert on Roman Britain, Romano-British pottery, and the archaeology of the Roman provinces generally; excavated Jericho, finding some of the earliest farming settlements, and the earliest town; developed elaborate methods using pottery to analyze interpret occupation levels in archaeological sites; brought new understanding of archaeology at Jericho and Jerusalem to a wide audience. Wrote *Beginning in Archaeology* (1952); *Digging up Jericho* (1957); *Archaeology in the Holy Land* (1960).

Mortimer Wheeler

EXCAVATOR
EXTRAORDINAIRE

T he whole war cemetery lay before Mortimer Wheeler, exposed in a windy trench atop Maiden Castle, a great Iron Age hill fort in southern England. He had uncovered the casualties from a brutal Roman attack on the fort in AD 43. There were skeletons in profusion, displaying savage wounds from sword and lance. In his report on the discovery, he wrote of the aftermath of the attack, when the defenders crept up to the abandoned fort in the dark and buried their dead with simple food offerings while the Romans' campfires twinkled a short distance away. Mortimer Wheeler was a consummate excavator and an archaeologist of vivid imagination who used to proclaim that archaeology was often too dull. Flamboyant, volatile, and given to overstatement, Wheeler spent a lifetime making the past come alive.

Robert Eric Mortimer Wheeler was born in Edinburgh, Scotland, in 1890. The 85 years of his colorful life spanned the decades when archaeology changed from a largely amateur pastime into a scientific discipline. His father was a

Known for his meticulous methods and strictly organized digs, Mortimer Wheeler helped change archaeology from a hobby to a science. Using his military background, Wheeler, as in this 1945 excavation of Taxila-Sirkap, Pakistan, carefully examined each layer and documented even the smallest artifacts.

journalist with a background in classics, both interests that had a profound influence on his son. At age 17 young Wheeler won a scholarship to University College, London, to study Classics. He also took classes at the Slade School of Art, for he had ambitions to become an artist. After graduating with a B.A. in 1910 and an M.A. in 1912, he applied for a postgraduate studentship to study Roman pottery in Germany's Rhineland. He then joined the Royal Commission on Historical Monuments for England as an investigator, but entered the army at the outbreak of World War I. He served with distinction in the Royal Artillery, ending the war with the rank of major and receiving the Military Cross.

By the end of World War I Wheeler had acquired the background and experience that were to guide his career. He had a fluent writing style learned from his father, a background in classics and archaeology, and a gift for logistics and organization acquired in the army. For a short while he returned to the Royal Commission, but was appointed Keeper of Archaeology at the newly founded National Museum of Wales and Lecturer in Archaeology at University College, Cardiff, in 1920. Four years later he became director and set the museum on a sound financial basis.

Between 1920 and 1926 Wheeler and his wife Tessa revolutionized Welsh archaeology with a series of major excavations on Roman frontier forts. At the time, most archaeological excavation was still little more than an uncontrolled search for spectacular artifacts. The Wheelers adopted and refined the almost forgotten excavation methods of the Victorian excavator General Lane Fox Pitt-Rivers. They paid careful attention to observing even shallow layers in the soil, recovered the smallest of potsherds and other artifacts, and published technical reports promptly, illustrated with Wheeler's own fine drawings. But this was not enough for the energetic investigator, who believed the public had the right to know about his researches. He gave many public lectures and wrote a popular book, *Prehistoric and Roman Wales,* published in 1925.

Wheeler's apprenticeship in Wales established his credentials as a serious archaeologist. He was offered the first professorship of Prehistoric Archaeology at Edinburgh University, but turned in down in favor of a nonacademic career. In 1926 he came Keeper of the much neglected London Museum, which he promptly resuscitated. Every summer he continued excavations, each designed to clarify the relationships between indigenous and the occupying Roman society in Britain and to train a new generation of young archaeologists.

In 1928 and 1929 he worked at a Roman sanctuary at Lydney in Gloucestershire. Then he turned his attention to the late Iron Age and Roman city of Verulamium just north of London, where he spent four years from 1930 through 1933, training such future excavators as Kathleen Kenyon in the process. Verulamium lay in open country, unlike many Roman towns that are buried under modern cities. He and his wife Tessa exposed 11 acres (4.45 hectares) of the city, as well as tracing the complicated history of its outlying earthworks and the smaller forts and settlements that had preceded it. By the time his report on Verulamium was published in 1936, he was tired of the Romans and looking for new topics to research.

The pace of Wheeler's administrative life was as exhausting as his fieldwork. Once the London Museum was revived, he founded the Institute of Archaeology at London University in 1934 and lectured there part-time. Three years later he became director of the institute, which soon became renowned for its training in fieldwork and scientific methods.

Mortimer Wheeler

BORN
September 10, 1890
Glasgow, Scotland

DIED
July 22, 1976
Leatherhead, England

EDUCATION
University College, London
(B.A. 1910, M.A. 1912)

ACCOMPLISHMENTS
Developed modern excavation methods in Britain and India; revolutionized the study of Iron Age and Roman Britain with excavations at Roman Verulamium and Maiden Castle in southern England; made excavations in what is now Pakistan that transformed scientific knowledge of the Harappan (Indus) civilization; founded the London Institute of Archaeology. Wrote *Archaeology from the Earth* (1954); *Still Digging: Leaves from an Antiquary's Notebook* (1955); *Alms for Oblivion: An Antiquary's Scrapbook* (1966).

> *"Dead archaeology is the driest dust that blows."*
>
> —Mortimer Wheeler, *Archaeology from the Earth* (1954)

The culmination of Wheeler's British excavations came when he turned his attention to the enormous Iron Age hill fort at Maiden Castle in southern England. During the summers of 1934 to 1937, he and Tessa developed the art of archaeological excavation to heights never achieved before. They excavated deep trenches through Maiden Castle's multiple lines of earthen ramparts. They investigated broad sections of the interior with shallow area trenches. Hundreds of visitors toured the excavations each summer, for the Wheelers believed in keeping the public informed about their work. An entire generation of young archaeologists worked at Maiden Castle, among them J. Desmond Clark, later to become an internationally famous African archaeologist. Despite the tragic early death of Tessa and the advent of World War II, Wheeler published the final report on Maiden Castle in 1943.

With his bristling mustache and flowing hair, Wheeler was a formidable personality who tolerated little criticism and did not have patience with those he considered fools. He drove the paid workers and volunteers on his excavations very hard, with scant regard for their feelings. His colleagues trod carefully in his presence. With his brusque, authoritarian ways, Wheeler made many enemies. But no one denied his talents as an organizer and leader, as the archaeologist who brought British excavation and fieldwork into the modern world. Maiden Castle led to his first expedition abroad, an investigation of Iron Age hill forts across the English Channel in Brittany in 1938 and 1939. This was Wheeler at his best, formulating a specific research plan, then executing it with brilliant skill.

Wheeler returned to the Royal Artillery with the outbreak of World War II in 1939. His coolness and decisive leadership under fire led to rapid promotion. At the battle of El Alamein in North Africa in 1942, Wheeler spent much of his time in a truck surrounded by telephones directing antiaircraft fire. He also restored the confidence of his men by calmly shaving with a mirror propped up against his jeep while under artillery fire. He was soon promoted to Brigadier and would have risen higher, had he not been invited by the Viceroy of India to become Director General of the Archaeological Survey of India. He led his regiment in the initial stages of the Italian campaign, then sailed for India in 1944.

The Archaeological Survey of India confronted Wheeler with an extraordinary challenge. The survey was moribund, with an untrained and demoralized staff and an entire continent to cover. Wheeler arrived with a mandate to train an Indian staff in high standards of excavation and publication, and to provide a sound chronological framework for India's past. Fresh from military command, he strode into the survey offices to find people dozing at their desks. A loud shout woke them up. Within 10 days the office was functioning efficiently.

Wheeler then set off on a whirlwind tour of India to meet outlying staff and, like a general on a military campaign, devise a strategy for major changes. He started a rigorous six-month training program at Taxila, a city in northern India visited by Alexander the Great in the 4th century AD. The 61 students worked long hours and learned a standard of excavation unheard of in India. His methods are still faithfully used in India and Pakistan to this day. Wheeler also founded an academic journal, *Ancient India*, then excavated Arikamedu, a trading station on the southeast coast. This site yielded Roman pottery, allowing him to establish chronological connections with the Roman world of the day.

Harappa and Mohenjo-daro, two great prehistoric cities in the Indus Valley of what is now Pakistan, provided Wheeler's greatest challenge. He deployed his now skilled fieldworkers at both cities and uncovered great citadels and massive defense works, as well as standardized grids of streets and brick houses. The excavations applied all his experience with Roman sites in Britain to huge cities, whose size did not intimidate him in the least. His work culminated in a classic account of the so-called Indus Civilization, which appeared as part of the *Cambridge History of India* in 1950.

Wheeler served in India for five years, leaving a year after the country became independent in 1948. He returned to the continent on several occasions as an adviser to the government of Pakistan. A generation of Indian and Pakistani archaeologists perpetuated his research methods. Back in England, he spent five years as Professor of the Archaeology of the Roman Provinces at the London Institute of Archaeology. During these years he excavated the Iron Age hill fort at Stanwick in Yorkshire, another brilliant investigation of a hitherto unknown site. But he found academic life an inadequate challenge, so resigned in 1949 to become part-time administrator to another moribund institution, the British Academy.

Over the next 20 years he transformed the academy from an organization of tired, self-satisfied old men into a dynamic institution at the forefront of research in the humanities and social sciences. He paid particular attention to directing research money to scholars work-ing in remote parts of the world. To Wheeler, archaeology was an international endeavor, something much broader than merely Roman or Iron Age Britain.

At the same time, he continued to popularize archaeology at every possible opportunity. He was knighted for his services to archaeology by King George VI in 1952. In that year, the British Broadcasting Corporation launched a popular archaeology television series, *Animal, Vegetable, Mineral,* in which a panel of archaeologists identified objects from antiquity. Wheeler soon became a TV star, so much so that he was voted "television personality of the year" in 1954. His TV appearances and constant public lecturing did much to make archaeology a popular subject.

Wheeler himself believed that scholars have a moral obligation to share their scientific work with lay people. Later generations of archaeologists have taken his example to heart. He remained active until his death in 1976.

Mortimer Wheeler lived his life to the full. A brilliant excavator and superb administrator, the magnitude of his achievements speak for themselves. One of Wheeler's contemporaries, Near Eastern excavator Max Mallowan, aptly described him as "a fire-breathing giant who bestrode the world like a colossus."

An aerial view of Maiden Castle shows the steep earthworks built by the early inhabitants. Attackers had to make their way through the narrow passages, where the defenders could shower them with arrows and stones.

FURTHER READING

Hawkes, Jacquetta. *Mortimer Wheeler: Adventurer in Archaeology.* London: Weidenfeld and Nicholson, 1982.

Louis and Mary Leakey

THE FIRST FAMILY OF PALEOANTHROPOLOGY

T hey excavated surrounded by Dalmatian dogs, in tropical heat that would make normal people melt. Painstakingly, inch by inch, they exposed the fragile bones of long-extinct animals on some of the earliest archaeological sites in the world. Together, they searched for the earliest human ancestors for more than a quarter-century. And, in the end, they found not one but several of them. Few archaeological partnerships have been so successful and so enduring.

Louis Seymour Bazett Leakey was the son of a Protestant missionary. He spent his childhood among the Kikuyu of central Kenya and became interested in archaeology as a teenager. In 1922 he entered St. John's College, Cambridge, where he was sent off a university tennis court for wearing shorts, a near scandalous breach of propriety at the time. He graduated with an anthropology degree in 1926 and immediately mounted a shoestring archaeological expedition to Kenya. Leakey excavated a series of sites, including Gamble's Cave, where he found human occupation going back an estimated 20,000 years. He also married his first wife, Freda. His first book, *The Stone Age Cultures of Kenya Colony*, was published to much acclaim in 1930. In this now-classic volume, Leakey outlined a long sequence of Stone Age cultures in East Africa quite unlike those found in Europe. It was a major scientific advance for the time. He received a doctorate from Cambridge University in 1930 on the basis of his Kenya research.

In 1931 Leakey set out for East Africa again, this time with the intention of visiting Olduvai Gorge, a 25-mile (40-kilometer) slash through the Serengeti Plains of what is now northern Tanzania. He traveled with German paleontologist Hans Reck, who had previously visited the gorge and found fossil elephant remains there. Reck had bet Leakey the then huge sum of £10 (about $40) that he would not find any human artifacts in the gorge. Leakey collected the wager on the very first day and soon established that Olduvai offered a unique chance to study the very earliest humans of all.

Back in Cambridge in 1934, Leakey left his first wife for a young archaeological student, Mary Nicol, who possessed a remarkable talent for drawing stone artifacts. Born in 1913, Mary was the daughter of a landscape artist. She was a quiet, determined person who was the exact opposite of the flamboyant Leakey. They shared a passion for archaeology and were to work together for three decades. They were married in 1936.

The same year, Louis was given funds for a year's study of the Kikuyu people. While he worked with the Kikuyu,

Mary excavated a series of sites, among them Njoro River Cave, a cavern used by late Stone Age people as a cemetery for the cremated dead. When World War II broke out in 1939, Louis became involved in intelligence work, but the Leakeys never let the war, or a growing family, interfere with their archaeology. In 1943 they excavated a magnificent 300,000-year-old Stone Age site at Olorgesaillie, in the Rift Valley near Nairobi, where early humans had killed and butchered large animals, including rhinoceroses. Hand axes used for butchering were lying where their users had dropped them 1,000 centuries ago. The Leakeys turned the site into one of the world's first open-air museums in 1947.

The next year, the Leakeys turned their attention to Rusinga Island in northeastern Lake Victoria, where Mary walked through crumbling gullies that cut through 20-million-year-old Miocene deposits. She saw some skull fragments and a tooth lying on an eroding slope. She shouted for Louis, who came running. Together they brushed away dirt from what Leakey called in a letter the "better part of a skull" of an apelike creature known as *Proconsul africanus*. The new fossil threw fresh light on very early human ancestry.

In 1951 the Leakeys resumed their investigations at Olduvai Gorge, where Louis was absolutely certain they would find an early human fossil. Between 1951 and 1958 they worked on the five geological beds of the gorge, fine clays and sands laid down by a shallow lake at a time when the surrounding landscape teemed with animals. Instead of systematic collecting, they concentrated on locating ancient "living floors," places where early humans had camped or butchered animals. By 1958 they had recovered large numbers of stone tools and the remains of dozens of extinct animal species, some of them from locations where the animals were butchered with crude stone choppers and flakes. Except for a few

Louis S. B. Leakey

BORN
August 7, 1903
Kabete, Kenya

DIED
October 2, 1972
London, England

EDUCATION
St. John's College, Cambridge (B.A.
1926, M.A. 1929, Ph.D. 1930)

ACCOMPLISHMENTS
Established the Stone Age archaeology of Kenya; was one of the founders of African archaeology as a serious scientific pursuit; with Mary Leakey made fossil discoveries at Rusinga Island and Olduvai Gorge that revolutionized the study of human origins; advocated and popularized a multidisciplinary approach to investigating human origins. Wrote *The Stone Age Cultures of Kenya Colony* (1931); *Adam's Ancestors* (1934); *By the Evidence: Memoirs, 1932–1951* (1974); *Olduvai Gorge: A Report on the Evolution of the Hand-Axe Culture in Beds I–IV* (1951).

"We almost cried with sheer joy, each seized by that terrific emotion that comes rarely in life. After all our hoping and hardship and sacrifice, at last we had reached our goal— we had found the world's earliest human [Zinjanthropus]."

—Louis Leakey, "Exploring 1,750,000 Years Into Man's Past," *National Geographic Magazine* (1961)

fragmentary hominid (early human or prehuman) teeth, there were no traces of human fossils.

Then, on July 17, 1959, Louis was in bed back at camp with a slight fever. Mary went out with her two Dalmatian dogs to examine a location that had yielded tools back in 1931, but had not been examined closely since. She noticed a scrap of thick skull projecting from the sloping lake bed. Gently brushing away the soil, she saw two large teeth set in a curved hominid jaw. She jumped into her Land Rover and raced back to camp, bursting in on a dozing Louis. "I've got him!" she cried. His illness forgotten, they looked at the teeth with a wave of emotion. Louis recalled: "At last we had reached our goal—we had discovered the world's earliest known human." As soon as the many pieces were recovered from the soil, Mary reconstructed the skull of a robust-looking ape-human, which they named *Zinjanthropus boisei*, "Southern ape-human of Boise," after a benefactor, Mr. Boise). Mary nicknamed the fossil "Dear Boy."

Almost overnight, the Leakeys became international celebrities. They were adopted by the National Geographic Society, which published articles on Olduvai and *Zinjanthropus*, while giving them a large research grant for further work. Louis estimated that *Zinjanthropus* was about 600,000 years old. He, and the rest of the scientific community, were stunned when two geophysicists from the University of California, Berkeley, used the new potassium-argon dating method for measuring radioactive decay in volcanic rocks to date the *Zinjanthropus* site to 1.75 million years. At one stroke, human origins had become three times as old.

While Louis traveled in the United States and Europe, Mary undertook a major excavation of the *Zinjanthropus* site, which she excavated grid square by grid square with meticulous care. All the soil from the site was passed through fine-mesh screens to recover even the smallest rodent bones and other bits of evidence. From this remarkable excavation, Mary not only recovered thousands of bone fragments and stone tools, but also developed methods for excavating early human sites that are still in use today.

The 11-year-old Philip Leakey watches as his parents excavate the so-called "Pre-Zinj" floor at Olduvai Gorge, where the skull of *Homo habilis,* the first toolmaker, came to light. The family dog looks on.

ARCHAEOLOGISTS

Mary D. Leakey

BORN
February 6, 1913
London, England

DIED
December 9, 1996
Nairobi, Kenya

EDUCATION
Private; honorary doctorates from British and American universities and the University of Witwatersrand, Johannesburg, South Africa

ACCOMPLISHMENTS
The more scientific member of the Leakey partnership; skilled excavator and expert at drawing stone tools; made numerous Kenya excavations and human fossil discoveries with Louis Leakey; made other important fossil discoveries at Olduvai Gorge; discovered 3.6 million-year-old Laetoli hominid prints in Tanzania. Wrote *Olduvai Gorge: My Search for Early Man* (1979), *Olduvai Gorge, Vol 3: Excavations in Beds I and II, 1960–1963* (1971).

Larger-scale excavations at nearby locations yielded yet more hominid fossils, including an almost complete foot, this time from a more lightly built creature quite different from *Zinjanthropus*. The well-known South African biological anthropologist Philip Tobias named the new hominid *Homo habilis*, "handy person," the first toolmaking human. In 1960 Louis found a massive skull of an anatomically more advanced human,

Homo ergaster in modern classificatory terms, at a high level in the gorge.

By the 1960s, Mary bore the brunt of the field research, living almost full time at Olduvai Gorge. She wrote the definitive study of the earliest human culture in the world, named the Oldowan, after Olduvai Gorge. They had a simple tool technology of stone choppers and flakes. Now she was internationally recognized as a scientist

LOUIS AND MARY LEAKEY • 151

> *"We are having a wildly exciting time here with [the 3.6 million-year-old Laetoli] footprints that might have been made today . . . with toe impressions and all."*

> —Mary Leakey, letter (1978)

in her own right, as a more patient and thorough excavator than Louis ever would be. Meanwhile, Louis was always proposing new theories of human origins and surrounding himself with controversy, notably over an alleged early human site at Calico Hills, California, which a panel of experts declared to be of natural origin rather than of human manufacture. He was also becoming interested in research into living primates, sponsoring a number of soon-to-be-well-known researchers, among them Jane Goodall, who worked among chimpanzees in Tanzania, and Dian Fossey, who became world famous for her research on mountain gorillas.

Louis's health deteriorated in the late 1960s. He died in London in 1972, just as his son Richard was achieving international fame with new hominid discoveries in the East Turkana area of northern Kenya. Meanwhile, Mary quietly worked on the Olduvai artifacts and opened excavations at Laetoli in Tanzania in 1977. Here she amazed the world with the discovery of a trail of footprints left by two hominids preserved in hardened volcanic ash

dating to 3.6 million years ago. "Now this is really something to put on the mantelpiece," she once remarked of a particularly nice footprint. This remarkable discovery was the capstone of an archaeological career as illustrious as that of her husband. She left Olduvai Gorge for the last time in 1983, retired in Nairobi, was honored with honorary degrees by many universities, and died in 1996.

FURTHER READING

Cole, Sonia. *Leakey's Luck*. London: Collins, 1975.

Morell, Virginia. *Ancestral Passions*. New York: Simon & Schuster, 1995.

Poynter, Margaret. *The Leakeys: Uncovering the Origins of Humankind*. Berkeley Heights, N.J.: Enslow, 1997.

Willis, DeHa. *The Leakey Family: Leaders in the Search for Human Origins*. New York: Facts on File, 1992.

Grahame Clark

SURVEYOR OF ANCIENT ECONOMIES AND ECOLOGY

John Douglas Grahame Clark drove cars with apparently reckless unconcern, talking about archaeology while driving along country roads at more than 60 miles (90 kilometers) an hour. He had a relentless curiosity about the human past and such a single-minded dedication to archaeology that his students sometimes wondered whether he was a machine rather than a scholar. But underneath an austere facade was a kind and gentle man.

Grahame Clark became interested in archaeology as a teenager, when a neighbor showed him a collection of stone arrowheads. By the end of his long life he had become one of the 20th century's most successful archaeologists. The son of a stockbroker, he was born in 1907. His father died of influenza at the end of World War I, a loss that affected young Grahame severely. For the rest of his life, he remained a shy and reticent man who seemed aloof, when in fact he was a kindly person.

Here working at Mortimer Wheeler's Maiden Castle excavation as a student, Grahame Clark became a leading expert in classification and dating prehistoric cultures.

As a professor at Cambridge University, Grahame Clark created one of the leading archaeologist departments attracting students from all over the world. Here in May, 1964, Clark examines the stratification at Fromm's Landing, Austrailia, where one of his students, John Mulvaney did extensive work looking at Austrailian prehistory.

In 1920, he went to Marlborough College, a well-known English private school that encouraged both academic study and broader interests. Clark became interested first in butterflies, then in archaeology. He started collecting stone tools when at home in southern England, which led to developing a serious interest in the prehistoric past at school. In 1926

he went to Peterhouse, a Cambridge University college, to study history. After two years of history, he transferred into the newly founded Archaeology and Anthropology degree program and graduated with honors in 1930.

Peterhouse immediately awarded Clark a three-year research fellowship, which he devoted to a study of British Mesolithic (Middle Stone Age) cultures. These prehistoric societies were still little known except for dozens of small collections of stone tools. Clark published *The Mesolithic Age in Britain* in 1932, a book which earned him wide praise and his doctorate a year later. In 1935 he was appointed an Assistant Lecturer in Archaeology at Cambridge. He was to spend his entire career at the university.

The Mesolithic Age established Grahame Clark as an expert in the classification and dating of prehistoric cultures. His university duties left him free to excavate during the summers, using skills he had learned working on Iron Age hill forts in southern England. He now expanded his work in two directions. While writing *The Mesolithic Age*, he became a founding member of the Fenland Research Committee, a group of scholars from several disciplines who collaborated on studies of the ecology of the waterlogged fen (swamplike) country around Cambridge.

Clark worked closely with Harry Godwin, a young botanist who was an expert in the study of fossil pollen grains found in prehistoric swamps. The tiny pollens had fallen into the layers of the swamp over many thousands of years. Fortunately, plant pollens are easy to recognize under a microscope. Often, dramatic changes can be traced in vegetation around the swamp over long periods of time. Their greatest research was an excavation at

Peacock's Farm near Cambridge in 1934, where they discovered Mesolithic flint tools in peat dated to about 6500 BC, a first for Britain.

The fenland research made Clark highly conscious of the importance of reconstructing ancient environments and the ways in which ancient people adapted to changing ecological conditions. However, 10 years were to pass before he excavated a waterlogged Mesolithic site which contained abundant wooden artifacts and other perishable artifacts. He visited Scandinavia several times to see waterlogged settlements dating to 5000 BC and earlier that the Danes had excavated. He looked with envy at their fiber fishnets, wooden arrows, antler spearheads, and their exotic artworks, and wished he could find them in Britain. After two years of traveling in the north of the continent, he published his second book, *The Mesolithic Settlement of Northern Europe* (1936). This was a masterly survey of the first settlement of northern Europe by humans after the Ice Age. It described not only the Stone Age cultures, but also the environmental changes that formed the backdrop to human life in the region. *The Mesolithic Settlement* soon became a classic, and a basic textbook on the subject for a generation.

By the outbreak of World War II in 1938, Grahame Clark was regarded as one of the rising stars of his archaeological generation. He had written a popular textbook, *Archaeology and Society* (1939), one of the first essays on the place of archaeology in modern society. His first students were already working in Africa and doing fundamental research. His career was stopped short by the war, which he spent like many other archaeologists, in aerial photographic interpretation. At the same time, he devoted many hours to an intensive study of ancient economic life, especially of the ways in which people acquired food.

A stream of papers flowed from his pen during these years, many of them, as he recalled, written on the train as he commuted to and from London. The first was on bees and ancient beekeeping. It set the blueprint for a series of publications that covered such diverse topics as whaling and shifting agriculture. In each he described the archaeological evidence from Europe, then bolstered it with analogies taken from European folk culture. Soon after the war he made a long journey through Norway, in which he observed Scandinavian fishing families still using the same artifacts as prehistoric fishers. All these papers culminated in one of Clark's greatest books, *Prehistoric Europe: the Economic Basis* (1952). In it he described ancient European societies: how prehistoric people had hunted animals, gathered plant foods, fished, and farmed—made their livings in different ways through time—as a way of convincing his colleagues that there was more to prehistoric Europe than just potsherds and stone artifacts. The book was, he said, "essentially an act of propaganda."

While writing *Prehistoric Europe,* Clark was also engaged on his greatest excavation. In 1947 an amateur archaeologist found some Mesolithic stone tools and antler fragments at Star Carr in northeastern England. Clark realized at once that this might be the waterlogged site with well-preserved artifacts he was looking for, and excavated there for three seasons between 1949 and 1951. Working with students and a minute budget, he recovered a small Stone Age hunting site with almost perfect preservation. The site

Grahame Clark

BORN

July 28, 1907
Bromley, Kent, England

DIED

September 12, 1995
Cambridge, England

EDUCATION

Peterhouse College, Cambridge
(B.A. 1930, M.A. 1933, Ph.D. 1934)

ACCOMPLISHMENTS

Pioneered in studying the effects of ancient ecology and environmental change on prehistoric economic life; excavated the Star Carr Mesolithic site; published the first prehistory of humankind based on radiocarbon dating. Wrote *The Mesolithic Age in Britain* (1932); *The Mesolithic Settlement of Northern Europe* (1936); *Archaeology and Society* (1939); *Prehistoric Europe: The Economic Basis* (1952); *Excavations at Star Carr* (1954); *World Prehistory* (1961, 1977); *Archaeological Researches in Retrospect* (1974), *Archaeology at Cambridge and Beyond* (1989). Awarded the Erasmus Prize in 1990 for his work in bringing archaeology to a broad audience.

> *"If anyone were to ask me why I have spent my life studying Prehistory, I would only say that I have remained under the spell of a subject which seeks to discover how we became human beings endowed with minds and souls before we had learned to write."*
>
> —Grahame Clark, in *Archaeological Researches in Retrospect* (1974)

was centered on a crude birchwood platform set in the reeds at an edge of a long-vanished glacial lake. Harry Godwin used pollen grains to reconstruct the vegetation that once surrounded Star Carr.

Clark himself described a Stone Age hunting society whose artifacts bore some similarity to those of the Maglemose culture across the North Sea. He also obtained a radiocarbon date of 7538 BC, ±350 years, for Star Carr, one of the first carbon dates for a Stone Age archaeological site ever processed. In his *Excavations at Star Carr* (1954), Clark set a small Stone Age site in a remarkably precise environmental context, as vivid a piece of archaeological reporting as any in the 20th century. Fifty years later, a team of experts applied the latest archaeological and environmental methods to Star Carr and proved the essential accuracy of Clark's findings.

In 1952 Grahame Clark was appointed Disney Professor of Archaeology at Cambridge, following Dorothy Garrod in the position. Although he was too shy to make a notable teacher and was uncomfortable with university administration, he threw himself into creating an archaeology department devoted to the study of world archaeology. Many students from as far afield as Australia came to Cambridge. The faculty excavated sites in North Africa and elsewhere. Between 1952 and his retirement in 1974, Clark and his colleagues trained a generation of young archaeologists who went out to work in distant lands—Africa, Australia, New Zealand, southwestern Asia, and the Americas.

He also began to travel widely, as a result of which he wrote one of his best-known volumes, *World Prehistory*, which appeared in 1961. This was the first synthesis of human prehistory that relied on radiocarbon dating; it attracted wide attention and went into three editions, the last in 1977.

After his retirement, Clark continued to travel. He also wrote a stream of books, the best known of which is *Archaeology at Cambridge and Beyond* (1989), an account of the Cambridge archaeology department and of its involvement in world prehistory. He also became Master of Peterhouse, his Cambridge college, an appointment that gave him great satisfaction. The culminating moment of his career came in 1990 when he was awarded the prestigious Erasmus Prize for his contributions to making prehistory known to a wide audience. This perhaps was Clark's greatest achievement, but he is also remembered as one of the outstanding pioneers of ecological archaeology, the study of how humans adapted to changing environments. Few scholars leave such a lasting impact on their field of study.

FURTHER READING

Fagan, Brian M. *Grahame Clark: An Intellectual Biography of an Archaeologist.* Boulder, Colo.: Westview, 2001.

John Desmond Clark

AUTHORITY OF
AFRICAN PREHISTORY

M useum director, researcher, and distinguished professor, John Desmond Clark was remarkable for his keen archaeological eye. In 1938 he picked up half of a small, 40,000-year-old stone scraping tool at an archaeological site in the Zambezi Valley. In 1959, he returned to the same site and promptly recognized the other half lying on the ground. Back at his museum, he reunited them for the first time in 40,000 years.

Clark was born in London in 1916, and entered Christ's College, Cambridge to study history in 1933. He was already interested in archaeology, thanks to a teacher at school. At Cambridge he studied Stone Age archaeology under Grahame Clark and learned excavation under Mortimer Wheeler at Iron Age hill fort at Maiden Castle in southern England. After graduation in 1937, he applied for three museum posts in England but was unsuccessful. Fortunately for African archaeology, he received a three-year appointment as administrator of the Rhodes-Livingstone Institute in Livingstone, close to the Victoria Falls in Northern Rhodesia (now Zambia). He was also appointed Curator of the Rhodes-Livingstone Museum, then housed in an old clubhouse.

From left to right, Desmond Clark, Mary Leakey, and Jack Harris at the hominid footprint site of Laetoli, Tanzania, in 1978.

Desmond Clark arrived in Livingstone in 1938 accompanied by his new wife Betty, who had a profound influence on his career. He was one of the very few professional archaeologists working in southern Africa at the time, and almost nothing was known of the prehistoric societies of the region. His first task was to set up and organize a proper museum, which he completed by the end of 1939. He also collaborated with a young geologist, Basil Cook, on a study of the geology, prehistoric stone tools, and fossil animal bones from the ancient gravels of the Zambezi River upstream of the Victoria Falls. This was Clark's first independent fieldwork, followed by an important excavation into the occupation deposits of Mumbwa Cave in the central part of the country. With these excavations, he began to put together the first sequence of prehistoric societies in northern Rhodesia.

During World War II Clark served as a sergeant in an ambulance unit in Ethiopia and what was then British Somaliland. He took advantage of every opportunity to collect Stone Age artifacts from river gravels, open sites, and rock shelters. After service in Madagascar and Kenya, he was posted to Somalia as a Civil Affairs Officer, a job that involved much travel. He made extensive archaeological collections, enough material for him to write what is still an authoritative book on the archaeology of the region, *Prehistoric Cultures of the Horn of Africa,* published in 1954. This provided the first description of what had happened in prehistoric times in northeast Africa. Half a century later, we know that Ethiopia was home to some of the earliest humans in the world.

Back in Livingstone, Clark planned and built a new building for the Rhodes-Livingstone Museum in 1951 and also established the Northern Rhodesia National Monuments Commission to administer archaeological and historic sites in the country. He was also astonishingly productive in the field, publishing *The Stone Age Cultures of Northern Rhodesia* in 1950, at the time a fine model of river valley archaeological study. His travels took him throughout the country and resulted in the discovery in 1953 of the now famous Kalambo Falls Stone Age site, which lies on the Zambia-Tanzania border.

Until Kalambo Falls, Clark was regarded as a competent archaeologist working in a remote backwater of the world. His work had local interest, but little more. Kalambo Falls changed all that. In a series of meticulous field seasons between 1956 and 1959, he excavated a long sequence of layers showing cultural change, including several Early Stone Age living surfaces, where fine hand axes used for butchering game lay where they had been used over 230,000 years ago. The site, just upstream of a spectacular waterfall, also contained extensive Middle Stone Age occupations, and a important early metal workers' settlement of the first millennium AD. The Kalambo excavations involved scholars from other disciplines who studied the geology and ancient environments, and many young archaeologists who went on to become distinguished excavators in their own right.

The Kalambo excavations unfolded at a time of great interest in Africa and early human evolution overseas, which brought a flood of American scholars to Central Africa. Clark became an international figure. With his open manner, intense curiosity and enthusiasm, and constant encouragement of less experienced fieldworkers, he became a much-loved mentor of young archaeologists from many parts of the world. His academic interests widened significantly, especially with the publication of his *Prehistory of Southern Africa* (1959), an engaging and still quoted synthesis of the subject. He was a whirlwind of new projects, including one to survey the archaeological sites of the Middle Zambezi Valley before this remote area was flooded by the rising waters of human-created Lake Kariba.

In 1961 Clark was invited to become a Professor of Anthropology at the University of California, Berkeley, where an important multidisciplinary group of African scholars was formed. This was a fortunate move both for Clark and for African archaeology, coming as it did two years after the Leakeys found *Zinjanthropus boisei* at Olduvai Gorge, Tanzania. The ample research funds available in the United States allowed Clark to expand his researches dramatically without the distractions of running a major museum. With the assistance of others, including the young paleoanthropologist Glynn Isaac, he trained not only a generation of American graduate students, but also more than 10 Africans who are now important figures in archaeology and antiquities administration in their own countries.

Clark's own interests now focused more on very early human evolution. His 1960s excavations extended from Zambia to neighboring Malawi, where he searched for evidence of very early hominids, without much success except for the discovery of an elephant that was surrounded by the stone tools used to butcher it. He also worked with multidisciplinary teams on Stone Age sites in the heart of the Sahara Desert and, in 1971, along the Upper Nile in the Sudan, where he searched for early farming villages.

The year 1974 saw Clark working extensively in Ethiopia, excavating a 75,000-year-old Middle Stone Age cave in the Ethiopian Rift, and Stone Age camps dating to about 1.5 million years ago at over 7,800 feet (2,400 meters) above sea level. Unfortunately, a deteriorating political situation made it impossible for him to work in the human fossil-rich Awash region, which he had planned to do in the 1980s. Africa was in such turmoil that Clark turned his attention to research projects in China and India, where he excavated early Stone Age sites.

Clark retired from teaching in 1986, but continued to carry out active fieldwork in China until the 1990s. He continued active research until his death in 2002. He remained the paragon of African archaeology. Always cautious and conservative in his interpretations, Clark had more firsthand knowledge of the prehistory of Africa than any person living. His boundless enthusiasm for archaeology brought dozens of young archaeologists into Africa and the study of early human evolution. He encouraged new methods for teasing information from stone tools, food remains, and environmental data. Few archaeologists worked in so many places and with such sustained effort as Desmond Clark. His influence on African archaeology will continue to be felt well into the 21st century.

FURTHER READING

Daniel, Glyh and Christopher Chippendale, eds. *The Pastmaster: Eleven Modern Pioneers of Archaeology.* London: Thames and Hudson, 1989.

Murray, Tim, ed. *Encyclopedia of Archaeology: The Great Archaeologists.* Santa Barbara, Calif.: ABC-Clio, 1999.

John Desmond Clark

BORN
April 10, 1916
London, England

DIED
February 14, 2002
Oakland, California

EDUCATION
Christ's College, Cambridge
(B.A. 1936, M.A. 1940, Ph.D. 1950)

ACCOMPLISHMENTS
Considered to be the leading 20th-century African prehistorian; carried out major researches in Zambezi Valley in Central Africa, Somalia, and Ethiopia before 1950; excavated Kalambo Falls site, transforming modern knowledge of Early Stone Age societies in Central Africa; made major contributions to the study of early human evolution, trained Africans to serve as archaeologists in their own countries. Wrote *The Stone Age Cultures of Northern Rhodesia* (1950); *Prehistoric Cultures of the Horn of Africa,* (1954); *The Prehistory of Southern Africa* (1959), *The Kalambo Falls Prehistoric Site* (1969, 1974, 2001).

Gordon R. Willey

MASTER OF MAYAN ARCHAEOLOGY

The genial Gordon Willey was a mentor and archaeological father to generations of young archaeologists. He was also a talented author of detective stories. Gordon Willey was born in Chariton, Iowa, in 1913, but grew up in Long Beach, California. After taking an undergraduate degree in archaeology at the University of Arizona, Tucson, in 1933, he took a master's degree in 1935. Willey studied under archaeologist Duncan Strong at Columbia University and earned a doctorate in Peruvian archaeology in 1942. While still a graduate student, Willey and his colleague Richard Woodbury carried out a major archaeological survey of sites along the northwestern coast of Florida between Pensacola and St. Marks. They found 87 sites, excavated six of them, and used their research to develop a regional chronology so important that it is still consulted today.

In 1943 Willey was appointed to the Smithsonian Institution in Washington D.C., to help the anthropologist Julian Steward edit the monumental *Handbook of South American Indians*. He came under the intellectual influence of Steward, a gifted fieldworker who had studied Shoshone Indian hunter-gatherers in the Great Basin of the western United States. These people lived in small groups and ranged widely over large home territories. Steward had proclaimed that archaeologists should spend less time looking at single sites and look at them set in their landscapes as these changed over time.

After World War II, Willey applied Steward's settlement and landscape approach to the Virú Valley on Peru's North Coast. There he studied an entire river valley's changing settlements through more than 1,500 years of prehistoric time, using aerial photography, surveying on foot, and limited excavations. Willey believed one could not study ancient societies without looking at them as part of complex economic, political, and social landscapes. The Virú research, published in 1953, helped found a new field of settlement archaeology in the 1950s and 1960s, which was based on large-scale archaeological surveys of such areas as the Valley of Mexico before Aztec civilization, ancient Nubia (Sudan), and Mesopotamia.

On the strength of his Virú research, Willey was appointed the Bowditch Professor of Central American Archaeology and Ethnology at Harvard University in 1950, a post he held for the remainder of his career. He was already working on a series of publications with his colleague Philip Phillips, identifying the economic and technological factors that distinguished hunters and gatherers from farmers. In their

Gordon R. Willey

Gordon Willey records data in a survey pit during the Belize Valley project of 1953–56. Willey's Belize research focused as much on site survey as on excavation. By looking at entire areas such as the Belize Valley, he was able to study changing Maya life over many centuries against a consistent landscape.

BORN
March 7, 1913
Chariton, Iowa

DIED
April, 28, 2002
Cambridge, Massachusetts

EDUCATION
University of Arizona (B.A. 1933, M.A. 1935); Columbia University (Ph.D. 1942)

ACCOMPLISHMENTS
Pioneered systematic use of archaeological survey in North America, the Maya lowlands, and coastal Peru; carried out large-scale investigations in river basins in the southeastern United States and a pioneer settlement survey in the Virú Valley, Peru; introduced settlement archaeology to the study of Maya civilization with notable researches at Barton Ramie, Belize, Seibal, Guatemala, and Copán, Honduras. Wrote *Archaeology of the Florida Gulf Coast* (1949); *Method and Theory in American Archaeology* (with Philip Phillips, 1958); *Prehistoric Settlement Patterns in the Virú Valley, Peru* (1953); *An Introduction to American Archaeology* (1966, 1971), *A History of American Archaeology* (with Jeremy A. Sabloff, 1974).

classic book, *Method and Theory in American Archaeology*, published in 1958, they argued that ancient American societies had changed through long periods of time as a result of a multitude of interacting factors, among them environmental change, population growth, and group and individual identities. Willey and Phillips argued that American archaeology had close ties to anthropology: it is "anthropology or it is nothing." This close marriage between anthropology and archaeology has become one of the cornerstones of American archaeology.

Gordon Willey either directed or carried out fieldwork in eight countries during his long career. The Bowditch professorship at Harvard carried the expectation that the holder would work in Central America, specifically on Maya civilization. Willey was appointed to the post on the basis of his general archaeological experience, having previously been only one season in Panama. He spent 1952 and 1953 working on shell middens in that country, but his

Bowditch predecessor, Alfred M. Tozzer, soon made it clear to him that he was supposed to work on the Maya.

Willey felt somewhat intimidated by the presence of Alfred Kidder, J. Eric Thompson, and other eminent archaeologists working on the subject. So he began with a settlement survey at Barton Ramie in the Belize River Valley. Here, farmers had cleared the forest for their fields, so Willey and his students were able to walk freely across the landscape. Willey spotted some promising house mounds in 1953 and returned a year later for a larger-scale survey. The result was one of the first Maya settlement patterns ever to be mapped.

Willey expanded his settlement researches to other sites, first at Altar de Sacrificios in Guatemala's Petén in 1959, where a Maya ceremonial center lay on an island in a swamp. The forest cover was thick and the survey yielded few house mounds. So the team moved to Seibal farther upstream on the Pasion River, where the ceremonial center lay on higher, better drained ground. Willey laid out a 3-mile-by-3-mile (5-kilometers-by-5-kilometers) square, which he surveyed intensively while training a generation of now distinguished Maya archaeologists. By the time the fieldwork at Altar de Sacrificios and Seibal ended in 1968, Willey had founded a new tradition in Maya archaeology. In all his researches, the focus of the surveys and excavations was not only on the city itself, but on the outlying areas as well, on the hierarchy of lesser settlements that flourished in the shadow of the larger centers. His successors carry on the tradition. Such settlement research continues to be a major part of Maya archaeology. The result is a much better understanding of the changing fortunes of individual Maya centers.

Willey next moved on to Honduras where, in 1975, he was invited by the Honduran government to carry out a settlement survey around the great Maya city of Copán, first investigated by John Lloyd Stephens in 1839. He directed the first two years of the survey, from 1975 to 1977, which was then continued by Claude Baudez and William Sanders with a Pennsylvania State University team. Years of meticulous survey have produced an unrivaled chronicle of the rise and fall of one of the greatest of all Maya cities.

Even while directing these large field surveys, Willey was busy writing up not only his fieldwork, but also engaged in compiling a massive summary of the archaeology of the Americas, the first ever attempted. He surveyed North and Central America in 1966, and South America in 1971. *An Introduction to American Archaeology* (1966–1971) drew on Willey's broad field experience and lifetime of archaeological study, as well as using the principles of culture history he had outlined with Philip Phillips in 1958. This magisterial, two-volume work rapidly became a classic, laying the foundations for new generations of field research throughout the Americas. Today it is largely outdated, in considerable part because of the fine training Willey gave his students. Willey was also co-author of *A History of American Archaeology* with his former student Jeremy A. Sabloff in 1974, a book widely used in college classrooms.

Gordon Willey spent much of his career developing culture histories and supervising studies of entire ancient landscapes. His later career unfolded during the theoretical ferments that enveloped archaeology in the 1960s (see Part 5), many of which revolved around the need to explain rather than describe the past. Willey himself urged caution, for he was wary of attempts to explain the creative ideas that once lay behind the material remains found by the archaeologist. Therein lay his greatest contribution, for Willey trained an entire generation of Maya archaeologists and others whose work was based firmly in descriptive archaeology and settlement studies. At the same time, the new generation, taught by Willey that solid data are the basis for sound theoretical reasoning about the past, has embarked on careful searches for explanations of such phenomena as the collapse of classic Maya civilization in AD 900. Willey himself carried his detective skills into retirement and was the author of several excellent crime novels before his death in 2002.

FURTHER READING

Daniel, Glyn, and Christopher Chippindale, "Gordon R. Willey," in *The Pastmasters*. London: Thames and Hudson, 1989.

Vogt, Evan Z., and Richard M. Leventhal, eds. *Prehistoric Settlement Patterns: Essays in Honor of Gordon R. Willey*. Albuquerque: University of New Mexico Press, 1983.

More Archaeologists to Remember

Edward H. Thompson (1860–1935) was a Maya archaeologist who investigated the mysterious Sacred Cenote at Chichén Itzá in Mexico's Yucatán region. Thompson recovered numerous gold offerings and figurines from the dark waters, using primitive diving technology.

O. G. S. Crawford (1886–1957) was a British archaeologist who pioneered landscape archaeology and archaeological survey. He was also an early user of aerial photographs to identify and study archaeological sites from the air. Crawford founded *Antiquity* in 1927, an archaeological journal with an international perspective still widely read today.

Gerhard Bersu (1889–1964), a German archaeologist, worked extensively in southern Britain. Bersu developed meticulous excavation methods for studying prehistoric dwellings, notably at the Little Woodbury Iron Age village of the first millennium BC. He also worked in Ireland and on the Isle of Man.

Li Chi (1895–1979) was the "father of modern Chinese archaeology." Trained in anthropology at Harvard University, he was responsible for the excavation of an early farming village at Yangshao in northern China, the first dig by a Chinese scholar. His most famous excavations investigated the Shang civilization capital at Anyang on the Hwang Ho (Yellow River) during the 1930s. Li Chi spent his later career in Taiwan.

Edward H. Thompson's 1890 office was once a palace room at the Maya site of Labna, Yucatán, Mexico. Like other early archaeologists, Thompson used temples and other ancient buildings as laboratories and living space.

William Albright (1891–1971) worked in southwestern Asia for his entire career. He was a pioneer of stratigraphic and biblical archaeology. His *Archaeology of Palestine* (1949) was for a long time a classic work.

Raymond Dart (1893–1988) achieved world fame for his discovery of the southern ape-human *Australopithecus africanus* at Taung, South Africa in 1924. Dart claimed the fossil was a human ancestor, but this was rejected by the wider scientific community until the 1950s, when he was vindicated by other discoveries.

J. Eric Thompson (1898–1975) was a British Maya archaeologist who exercised a strong influence on the decipherment of Mayan writing. His strongly expressed belief that the Maya rulers were peaceful astrologer priests obsessed with calendars and the passage of time held back decipherment for a considerable time. In fact, the script was phonetic and the Maya rulers were warlike, ambitious lords with little respect for human life.

William Duncan Strong (1899–1962) was a self-trained archaeologist. During his two years as professor of anthropology at the University of Nebraska from 1929 to 1931, Strong revolutionized the archaeology of the Great Plains by investigating settled agricultural villages. He used anthropological sources to do so, working back from the present into the past. In 1937 he became professor of anthropology at Columbia University, where he trained many later well-known archaeologists. His later career was spent in Peruvian archaeology.

Emil Haury (1904–92) was an expert in the archaeology of the American Southwest, and professor of anthropology at the University of Arizona, Tucson. He defined the well-known Hohokam culture of the southern desert. His excavations at Snaketown in Arizona achieved worldwide fame.

Christopher Hawkes (1905–92) was a British archaeologist responsible for detailed classifications and dating of Bronze Age and Iron Age societies. As a professor of European archaeology at Oxford University, he did much to integrate British prehistoric cultures with their contemporaries on the continent.

James B. Griffin (1905–97), was the leading authority on the archaeology of eastern North America for over 40 years. He was an expert on artifact styles, especially pottery, and developed classification schemes for the region that are still in use today. Griffin also studied relationships between eastern North America and neighboring regions like the Great Plains and the St. Lawrence Valley. He trained several generations of now well-known archaeologists.

Robert Braidwood (b. 1907) professor of anthropology at the University of Chicago, pioneered multidisciplinary research into the origins of food production in the Near East during the 1950s. His best known excavation was of the early farming village at Jarmo in northern Iraq in 1959 and 1960, which produced radiocarbon dates earlier than 6000 BC, a sensational reading at the time.

Eric Higgs (1908–76) was a sheep farmer who became an archaeologist in his 50s. After training at Cambridge University, he headed a major project on the origins of agriculture in the early 1970s, making use of innovative approaches such as studies of the surroundings of ancient settlements and flotation methods for recovering seeds from archaeological levels. Flotation, which involves passing soil samples through fine screens and water, has revolutionized the study of early agriculture by multiplying the number of seeds available for study from early farming settlements.

Aleksei Pavlovich Okladnikov (b. 1908), a Soviet archaeologist of great distinction, achieved international fame for his excavations in Mongolia and northeastern Asia. He discovered the well-known, 21,000-year-old Stone Age hunting camp at Mal'ta on Lake Baikal, and the Neanderthal burials at Teshik-Tash cave in the Crimea, which date to over 50,000 years ago.

Tatiana Proskouriakoff (1909–85) was a brilliant artist who is still remembered for her meticulous artistic reconstructions of Maya cities and monuments. She also made serious contributions to the decipherment of Mayan script with her work on the royal stelae at the Maya center of Yaxchilán.

Jesse D. Jennings (1909–97), professor of anthropology at the University of Utah, Salt Lake City, was a dominant figure in the study of Great Basin archaeology. Jennings excavated Danger Cave in Utah, which contained evidence of thousands of years of human occupation, and was a pioneer in salvage archaeology, carried out before the construction of major dams. He also worked in the Pacific area.

Xia Nai (1910–85), of the Institute of Archaeology of the Chinese Academy of Sciences, learned excavation under Mortimer Wheeler at Maiden Castle, England. He investigated numerous Chinese sites, among them the Shang civilization's city of Erligang on the Hwang Ho (Yellow River). He also excavated the early farming village at Banpo, which dates to about 4000 BC. Xia trained hundreds of archaeologists during his long career.

Stuart Piggott (1910–96), an expert on Stone Age farming cultures and European prehistory, was the first archaeologist to develop a classification of Neolithic pottery in Britain. His

Ancient Europe (1965) was an elegant summary of European prehistory. Piggott was also the biographer of William Stukeley and an expert on the Druids, ancient British priests described by Julius Caesar.

Walter W. Taylor (1913–97) achieved fame and notoriety for his *Study of Archaeology*, published in 1955. This book was a scathing critique of North American archaeology as practiced at the time and was widely considered to be a personal attack on eminent colleagues. Taylor claimed that archaeologists of the day were little more than technicians, and advocated multidisciplinary research in field and laboratory. In this he was a decade ahead of Lewis Binford's "new archaeology" (see Part 5).

Charles McBurney (1914–79) was a Stone Age archaeologist best known for his excavations at the Haua Fteah in what is now Libya. He also worked on Le Cotte de St. Brelade cave on the island of Jersey in the English Channel.

Thurstan Shaw (b. 1914), a distinguished African archaeologist, worked on the Later Iron Age societies of West Africa. A meticulous fieldworker, Shaw excavated the remarkable royal burials of the 9th century AD at Igbo Ukwo in Nigeria and wrote a monograph on the spectacular bronze artifacts and other finds. His *Nigeria: Its Archaeology and Early History* (1978) is a classic work. He also founded the department of archaeology in Nigeria's University of Ibadan, a major center for archaeological training in Africa.

Robert Heizer (1915–79) was a North American archaeologist who specialized in the archaeology of California and the desert West. He was also an expert on modern Native American groups. He excavated numerous sites during his long career, including Lovelock Cave in Nevada, uncovering a

long chronicle of Great Basin occupation. Heizer was also a pioneer of economic archaeology and the study of early life ways.

John Rowe (b. 1918), professor of anthropology at the University of California, Berkeley, carried out pioneer researches on the Inca of highland Peru and their ancient capital at Cuzco. His *Introduction to the Archaeology of Cuzco* (1944) remains a definitive account of Inca civilization.

François Bordes (1919–81) became famous for his excavations in French late Ice Age caves. He was an expert on the classification of stone tools who developed elaborate methods for doing so that are still in use today.

Marion White (1921–75) spent her career working in western New York State. She was the first woman to earn a Ph.D. in anthropology from the University of Michigan (1956) and subsequently joined the faculty at the State University of New York, Buffalo. White developed an extraordinary database of archaeological sites and collections from western New York. She was also a pioneer of salvage archaeology, carried out in advance of road construction and dam projects.

Raymond Dart (far left) with his ardent supporter Robert Broom, French prehistorian Abbé Henri Breuil, and South African archaeologist C. Van Riet Lowe examine the skull of Australopithecus africanus which Dart discovered in 1924.

Charles Higham (center), with graduate students Beatrice Hudson (left) and Famaanu Mualia, excavates the prehistoric site of Ban Non Wat, Thailand, in February 2002. Here they have uncovered a unique Neolithic jar burial dating from about 2000 BC.

5 Team Players

Until the 1960s, the world of archaeology was a small one. The entire population of professional archaeologists was never more than about 2,000. Most of them worked alone, or nearly alone, making often dramatic discoveries with almost no money at all. Even as late as the early 1960s, it was possible to go out and find entire ancient societies whose existence was completely unknown.

Then came the 1960s, and a massive population explosion of archaeologists. The individual excavator of earlier generations gave way to large and small field projects involving teams of scientists, many of them nonarchaeologists. For example, in addition to one or more archaeologists, even a modest-sized excavation of a Stone Age hunting camp can now involve experts on ancient environments, local geology and geomorphology, animal bones, soil science, and human fossils—some of these experts have significant archaeological expertise as well. Almost all of today's archaeologists are specialists, either in a particular ancient society or some highly technical archaeological method. Generalists like Flinders Petrie or Louis Leakey are almost unknown.

In Part 5, we move from individual biographies to short portraits of still-living archaeologists who have had a profound influence on the subject or have made important discoveries. Even these portraits are incomplete, for today's archaeological world is large, complex, and to a large extent anonymous. For example, 50 years ago, nearly everyone working on ancient Egypt knew one another. Today, many are strangers to one another.

The great growth in archaeology resulted from a combination of factors, including an expansion in university departments and graduate programs in archaeology and the building of new museums. At least equally as important, there was a growing demand for archaeologists in colonial territories around the world to run museums, staff antiquities services, and investigate the past. The expansion was rapid. For example, in 1960 there were about nine professional archaeologists working in Africa south of the Sahara Desert. Today there are over 100 in South Africa alone. Until the early 1960s most archaeologists concentrated primarily on highly specific, detailed studies of artifacts of all kinds, and with dating the past by cross-comparison of bits of evidence. Archaeology was by and large a descriptive activity—descriptions of artifacts, houses and other structures, and records and descriptions of the contents of stratigraphic layers. Archaeologists were concerned not with patterns of human settlement or the ways people made their livings, but with objects. There were exceptions, of course, notably Gordon Willey's Virú Valley survey in Peru, and Grahame Clark's Star Carr excavations in Britain, but they were few. Inevitably,

IN THIS PART

HASMUKH SANKALIA

ROBERT MCADAMS

LEWIS BINFORD

JAMES DEETZ

HESTER DAVIS

STUART STRUEVER

ROGER GREEN

PATTY JO WATSON

GEORGE BASS

KENT FLANNERY

DAVID CLARK

GLYNN ISAAC

CHARLES HIGHAM

COLIN RENFREW

LINDA SCHELE

DON JOHANSON

RICHARD LEAKEY

OLGA SOFFER

ZAHI HAWASS

MARGARET CONKEY

CHRIS DONNAN

JEAN CLOTTES

CLIVE GAMBLE

IAN HODDER

PATRICK KIRCH

DAVID LEWIS-WILLIAMS

IVOR NOEL HUME

a powerful reaction developed against the narrow approaches to the past that marked most of archaeology. The reaction was fueled in part by the scientific developments such as radiocarbon and potassium-argon methods that made dating very early human sites a matter of precision rather than educated guesswork, and by a greatly broadened perspective on cultural development.

The 1960s were a time of dramatic social protest in many parts of the western world. These spilled over into archaeology in calls for a "new archaeology" based on formal scientific methods and approaches that stressed the complex relationships between ancient human societies and their natural environments. The new archaeology was in large part the brainchild of Lewis Binford, who argued passionately for new perspectives on archaeology that emphasized explanation and interpretation of the past in place of the descriptive approaches of earlier generations. His "processual approach" placed an emphasis on the study of the processes of human cultural change; it continues to dominate much archaeological thinking.

The 1960s and 1970s saw a new generation of fieldworkers, notably in Central America, who put many of the principles of processual archaeology into practice. University of Michigan archaeologist Kent Flannery led the way with important surveys and excavations in the Valley of Oaxaca, home of the ancient Zapotecs. He, with his wife Joyce Marcus and many students, carried out the fieldwork as a form of dialogue between more traditional approaches to archaeology and processual research. Simultaneously, a team of archaeologists from Pennsylvania State University carried out a 10-year survey of the Valley of Mexico, plotting site distributions and studying settlement changes in the millennia before the appearance of the Aztec civilization.

Grahame Clark of Cambridge University and his colleagues trained a generation of young archaeologists to work overseas, in lands far from Europe. Clark's students, notably John Mulvaney, started the systematic study of Australian prehistory. Charles Higham, another Cambridge product, has made a lifetime study of the archaeology of southeast Asia and of the ancestry of the spectacular Angkor civilization of about AD 1100, which was located in present-day Cambodia. Many Cambridge students also worked in tropical Africa, among them the paleoanthropologist Glynn Isaac, and John Parkington, a notable expert on late prehistoric hunter-gatherers in southern Africa.

The new archaeology in North America coincided with the expansion of jet travel around the world. Until the 1960s, contacts between American and European archaeologists were sporadic at best. Air travel allowed archaeologists to have face-to-face contact and helped facilitate debate and the exchange of ideas. The British archaeologist David Clark was criticizing the current state of European archaeology at the same time as Lewis Binford was advocating new theoretical approaches in North America. Also at the same time, young archaeologists like Colin Renfrew were applying new high-technology methods to the past. Renfrew and some scientist colleagues used the telltale trace elements in obsidian (volcanic glass), which vary from one source to another, to trace long-distance trade routes across the eastern Mediterranean as early as 6000 BC.

Computers, spectrometers, tree-ring calibration of radiocarbon dates, flotation methods for recovering tiny seeds—these and other truly amazing technological advances propelled archaeology into the late 20th century. As the number of archaeologists increased greatly, so did their discoveries and the complexity of the data. The 1970s and 1980s saw major advances in the study of human origins, with new fossils dating back as far as 3.5 million years, notably the celebrated fossil in Ethiopia found and named Lucy by paleoanthropologists Don Johanson and Tim White. The discovery of Chinese emperor Qinshihuangdi's terra-cotta regiment was another highlight, as was the excavation of a Bronze Age shipwreck at Uluburun off southern Turkey by George Bass and his colleagues. The late 1980s saw the discovery of the Moche Lords of Sipán on Peru's North Coast, gold-clad warrior priests whose riches rivaled those of the Egyptian pharaoh Tutankhamun. By the 1980s, too, teams of experts, notably Linda Schele, had deciphered ancient Maya writing, a puzzle that had mystified scholars for centuries. Now Maya archaeologists dig cities and temples with translations of inscriptions to guide them.

Archaeology has truly come of age in the early 21st century, not only with a battery of new scientific methods that allow us to identify the first domesticated seeds, or beetles found in house middens, but also with a new generation of theoretical approaches that extend the horizons of archaeology in new directions. The processual archaeology of the 1960s and 1970s was concerned primarily with how human societies changed over time. But the concept and interpretation of these processes of change became more and more mechanical and impersonal to many people. A new generation of theory emerged, this time concerned with people, both as groups and individuals, rather than process. These "post-processual" approaches focus on how people interact with one another, and with their natural and supernatural worlds, as they do on cultural change. Examples include studies of male and female gender roles, and the reconstruction of sacred landscapes around such well-known sites as Avebury, Stonehenge, and the Maya city of Copán in Honduras. Increasingly, too, archaeology is becoming a multidisciplinary enterprise, where fieldworkers draw on experts from many other disciplines to solve specific problems. For example, an archaeologist working on the origins of agriculture in southwestern Asia some 12,000 years ago would rely on the expertise of botanists, climatologists, animal bone experts, and radiocarbon dating specialists, to mention only a few.

In recent decades archaeologists have invested more and more time in saving the past for the future. The ravages of treasure hunters and looters, and a tidal wave of urban development, deep plowing, strip mining, and road construction, have destroyed thousands of archaeological sites around the world. Increasingly, archaeological discoveries have come from excavations carried out a few days ahead of bulldozers on sites threatened with destruction. Increasingly, too, archaeologists have become concerned with conservation and management of archaeological sites and artifacts, for unlike many other resources, the fragile records of the human past are finite. Once a site is destroyed, an artifact wrenched from its find spot, it is gone forever. Archaeological excavation, however scientific, is destruction, so recording and managing the past for the future is of overwhelming importance. Within another generation, most archaeologists will be as much concerned with the conservation and management of archaeological sites as with actual discovery.

Today's archaeology is highly complex, very specialized, and concerned with every period of human history, from our origins among East African primates some 2.5 million years ago to historical neighborhoods in U.S. cities. Modern archaeologists are students of the human past, and of human behavior in the broadest possible sense; they are practitioners of a science that provides a unique and fascinating way of studying the changes in human societies over very long periods of time.

Even a generation ago, archaeology was dominated by a few world-famous scholars whose discoveries often became household words. Today, archaeological excavations and surveys involve the teamwork of many scientists. Even modest discoveries are the work of several archaeologists, and no one person dominates even a small area of the field. For this reason, here are short biographies of archaeologists whose work has wide influence, instead of longer profiles of only a handful of celebrated excavators.

Some Prominent Archaeologists of Our Time

Hasmukh Sankalia (1908–89) was an Indian archaeologist who learned excavation from Mortimer Wheeler and pioneered the teaching of archaeology at Deccan College, where he served as professor of proto-Indian and Indian history from 1939 to 1973. Sankalia excavated both Stone Age and historical sites throughout India. He did much to raise public consciousness of archaeology in India.

Robert McAdams (b. 1926), a Near Eastern archaeologist, pioneered settlement surveys in Mesopotamia. In these, he traced the dramatic changes resulting from intensive irrigation agriculture, then rising salt levels in the soil. Adams has also made important contributions to the study of the origins of civilization.

Lewis Binford (b. 1929) is arguably the most influential archaeologist of the 20th century. Binford developed new theoretical approaches to archaeology in the 1960s that advocated more scientific approaches and an emphasis on human societies as constantly changing systems. This so-called new archaeology, described in his book *In Pursuit of the Past* (1973), triggered a major change in archaeological research in the 1960s and 1970s that is still influential today. Binford is also famous for his studies of animal bones and of hunter-gatherer societies, ancient and modern.

James Deetz (1930–2001) was a brilliant teacher and world-famous historical archaeologist. He worked on California mission archaeology, at Plimoth Plantation, and on other colonial American sites. Deetz's *Invitation to Archaeology* (1967) and *In Small Things Forgotten* (1991), although short paperbacks, are among the most influential books on archaeological practice ever written.

Hester Davis (b. 1930) was trained at the University of North Carolina and has spent her career in Arkansas, where she was one of the organizers of the Arkansas Archaeological Survey. Davis is internationally famous for her efforts to develop legislation to protect archaeological sites both in Arkansas and nationally.

Stuart Struever (b. 1931) is a North American archaeologist famous for his enormous excavations at Koster in the Midwest's Illinois Valley. Here, successive groups of ancient native Americans settled at the same location from about 10,000 years ago to the threshold of historic times. Struever also pioneered the use of computers to record and classify data recovered from archaeological excavations.

Roger Green (b. 1932), a pioneer in the development of Pacific prehistory, is well known for identifying the famous Lapita culture in the eastern Pacific. This culture is associated with the spread of human settlement as far east in the Pacific as Fiji and Tonga.

Patty Jo Watson (b. 1932) of Washington University, Saint Louis, is famous for her research at Mammoth Cave, Kentucky. There, she pioneered the use of flotation methods to recover large numbers of seeds by passing them through water. These researches have shown that the inhabitants of Mammoth Cave used all kinds of wild plant foods, to the point that they were easily able to grew domesticated maize after AD 1000.

George Bass (b. 1934) is effectively the founder of underwater archaeology. He has developed scientific methods for excavating and recording sites on the sea bed that are used internationally today. Bass is famous for several shipwreck excavations, notably the Uluburun Bronze Age shipwreck off southern Turkey, dating to about 1310 BC, excavated with Äemal Pulak. This remarkable excavation of the 1980s revolutionized our knowledge of commercial life in the eastern Mediterranean more than 3,000 years ago.

Kent Flannery (b. 1934) has spent his career working in Central America and, on one occasion, in Peru. His most important work, on the origins of agriculture and the beginnings of Mesoamerican civilization, is in the Valley of Oaxaca, Mexico. Flannery's *The Early Mesoamerican Village* (1976) is an influential book that contrasts the older and newer ways of carrying out archaeological research.

David Clark (1937–76), a Cambridge University archaeologist, acquired notoriety at an early age for his remarkable and critical theoretical studies. His book *Analytical Archaeology* (1968) foreshadowed many of the major theoretical advances in archaeology that unfolded in the late 1960s and the 1970s.

Glynn Isaac (1937–85) was a young paleoanthropologist and archaeologist

of great brilliance who died at a tragically young age. He excavated at the famous 300,000-year-old Olorgesaillie Stone Age site in Kenya's Rift Valley, and at early hominid sites in East Turkana in northern Kenya. Isaac is mainly remembered for his theories about early human behavior, which saw our earliest ancestors as opportunists. They survived by taking advantage of food supplies of all kinds when they encountered them, and also used base camps.

Charles Higham (b. 1937) is an expert in southeast Asian archaeology who has excavated extensively in Thailand, investigating the origins of rice agriculture and civilization in that

Shipwreck excavations, such as those undertaken by George Bass, require not only diving expertise but all manner of special recovery and recording methods. Larger artifacts, such as these containers, are usually taken to the surface in large baskets.

region. His *Archaeology of Mainland Southeast Asia* (1989) was the first scientific account of an area vital to our understanding of early Asian civilization.

Colin Renfrew (b. 1937), a leading European archaeologist, was one of the pioneers of studying ancient trade in the Near East using minute trace elements in widely traded volcanic glass. Renfrew excavated a celebrated Mycenaean shrine at Phylakopi on the island of Melos in the Aegean Sea and has worked extensively on the history of European languages and genetics.

Linda Schele (1942–98) was an epigrapher, one who studies and deciphers inscriptions. In the 1970s and 1980s she was deeply involved in the decipherment of Mayan writing. She did much to disseminate knowledge of Maya art, culture, and writing to a wider audience, especially through the book *A Forest of Kings*, written with Maya archaeologist David Freidel in 1990.

Don Johanson (b. 1943), a palaeoanthropologist, is world famous for his discovery in 1974, with biological anthropologist Tim White, of the 3.5 million-year-old fossil of *Australopithecus afarensis* known as "Lucy." The small, lightly built Lucy is one of the earliest upright walking hominids in the world.

Richard Leakey (b. 1944) is a palaeoanthropologist famous for his remarkable hominid discoveries at East Turkana on the eastern shores of the lake of that name in northern Kenya, East Africa. Leakey, the son of Louis and Mary, found the famous Skull 1470 in the 1970s, the remnant of an ancestral human dating to over 2 million years ago. Leakey has also had a distinguished career in museum administration, politics, and wildlife conservation.

Olga Soffer (b. 1944) is famous for her excavations at the late Ice Age camp at Mezhirich in Ukraine, dating to about 14,500 BC. The site yielded the remains of dome-shaped mammoth bone houses inhabited by prehistoric big-game hunters. Soffer has also worked on late Ice Age sites in Moravia, central Europe, and is an expert on ancient storage methods.

Zahi Hawass (b. 1947), an Egyptologist, has devoted much of his career to excavations in the surroundings of the pyramids of Giza. He discovered a rock-cut harbor for barges close to the pyramids, and a workers' cemetery outside the sacred precincts. In recent years he has been involved in the excavation of a huge cemetery of mummified Egyptians of about 2,000 years ago, the Valley of the Golden Mummies, in the Bahariya Oasis west of the Nile River.

Margaret Conkey (b. 1944), of the University of California at Berkeley, is a world authority on late Ice Age art in Europe. She has also worked on gender in the past and is co-editor with

A panel from Temple XIV at Palenque shows Lord K'inich Kan B'alam II dancing on a surface covered with symbols for water. Such ceremonies linked the ruler to the Maya cosmos and to rain making.

Joan Gero (b. 1940) of *Engendering Archaeology*, a classic set of essays on the subject.

Chris Donnan (b. 1941) is an expert on the Moche civilization of Peru's North Coast. He is famous for his work on Moche painted pots, which record religious ceremonies that included human sacrifices presided over by Moche warrior priests. Donnan was involved in the excavation of the sensational Lords of Sipán burials in 1989, and has recently found even earlier, gold-adorned Moche rulers.

Jean Clottes (b. 1933), France's leading expert on late Ice Age cave art, has studied the newly discovered cave paintings in the Grotte de Chauvet in southeastern France. Some of these paintings date to over 30,000 years ago. Clottes has worked with David Lewis-Williams on interpretations of Chauvet and other painted caves, which attribute many of the paintings to the work of shamans.

Clive Gamble (b. 1951) is a Stone Age archaeologist who has written influential studies of the first human settlement of Europe. His book *The Palaeolithic Societies of Europe* (1999) is an influential account of Stone Age life before, during, and after the late Ice Age.

Ian Hodder (b. 1949) is both a theoretician and a basic researcher. He was responsible for a revolt against Binford's processual archaeology in the late 1970s and 1980s, advocating more diverse approaches to the study of the past. These post-processual approaches combine science with more instinctive interpretations of the past. In recent years Hodder has been involved in an international excavation at the early farming village of Çatalhöyük in central Turkey, which dates to about 6000 BC.

Patrick Kirch (b. 1950), an archaeologist of Pacific Ocean cultures, is well known for his researches into the first settlement of Polynesia and for his studies of the nature of chiefdoms in the ancient Pacific.

David Lewis-Williams (b. 1934) is a South African prehistorian and rock art expert who has devoted his career to the study of San hunter-gatherer art in southern Africa. Lewis-Williams rediscovered the linguistic and ethnographic researches of 19th-century German scholar Wilhelm Bleek, who interviewed San informants. From this work, Lewis-Williams developed new interpretations of their rock art, which attribute much of it to the work of shamans in hallucinogenic trances.

Ivor Noel Hume (b. 1927) is a historical archaeologist who excavated the Colonial American village at Martin's Hundred, Virginia, which was attacked by local American Indians in 1623. He has also carried out extensive excavations at Jamestown and Williamsburg, Virginia, and he is an expert on ceramics.

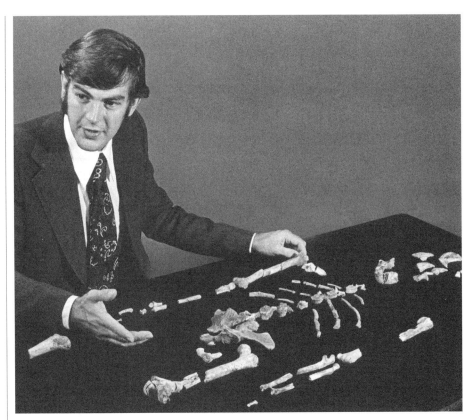

Donald Johanson displays the partial skeleton of Lucy, *Australopithecus afarensis*, soon after its discovery in the Hadar region of Ethiopia.

Major Events in the History of Archaeology

1586
Publication of William Camden's Britannia

1649
John Aubrey visits Avebury

1720–24
William Stukeley maps Avebury and Stonehenge

1738
First excavations at Herculaneum, commissioned by the king of Naples

1798
General Napoleon Bonaparte invades Egypt, taking scientists with him

1799
Napoleon's troops discover the Rosetta Stone

1822
Jean François Champollion deciphers Egyptian hieroglyphs

1839–42
John Lloyd Stephens and Frederick Catherwood explore Maya sites in Central America and reveal Maya civilization to an astonished world

1843–45
Paul Emile Botta excavates Assyrian King Sargon's palace at Khorsabad, Iraq

1845–50
Austen Henry Layard excavates Assyrian cities in northern Iraq and unearths the Assyrian civilization

1856
Neanderthal skull discovered in the Neander Valley, Germany

1859
Establishment of human antiquity, the association of extinct animals and humanly made artifacts Publication of Charles Darwin's Origin of Species

1863–71
Edouard Lartet excavates Cro-Magnon, late Ice Age caves in southwestern France

1867
Charles Warren excavates beneath Jerusalem

1871
Heinrich Schliemann excavates Homeric Troy

1872
George Smith discovers, among artifacts in the British Museum, the "Deluge Tablets" with an account of a Babylonian flood

1875–81
Ernst Curtius excavates Olympia, Greece, with new scientific methods

1876
Heinrich Schliemann digs Mycenae, Greece

1879
Altamira Stone Age cave paintings found, northern Spain

1881
General Augustus Lane Fox Pitt-Rivers begins Cranborne Chase excavations, southern England

1899–1912
Robert Koldeway's Babylon excavations revolutionize mud brick excavation

1900
Arthur Evans starts excavations at Knossos, Crete, palace of the Minoan civilization

1908

Cowboy George McJunkin finds the Folsom site, New Mexico

1912

Hiram Bingham visits Macchu Picchu, Peru

1917–22

Manuel Gamio surveys the city of Teotihuacán, Mexico

1922

Discovery of the tomb of the pharaoh Tutankhamun by Howard Carter and the Earl of Carnarvon

1924

Raymond Dart discovers *Australopithecus africanus*, the southern ape-human

1926

Leonard Woolley excavates the Royal Cemetery at Ur, Iraq (excavations in Ur from 1922 to 1934)

1927

Co-existence of humans and extinct bison established by excavations at Folsom, New Mexico

1946

Virú Valley project, coastal Peru

1947

Discovery of the Dead Sea Scrolls, Jordan

1949

Development of radiocarbon dating, University of Chicago

1949–52

Star Carr excavations, England

1959

Discovery of *Zinjanthropus boisei*, Olduvai Gorge, Tanzania

1961

Discovery of *Homo habilis*, Olduvai Gorge, Tanzania

1960S ONWARD

Development of the "new archaeology," often called processual archaeology

1970S ONWARD

Emergence of post-processual archaeology as an alternative to processual archaeology

1974

"Lucy," *Australopithecus afarensis*, found in Ethiopia's (Djibouti) Afar region

Discovery of the terra-cotta regiment of Emperor Shihuangdi, China

1977

Han royal burials unearthed in China

1978–82

Excavations at the Aztec Temple of the Sun God Huitzilopochtli, the "Templo Mayor," Mexico City

1982

Discovery of the Uluburun ship, Turkey

1989

Discovery of the Moche lords of Sipán, Peru

1991

Discovery of the Bronze Age "Ice Man" in the Italian Alps.

1994

Discovery of 31,000-year-old Cro-Magnon paintings in the Grotte de Chauvet, France

1995

Excavation of the tomb of Rameses II's sons, Valley of the Kings, Egypt

Major Events in Prehistoric Times

KEY

AD Anno Domini (year of our lord)

BC Before Christ

BP Before present

MYA Million years ago

ABOUT 5.0 MYA

Humans split off from nearest living primate relatives, the ancestors of chimpanzees

2.5 MYA

Homo habilis and the first simple toolmaking culture

1.9 MYA

First appearance of *Homo ergaster* (*Homo erectus*) in tropical Africa

Development of the handax, an artifact flaked on both sides

1.8 MYA

First human settlement of southern and eastern Asia perhaps by *Homo erectus*

ABOUT 650,000 BP

First human settlement of Europe by *Homo erectus*

ABOUT 175,000 BP

First modern humans evolve in tropical Africa

100,000 BP

Neanderthals widespread in Europe

Modern humans first appear in southwestern Asia and coexist with Neanderthals

42,000 BP First modern humans (Cro-Magnons) appear in Central Europe

35,000 BP First colonization of Australia and New Guinea by this date

30,000 BP

The last Neanderthals become extinct; cave art appears in Europe just before this date

18,000 BP

Cro-Magnon cultures flourish in Europe and Eurasia

15,000 BP

Approximate date for the first settlement of the Americas across the Bering Land Bridge and by adjacent waters

End of the Great Ice Age

10,000 BC

First domestication of plants in southwestern Asia; animal domestication follows soon afterward

6000 BC

Widespread farming villages between Greece, Turkey, Mesopotamia, and the Nile Valley

5800 BC

A rising Mediterranean Sea floods the freshwater Euxine Lake, forming the Black Sea

5500 BC

Agriculture spreads into temperate Europe

3100 BC

Unification of Egypt into a single state by the pharaoh Narmer

Founding of Sumerian city-states

Maize domesticated in Central America by this date

Complex hunter-gatherer societies developing in parts of North America

2550 BC

Avebury stone circles in use, England

2550 BC

Pyramid building in Old Kingdom Egypt

2300 BC

Major construction at Stonehenge, England

Third Dynasty at Ur extends Sumerian civilization from Mesopotamia to the Mediterranean

2180 BC

Major famines in Egypt, which breaks down into provinces

1900 BC

Harappan civilization flourishes in the Indus River, Pakistan

1600 BC

Minoan civilization on Crete and Aegean islands

Shang civilization in northern China

Middle Kingdom pharaohs reunite Egypt

1500 BC

Olmec civilization in lowland Mesoamerica

Mycenaean civilization in mainland Greece and Aegean

1275 BC

New Kingdom Egypt at the height of its power

The heretic pharaoh Akhenaten rules Egypt

1200 BC

Widespread disorder in the eastern Mediterranean world

Collapse of Hittite civilization

1070 BC

End of New Kingdom Egypt and Egypt's greatest political power

Settlement of offshore Pacific islands begins

850 BC

Etruscan civilization in Italy

753 BC

Founding of Rome

ABOUT 700 BC

Assyrian civilization at its height

612 BC

Nineveh sacked by Babylonians and others

580 BC

King Nebuchadnezzar's Babylon

450 BC

Classical Greece at its height

200 BC

Carthaginian wars end in Rome's victory

55 BC

Roman general Julius Caesar lands in Britain

30 BC

Egypt becomes a province of the Roman Empire

AD 200

Classic Maya civilization expands

AD 600

Moche civilization of northern coastal Peru at its height

City of Teotihuacán, highland Mexico, rises to its greatest power

AD 900

Collapse of classic Maya civilization in the southern Maya lowlands

AD 1000

Norse voyagers in touch with Newfoundland

By this date, the first settlement of New Zealand

Tiwanaku state at its height, Lake Titicaca, Bolivia

AD 1200

Toltec civilization of Mexico

Mississippian chiefdoms of North American approach their greatest power

AD 1400

Chimu civilization of coastal Peru

AD 1492

Christopher Columbus lands in the Bahamas

AD 1519–21

Hernan Cortés lands in Mexico and conquers the Aztec civilization, reducing their capital, Tenochtitlán, to rubble

AD 1531

Francisco Pizarro encounters and conquers the Inca civilization of Peru

Glossary of Archaeological Sites and Terms

Abu Simbel—Temple built by the ancient Egyptian pharaoh Rameses II on the banks of the Nile in Nubia (Sudan), about 1270 BC.

Abydos—Sacred community and burial place of early Egyptian kings, believed to be close to the gateway to the underworld.

Accelerator Mass Spectrometry (AMS) dating—Refined method of radiocarbon dating which counts the number of carbon-14 atoms present, using a high-energy mass spectrometer.

Acheulian—Term applied to cultures that made distinctive stone axes between about 1.9 million years ago and 200,000 years before the present. Named after the town of St. Acheul in northern France, where many hand axes were found.

Agricultural (Neolithic) Revolution—Term coined by archaeologist Vere Gordon Childe to refer to the appearance of animal and plant domestication in the Near East. Characterized by settled village life, pottery, and other innovations.

Altamira—Cave in northern Spain where 15,000-year-old Cro-Magnon rock paintings were first discovered in 1879.

Angles-sur-L'Anglin—Late Ice Age cave in southwestern France that yielded 16,000-year-old reliefs of animals and women.

Angkor civilization—Khmer civilization in Cambodia, dating to the early first millennium AD, remarkable for its elaborate palaces and temples.

anthropology—The study of humanity in the widest possible sense. Includes archaeology, the study of ancient cultures.

Anyang—Capital of the Shang civilization in northern China, about 1500 BC.

archaeology—The study of the human past and ancient human behavior using material remains.

Arikamedu—Southern Indian settlement with connections with the Roman Empire dating to the first century AD.

Avebury—Large stone circle complex in southern England built by Stone Age farmers in about 2500 BC.

Banpo—Stone Age farming village in northern China dating to about 4000 BC.

Barton Ramie, Belize—Maya center in Honduras dating to the seventh century AD.

Behistun (Bisitun)—Ruined city, site of a famous trilingual inscription on an cliff face in Iran, commemorating Persian King Darius's victory over rebels in 522 BC. The inscription helped in the decipherment of cuneiform script.

Beni Hassan—Cemetery in Middle Egypt famous for its wall paintings of important provincial governors from about 2000 BC.

Birbinkilise—Site of the so-called Thousand-and-One Byzantine churches in Turkey, now largely destroyed. Dates to the first millennium AD.

Brixham Cave—Late Ice Age cavern in southern England with occupation dating to about 18,000 years ago.

Carchemish—Major Hittite city on the Euphrates River that guarded a major river crossing. Also occupied by the Romans as a frontier post.

Çatalhöyük—Early farming village in Turkey famous for its household shrines, dating to about 6000 BC.

Chichén Itzá—Late Maya city in northern Yucatán, Mexico, celebrated both for its architecture and its Sacred Cenote, an offering pool; flourished about AD 1200.

Cissbury Hill—Iron Age hill fort in southern England dating to the late first millennium BC.

context—In archaeology, the exact physical position of an artifact or other archaeological find in a site and its date or age in time.

Copán—Major Maya city and ceremonial center in Honduras; flourished before AD 900.

Cro-Magnon—Generic name given the anatomically modern humans who lived in Europe during the late Ice Age, after about 40,000 years ago. Named after the Cro-Magnon rock shelter near Les Eyzies, France.

cross-dating—Method that uses artifacts of known age, such as coins, to date sites where they are found far from the objects' places of origin.

culture history—The study of prehistoric societies using artifacts and their location-age contexts to place them in order through time and across the landscape.

cuneiform—Wedge-shaped script used by early Mesopotamian civilizations, written on clay. Cuneiform became the diplomatic script of eastern Mediterranean states, including Egypt, for many centuries.

cylinder seal—Small stone cylinder carved with distinctive script that was rolled into clay or wax to leave an impression; used by the Minoan civilization, first millennium BC.

Danger Cave—Dry cave in Utah that was occupied by humans from before 9000 BC until recent times. During this long occupation, the tools and lifestyle of the inhabitants changed little.

Deir el-Bahari—Burial area on the west bank of the Nile opposite Luxor; location of the mortuary temple of Queen Hatshepsut (about 1400 BC).

dendrochronology—Dating method based on counting and matching the growth rings of tree trunks.

Devil's Tower—Cave on the Rock of Gibraltar at the southern tip of Spain that has yielded Neanderthal fossils.

Direct Historical Method—Approach to archaeology that involves working with artifacts and stratified occupation layers from the present back into the past. First pioneered in the American Southwest.

Druids—Prehistoric British priests; observed by the Roman general Julius Caesar in 55 BC.

el-Amarna—Short-lived royal capital of the heretic Egyptian pharaoh Akhenaten, occupied about 1350 BC.

el-Kahun—Middle Kingdom Egyptian community in Upper Egypt that housed the funerary workers of King Senusret II (1897–1878 BC).

Fayum Depression—Low-lying area west of the Nile River in Lower Egypt, once a lake surrounded by fertile land. Site of early agricultural settlements dating to about 4000 BC and later a major center of ancient Egyptian agriculture.

flotation—A method of recovering tiny plant remains by passing them through water and fine screens. The seeds float to the top and are trapped in the screen mesh; the residue falls through.

Font de Gaume—Cro-Magnon rock shelter with mammoth paintings about 18,000 years old, located near Les Eyzies, France.

Gamble's Cave—Stone Age cave in central Kenya occupied from as long ago as 20,000 years before the present.

Giza, Pyramids of—Royal burial places for Egypt's Old Kingdom pharaohs, about 2550 BC.

Gournia—Minoan community in northern Crete dating to about 1500 BC.

Hadrian's Wall—Defensive wall against northern Britons built in England by Roman emperor Hadrian between AD 122 and 130.

Harappa—Major city of the Harappan civilization (named after the city) in the Indus River Valley, dating to about 1700 BC.

Haua Fteah—Large cave in northern Libya that yielded traces of human occupation from at least 50,000 years ago up to 10,000 BC.

Hawara—Roman-Egyptian cemetery of AD 100–250 in the Fayum Depression west of the Nile River. Many of the mummies in the cemetery bore portraits of the deceased.

Herculaneum—Roman city near Naples, Italy, destroyed by an eruption of Mt. Vesuvius in AD 79.

hieroglyphs—Literally, picture signs, which formed the basis of Ancient Egyptian and Mayan scripts, although the two are not related.

Hissarlik—Ancient city mound in northeastern Turkey, the site of Homeric Troy. A major Bronze Age city in the second millennium BC.

Hittite civilization—Major civilization centered on Turkey; it was a major political and economic presence in the eastern Mediterranean world, 1700 to 1200 BC.

hominid—A member of the family Hominidae, represented today by one species, modern humans (*Homo sapiens*).

Igbo-Ukwu—Site of important royal burials of the 9th century AD in Nigeria, famous for their lavish adornments.

Jericho—Biblical city in Jordan, the lower levels of which comprise some of the earliest farming villages in the world, about 9000 BC. One of the settlements is fortified with a stone wall and watchtower.

Kalambo Falls—Major Stone Age site on the Tanzania-Zambia border in Central Africa, with human occupation dating back at least 300,000 years.

Kanam and Kanyera—Two human fossil-bearing locations in East Africa found in 1933, claimed to be of high antiquity but subsequently discredited.

Karnak—Elaborate temple to the ancient Egyptian god Amun at Luxor; flourished in the second millennium BC.

Kharga Oasis—Oasis west of the Nile River in Egypt that contains signs of extensive Stone Age occupation dating to at least 300,000 years ago.

Khorsabad—Capital of Assyrian King Sargon II (721–705 BC) in northern Iraq.

Khotan—Important empire of the first millennium AD on the China-India border.

Knossos—Site of the famed Palace of Minos, capital of the Minoan civilization; occupied between about 2000 and 1400 BC.

Koster—Prehistoric site in the Illinois River Valley, with human occupation from before 8000 BC to AD 1200.

Kuyunjik—A palace mound at Nineveh.

La Cotte de St. Brelade—Cliff face on the island of Jersey in the English Channel over which Neanderthals drove mammoth and rhinoceros more than 100,000 years ago to kill them for food, tusks, and hides.

Laetoli—Site of sets of 3.6 million-year-old hominid footprints in Tanzania, East Africa.

Le Moustier—French rock shelter inhabited by Neanderthals about 75,000 years ago.

Les Combarelles—Deep Cro-Magnon cave with rock engravings about 15,000 years old, located near Les Eyzies, France.

Linear A and B—Minoan scripts. Recovered examples are mainly records of commercial transactions. Linear A has not yet been deciphered.

Long Count—The linear calendar developed by the Maya civilization of Central America.

Lydney—Roman-British sanctuary in western England dating to the 2nd century BC.

Maglemose culture—Scandinavian Mesolithic culture that placed a major emphasis on fishing and bird hunting. Dates from before 6000 to 5000 BC and later.

Maiden Castle—British Iron Age hill fort in southern England besieged and captured by a Roman legion in AD 43.

Mal'ta—Important Siberian hunting camp at the southern end of Lake Baikal, occupied about 21,000 years ago.

Martin's Hundred—Colonial village in Virginia attacked by Native Americans in 1623.

Meilgaard—Famous shell midden site in Denmark occupied by people of the Stone Age Maglemose culture, about 7000 BC.

Meroe—African state and city centered on the Sudan and the Nile Valley that flourished from about 590 BC to AD 350. The people and their culture are termed *Meroitic*.

Mesolithic—Term used to refer to hunter-gatherers who flourished in Europe after the Ice Age.

Mesoamerica—Area of Central America where advanced civilizations arose after 1000 BC.

Mesopotamia—Greek for "the land between the rivers," applied to the flat lands between the Euphrates and Tigris rivers in southern Iraq. Cradle of some of the world's earliest civilizations.

midden—An accumulation of human garbage of all kinds.

Minoan civilization—Cretan Bronze Age civilization; flourished between about 2000 and 1400 BC.

Moche civilization—Elaborate coastal river valley civilization in northern Peru, dating to the mid–first millennium BC.

Mohenjo-daro—Major city of the Harappan civilization of the Indus River Valley in Pakistan, dating to about 1700 BC.

Mount Carmel caves—Important Stone Age caves on the coast of present-day Israel; they provide a sequence of Neanderthal and modern human occupation from about 70,000 years ago until 10,000 years before the present.

Mugau—Buddhist cave shrines of the first millennium AD in eastern China, famous for their paintings and statuaries.

Mycenae—Bronze Age citadel in southern Greece built by a chiefly dynasty of the Mycenaean civilization, about 1300 BC.

Neolithic—"New Stone Age"; term used to refer to Stone Age farmers. Now somewhat outdated, but a convenient label.

Niaux—Cro-Magnon painted cave in southern France, about 14,000 years old, famous for its magnificent bison paintings.

Naqada—Early Egyptian town associated with extensive desert cemeteries dating to before dynastic Egyptian times of 4,000 BC and later.

Nimrud—Assyrian city in northern Iraq also known as Calah, once the palace of the Assyrian King Esarhaddon (680–669 BC) and two other Assyrian monarchs. Famous for its magnificent ivories.

Nineveh—Biblical city in northern Iraq associated with Assyrian King Assurbanipal (668–627 BC). Sacked by the Babylonians and others in 612 BC.

Njoro River Cave—Stone Age cave in Kenya with human occupation dating to about 3,000 years ago.

Olorgesaillie—A 300,000-year-old Stone Age kill and butchery site in Kenya's Rift Valley.

Olduvai Gorge—Deep gorge on the edge of Tanzania's Serengeti Plains, with evidence of human occupation from about 2 million years ago to 100,000 years before the present. Known for its early hominid fossils, which write much of the history of early human evolution.

Pachamacac—Important Inca ceremonial center in southern coastal Peru dating to the 15th century AD.

Palaeolithic—"Old Stone Age"; prehistoric times before the advent of agriculture. A now seldom used term.

Palenque—Important Maya city associated with a dynasty of powerful rulers who reigned from AD 431 to 799.

paleoanthropology—The multidisciplinary study of early human evolution, including archaeology.

Peacock's Farm—Mesolithic site in eastern England celebrated for its association of flint tools with swamp levels, dated to 6500 BC.

Pecos—Long-inhabited pueblo in northern New Mexico that provided the first stratigraphic sequence for the Southwest. Famous also for its early Spanish mission.

Persepolis—Palace complex in central Iran built by King Darius the Great in about 518 BC. It was looted and burned by Alexander the Great in 331–330 BC.

Petra—Famous Nabatean and Roman caravan city in Jordan famous for its narrow entrance and fine temples.

Philae—Island in the Nile in Upper Egypt famous for a magnificent temple to the goddess Isis.

Phylakopi—Mycenaean village and shrine on the island of Melos in the Aegean, about 1300 BC.

Pompeii—Roman town near Naples, Italy, destroyed by an eruption of Mt. Vesuvius in AD 79.

post-processual archaeology—A series of theoretical approaches to archaeology that argue for the importance of individual and group interactions in changing human cultures and societies.

potassium-argon dating—Method that uses the decay rates of radioactive elements in volcanic rocks to date early human and geological sites.

prehistory—That period of the human past not covered by written records.

primate—Highest order of mammals; includes apes, humans, and monkeys.

processual archaeology—Archaeology based on the idea that human cultures are systems which interact with ecological systems. Focuses on explaining the processes of culture change.

radiocarbon dating—Method based on measuring the decay radioactive elements in organic materials like bone, charcoal, and wood to date sites up to about 40,000 years old.

rath—An earthen or stone enclosure that forms a hill fort.

Rollright Stones—Prehistoric stone circle in Oxfordshire, England, estimated to date to about 2,500 BC.

Saqqara—Burial place of ancient Egyptian pharaohs of the Old and Middle Kingdoms, also center of the cult of the bull god Apis.

Shang civilization—One of the first civilizations of northern China, dating to about 1766 to 1122 BC. Centered on Hwang Ho, the Yellow River.

shell midden—Accumulated pile of the remains of freshwater or saltwater shellfish gathered by humans, presumably for food.

Silk Road—Ancient trading route between China and the West that passed through Central Asia.

Sipán—Region of Moche burial sites in north coastal Peru dating to AD 400.

Skara Brae—Stone Age farming village in Scotland's Orkney Islands dating to about 2000 BC.

Snaketown—Large prehistoric town in Arizona occupied by Hohokam people from AD 500 to 1450. The Hohokam were expert irrigation farmers.

Somme River gravels—Sites celebrated for their abundance of Stone Age hand axes and other artifacts, and bones of extinct animals, dating mainly to about 300,000 years ago.

Star Carr—Mesolithic encampment in northeastern England now dated to about 9500 BC, which yielded evidence of deer hunting.

Stanwick—Iron Age hill fort in northeastern England dating to the 1st century BC.

Stonehenge—Stone circles erected by Stone Age and Bronze Age farmers after 2300 BC; flourished about 1800 BC.

Sumerian civilization—First urban civilization in Mesopotamia (southern Iraq), where a patchwork of city states, notably Sumer, formed a distinctive civilization after 3100 BC.

Three Age System—Classification system for Old World prehistory developed by Danish archaeologist C. J. Thomsen in 1807. The three ages, from the oldest, are Stone, Bronze, and Iron.

Tikal—Maya city in Guatemala that was one of the largest and most important of all Maya city-states; flourished in AD 600.

Trilithon—A stone arch formed by two uprights and a cross lintel. Found at Stonehenge, England.

typology—In archaeology, the study of artifact classification.

Uaxacatún—Large Maya center in Guatemala close to Tikal.

Ukhaidir—An Abbasid caliph's palace in northern Iraq dating to the 6th century AD.

Uluburun shipwreck—Bronze Age shipwreck off southern Turkey dating to about 1310 BC, remarkable for its cargo from nine countries in the eastern Mediterranean.

Ur (Ur-of-the Chaldees)—Important Sumerian city in southern Iraq occupied from the earliest stages of Mesopotamian civilization. Famous for its royal cemetery of about 2900 BC.

Urban Revolution—Term coined by archaeologist Vere Gordon Childe to identify the appearance of civilization in the Near East, marked by cities, metallurgy, writing, and other characteristics.

Uxmal—Classic Maya city in Mexico's Yucatán; reached its peak about AD 800. Famous for its fine architecture.

Valley of the Kings—Burial place of ancient Egypt's New Kingdom pharaohs, 1530–1070 BC.

Verulamium—Roman-British town north of London, England, which flourished in the 2nd century AD.

Virú Valley—Peruvian coastal river valley occupied by 2000 BC into the first millennium AD.

Yangshao—Chinese early farming village in the Hwang Ho (Yellow River) Valley dating to about 4000 BC.

Zimbabwe (or Great Zimbabwe)—Stone building complex in southern Africa built by Shona-speaking Africans between AD 1000 and 1450; the center of a powerful cattle kingdom and a major trade center.

Further Reading and Websites

Readings about the individual archaeologists in this book are included at the end of each profile. The following list offers a brief sampling of a vast amount of literature about archaeology. All of the sources here include bibliographies, which will lead you to the more specialized literature.

What Happened in the Past?

Clark, Grahame. *World Prehistory: A New Outline*. New York: Cambridge University Press, 1977.

Fagan, Brian. *People of the Earth*. 10th ed. Upper Saddle River, N.J.: Prentice Hall, 2001.

———. *World Prehistory: A Brief Introduction*. 5th ed. Upper Saddle River, N.J.: Prentice Hall, 2002.

Gamble, Clive. *Timewalkers*. Cambridge, Mass.: Harvard University Press, 1994.

Price, Douglas, and Gary Feinman. *Images of the Past*. 3rd ed. Mountain View, Calif.: Mayfield, 2001.

How Archaeology Works

Deetz, James. *In Small Things Forgotten*. Rev. ed. New York: Anchor/Doubleday, 1996.

———. *Invitation to Archaeology*. New York: Natural History, 1967.

Fagan, Brian. *Archaeology: A Brief Introduction*. 7th ed. Upper Saddle River, N.J.: Prentice Hall, 2000.

———. *In the Beginning*. 10th ed. Upper Saddle River, N.J.: Prentice Hall, 2001.

———. *Time Detectives*. New York: Simon & Schuster, 1995.

Sharer, Robert J., and Wendy Ashmore. *The Foundations of Archaeology*. 4th ed. Mountain View, Calif.: Mayfield, 1998.

Thomas, David Hurst. *Archaeology*. 3rd ed. Fort Worth: Harcourt College Publishers, 2000.

The History of Archaeology

Bahn, Paul, ed. *The Cambridge Illustrated History of Archaeology*. New York: Cambridge University Press, 1996.

Ceram, C. W. *Gods, Graves & Scholars*. 2nd ed. New York: Vintage, 1986.

Coe, Michael. *Breaking the Maya Code*. London: Thames and Hudson, 1992.

———. *One Hundred and Fifty Years of Archaeology*. London: Thames and Hudson, 1981.

Fagan, Brian. *The Adventure of Archaeology*. Washington D.C.: National Geographic, 1985.

———. *Elusive Treasure*. New York: Scribners, 1977.

———. *The Rape of the Nile*. New York: Scribners, 1975.

———. *Return to Babylon*. Boston: Little, Brown, 1979.

Larsen, Mogens Trolle. *The Conquest of Assyria*. London: Routledge, 1996.

Lloyd, Seton. *Foundations in the Dust*. London: Thames and Hudson, 1980.

Murray, Tim, ed. *The Great Archaeologists*. Santa Barbara, Calif.: ABC-Clio, 1999.

Reeves, Nicholas. *Ancient Egypt: The Great Discoveries*. London: Thames and Hudson, 2001.

Trigger, Bruce. *A History of Archaeological Thought*. New York: Cambridge University Press, 1989.

Willey, Gordon R., and Jeremy A. Sabloff. *A History of American Archaeology*. London: Thames and Hudson, 1974.

Archaeological Reference Books

Bahn, Paul, ed. *100 Great Archaeological Discoveries*. New York: Barnes and Noble, 1995.

Fagan, Brian, ed. *Eyewitness to Discovery*. New York: Oxford University Press, 1997.

Fagan, Brian, ed. *The Oxford Companion to Archaeology.* New York: Oxford University Press, 1996.

Scarre, Chris, ed. *Past Worlds: The Times Atlas of Archaeology.* London: Times Books, 1988.

General Surveys of Some Research Topics and Regions

Human Origins

Johanson, Donald C., and Maitland A. Edey. *Lucy.* New York: Simon & Schuster, 1981.

Leakey, Richard, and Roger Lewin. *Origins.* New York: Penguin, 1991.

Lewin, Roger. *Bones of Contention.* New York: Simon & Schuster, 1977.

The Neanderthals

Stringer, Christopher, and Clive Gamble. *In Search of the Neanderthals.* London: Thames and Hudson, 1993.

Origins of Modern Humans and the Human Mind

Mithen, Steven. *The Prehistory of the Mind.* London: Thames and Hudson, 1996.

Stringer, Christopher, and Robin McKie. *African Exodus.* New York: Holt, 1996.

Origins of Agriculture and Civilization

Redman, Charles L. *The Rise of Civilization.* San Francisco: Freeman, 1978.

Robinson, Andrew. *The Story of Writing.* London: Thames and Hudson, 1995.

Scarre, Chris, and Brian Fagan. *Ancient Civilizations.* 2nd ed. Upper Saddle River, N.J.: Prentice Hall, 2002.

Smith, Bruce D. *The Emergence of Agriculture.* New York: Scientific American, 1994.

Biblical and Classical Archaeology

Hornblower, Simon, and Anthony Spawforth, eds. *The Oxford Classical Dictionary.* 3rd ed. New York: Oxford University Press, 1996.

Levy, T. E., ed. *The Archaeology of Society in the Holy Land.* New York: Facts on File, 1995.

Historical Archaeology

Noel Hume, Ivor. *Historical Archaeology.* New York: Knopf, 1969.

————. *Martin's Hundred.* rev. ed. Charlottesville: University of Virginia Press, 1991.

Orser, Charles E., and Brian Fagan. *Historical Archaeology.* New York: HarperCollins, 1995.

Underwater Archaeology

Bass, George. *Archaeology Underwater.* London: Thames and Hudson, 1966.

————, ed. *A History of Seafaring Based on Underwater Archaeology.* London: Thames and Hudson, 1972.

————, ed. *Ships and Shipwrecks of the Americas.* London: Thames and Hudson, 1988.

African Archaeology

Connah, Graham. *African Civilizations.* New York: Cambridge University Press, 1987.

Phillipson, Davis W. *African Prehistory.* 2nd ed. New York: Cambridge University Press, 1994.

Oliver, Roland. *The African Experience.* London: Weidenfeld and Nicholson, 1991.

Oliver, Roland, and John Fage, eds. *The Cambridge History of Africa.* Vol. 1, *Prehistory.* New York: Cambridge University Press, 1981.

The Americas

Bernal, Ignacio. *A History of Mexican Archaeology*. London: Thames and Hudson, 1980.

Coe, Michael. *The Maya*. 6th ed. London: Thames and Hudson, 1999.

————. *Mexico*. 4th ed. London: Thames and Hudson, 1994.

Dillehay, Tom. *First Settlement of America: A New Prehistory*. New York: Basic Books, 2000.

Fagan, Brian. *Ancient North America: The Archaeology of a Continent*. 3rd ed. London: Thames and Hudson, 2001.

————. *Kingdoms of Gold, Kingdoms of Jade*. London: Thames and Hudson, 1991.

Feidel, Stuart J. *Prehistory of the Americas*. 2nd ed. New York: Cambridge University Press, 1992.

Meltzer, David. *The Search for the First Americans*. Washington D.C.: Smithsonian Books, 1994.

Moseley, Michael. *The Inca and their Predecessors*. 2nd ed. London: Thames and Hudson, 2001.

Australia and Pacific, Asia

Barnes, Gina L. *China, Korea, and Japan: The Rise of Civilization in East Asia*. London: Thames and Hudson, 1993.

Bellwood, Peter. *The Polynesians*. London: Thames and Hudson, 1987.

Chang, K-C. *The Archaeology of Ancient China*. 4th ed. New Haven, Conn.: Yale University Press, 1986.

Higham, Charles. *The Archaeology of Mainland Southeast Asia*. New York: Cambridge University Press, 1989.

Kirch, Patrick V. *The Lapita Peoples: Ancestors of the Oceanic World*. Cambridge, Mass.: Blackwell, 1997.

————. *On the Road of the Winds: An Archaeological History of the Pacific Islands*. Berkeley: University of California Press, 2000.

Possehl, Gregory, ed. *The Harappan Civilization*. London: Aris and Phillips, 1982.

White, J. Peter, and James O'Connell. *A Prehistory of Australia, New Guinea, and Sahul*. New York: Academic, 1982.

Egypt

Fagan, Brian. *Egypt of the Pharaohs*. Washington, D.C.: National Geographic Society, 2001.

Kemp, Barry. *Ancient Egypt: Anatomy of a Civilization*. London: Routledge, 1989.

Shaw, Ian, ed. *The Oxford History of Ancient Egypt*. New York: Oxford University Press, 2000.

Europe

Childe, V. Gordon. *The Prehistory of European Society*. Baltimore: Pelican, 1958.

Cunliffe, Barry, ed. *The Oxford Illustrated History of Prehistoric Europe*. New York: Oxford University Press, 1994.

Gamble, Clive. *The Palaeolithic Societies of Europe*. New York: Cambridge University Press, 1999.

Renfrew, Colin. *Before Civilization*. New York: Knopf, 1981.

Piggott, Stuart. *Ancient Europe*. Chicago: Aldine, 1965.

WEBSITES

American Museum of Natural History Resources for Learning
www.amnh.org/education/resources/index.html

This section of the AMNH website provides a collection of learning resources such as activities and articles in fields including anthropology and paleontology.

Archaeology Magazine
www.he.net/~archaeol/index.html

This online version of the official publication of the American Institute of Archaeology provides up-to-date information on digs and discoveries and the latest news. This site also has an archive of past articles organized by date and region.

ArchNet

http://archnet.asu.edu

ArchNet serves as the World Wide Web Virtual Library for archaeology. This site provides access to archaeological resources available on the Internet. Information is categorized by geographic region and subject and includes lists of excavation sites, museums, academic departments, and journals.

British Museum

www.thebritishmuseum.ac.uk

This site offers information about past and current British Museum sponsored excavations. Using the search feature, visitors can access hundreds of digital images of archaeological finds. Also, in the Education Department section, visitors can find links to pages with recommended books and educational resources.

Current Archaeology

www.archaeology.co.uk

This site for Britain's leading archaeological magazine is a gateway to the world of British archaeology. Visitors can take an online walking tour through a timeline of British archaeology, find information on over 900 archaeological organizations, inquire about education and careers in archaeology, and read current and back issues of *Current Archaeology*, which feature recent digs and discoveries, and the latest news.

Emuseum Virtual Archaeology

http://emuseum.mnsu.edu/archaeology/virtual/index.shtml

Virtual archaeology is used to help archaeologists manipulate and analyze materials using computers. This website gives a tutorial about virtual archaeology and offers a broad list of sites where visitors can experience virtual archaeology.

Field Museum of Natural History

www.fmnh.org

Since its founding the Field Museum has been an international leader in evolutionary biology and paleontology, and archaeology and ethnography. This site offers introductory notes to the various fields of natural history and offers helpful weblinks for more information.

National Museum of Natural History

www.mnh.si.edu

This Smithsonian Institution museum holds collections with more than 124 million objects and specimens. This site provides insight to the ongoing research with these collections and the various fields that comprise natural history.

Peabody Museum of Archaeology and Ethnology

www.peabody.harvard.edu/default.html

This site highlights one of the oldest museums in the world devoted to anthropology and houses one of the most comprehensive records of human cultural history in the Western Hemisphere. This site includes "virtual tours" through online exhibitions and online finding aids to the museum's archival collection, which holds millions of artifacts, photos, and papers.

University of Pennsylvania Museum of Archaeology and Anthropology Educational Department

www.upenn.edu/museum/PublicServices/edservices.html

This section of the museum's website offers interactive introductions to the field of archaeology and to many key geographical areas in archaeological study.

Index

References to main biographical entries are indicated by **bold** page numbers; references to illustrations are indicated by *italics*

Abu Simbel, 31
Abydos, 81, 133
An Account of the Danes and Norwegians in England, Scotland, and Ireland (Worsaae), 38, 39
Adam's Ancestors (Leakey, L.), 150
Africa, *11*, 73, 158–159, 165, 167, 168
African archaeology, 157, 159
Agasizz, Alexander, 102
Agricultural Revolution, 123, 124
Akhenaten, 80, 91
Akkadian language, 56
Albright, William, **164**
de Alcubierre, Rocque Joaquin, 16, 23
Alms for Oblivion: An Antiquary's Scrapbook (Wheeler), 145
Altamira Cave, 86
Amarna, 80, 91
American archaeology, 67, 68, 73, 102–104, 126–127, 160–161
American Southeast, 127
Amiens, 35
Amun's temple at Karnak, 59
An Introduction to American Archaeology (Willey), 162
Analytical Archaeology (Clark, D.), 171
The Ancient Bronze Implements, Weapons, and Ornaments of Great Britain and Ireland (Evans, J.), 35
Ancient Egypt and Ancient Israel (Flinders Petrie), 81
Ancient Europe (Piggott), 165
The Ancient History of Wiltshire (Colt Hoare), 42
Ancient India [journal] (Wheeler), 146
Ancient Khotan (Stein), 114
The Ancient Maya (Morley), 111
Ancient Monuments of the Mississippi Valley (Squier, Davis), 68
The Ancient Stone Implements, Weapons, and Ornaments of Great Britain (Evans, J.), 35
Angkor civilization, 168
Angles-sur-Anglin rock shelter, 139
Anyang, 163
Archaeological Reconnaissances in Southeastern Iran (Stein), 116
Archaeological researches in Retrospect (Clark, G.), 155
Archaeology and Society (Clark, G.), 155
Archaeology at Cambridge and Beyond (Clark, G.), 156
Archaeology at Cambridge and Beyond (Clark, G.), 155
Archaeology from the Earth (Wheeler), 145
Archaeology in the Holy Land (Kenyon), 143

Archaeology of Mainland Southeast Asia (Bass), 172
Archaeology of Palestine (Albright), 164
Archaeology of the Florida Coast (Willey), 161
Archaeology of the United States (Haven), 67
Arikamedu, 146
The Arts and Crafts of Ancient Egypt (Flinders Petrie), 81
The Aryans (Gordon Childe), 122, 123
Ashurbanipal's archives, 54
Asia, *13*, 164, 171
Assurbanipal's palace, 52, 70
Assurbanipal's royal library, 46, 56
Assyrians, 45–46, 52–54
Atwater, Caleb, **43**, 46
Aubrey, John, 16, **42**
Aurignacian culture, 88
Australian prehistory, 168
Australopithicus afarensis, 172, *173*
Australopithicus africanus, 164
Avebury, 16, 18–20, 42, 169
Avebury, A Temple of British Druids Described (Stukeley), 19
Avebury (Stukeley), 20

Babylon, 54, 126
Ban Non Wat, *166*
Banpo, 164
Bartram, William, **42**
Bass, George, 169, *171*, **171**
Baudez, Claude, 162
Beginning in Archaeology (Kenyon), 143
Bell, Gertrude, 72, 82, **82–85**, *84*
Belzoni, Giovanni Battista, 16, *29*, **29–32**, 45, 91
Beni Hasan tombs, 126
Bersu, Gerhard, 129, **163**
Biblical archaeology, 63
Biblical archaeology, 143
Binford, Lewis, 165, 168, **170**
Bingham, Hiram, 47, **69**
Biologica Centrali Americana (Maudsley), 126
Bleek, Wilhelm, 173
Boas, Franz, 103
Bonaparte, Napoleon, *44*, 45
Bordes, François, **165**
Botta, Paul Emile, 7, 45–46, 56, **68**
Boule, Marcellin, **126**
Bouyssonnie, Abbé, 87
Braidwood, Robert, **164**
Breasted, Henry, 93
Breuil, Abbé Henri, 73, 86, **86–89**, 137, 138
Britannia (Camden), 41
British Mesolithic culture, 154
British prehistoric cultures, **164**
Brittany, 146
Brixham Cave, 17, 35
Bronze Age, 106–108, 123, 125, 142–143, 164

The Bronze Age (Gordon Childe), 123
Brooches from the Bronze Age (Montelius), 106, 107, 108
Buonodelmonti, Cristoforo, 14
Burial mounds, 127

Cabot, Samuel, 50
Calah, 46, 53, 56
California, 165
Callendar, Alexander, 90
Camden, William, 16, **41–42**
Capitan, Louis, 87
Carchemish, *117*, 118–119
Carnarvon, Lord, 72, 92–93
Carter, Howard, 9, 72, 80, 90, **90–93**, *92*, 133
Çatalhöyük, 173
Catherwood, Frederick, 7, 47, 49, 50, **67**
Caton-Thompson, Gertrude, 72, 130, *132*, **132–135**, 139, 140, 143
The Cave of Altamira at Santillana del Mar, Spain (Breuil, Obermaier), 87
Caves of the Thousand Buddhas, *114*, 114–115
Central America, *10*, 49–50, 104–105, 109, 111, 112, 161, 162, 171
Central Asia, 73, 113–116
On Central Asian tracks (Stein), 116
Champollion, Jean François, 45, **67**
de Chardin, Father Teilhard, 87, **127**
Chase, George, 103
Chi, Li, **163**
Chichén Itzá, 50, 105, 109, 111, 163
Childe. See Gordon Childe, Vere
China, 73, 114–115, 116, 127, 159, 163, 164
Chippindale, Christopher, 21
Christie, Agatha, 119
Chronicles of the Kings of Kashmir (Stein), 114
Cisbury Hill Iron Age fort, 75
The Civilization of Sweden in Heathen Times (Montelius), 107
Clark, David, 168, **171**
Clark, Grahame, 129, 130, 131, *153*, **153–156**, *154*, 157, 167, 168
Clark, John Desmond, 131, 146, *157*, **157–159**
Cliff Palace at Mesa Verde, 73
Clottes, Jean, **173**
Colt Hoare, Sir Richard, 16, **42–43**, *43*
Conkey, Margaret, **172–173**
Conservation of archaeological sites, 169
Conze, Alexander, 71
Cook, Basil, 158
Copán, 111, 162, 169
Cozumel, 50
Crawford, O. G. S., 130, **163**
Crete, 72, 95, 98, 99
Cro-Magnon people, 138–139
Cross-dating method, 80

Cultural Resource Management (CRM), 8–9
Culture history, 122
The Cuneiform Inscriptions of Western Asia (Rawlinson), 57
Cuneiform script, 55–57
Cunnington, William, 16, **42**, *43*
Curtius, Ernst, **68**, 71
Cuvier, Jacques, 17
Cuzco, 165

Danger Cave, 164
The Danube in Prehistory (Gordon Childe), 122, 123
Dart, Raymond, **164**
Darwin, Charles, 7, 17, 35, 106
On the Dating of the Bronze Age, particularly in relation to Scandinavia (Montelius), 106, 107
Davis, Edwin, 46, 68
Davis, Hester, **170**
Davis, Theodore, 92
The Dawn of European Civilization (Gordon Childe), 121, 123
Dead Cities and Living Men (Woolley), 119
Deetz, James, **170**
The Desert and the Sown (Bell), 83
Desert West, 165
Destruction of archaeological sites, 8–9, 75, 169
Devil's Tower, 137
Digging up Jericho (Kenyon), 143
Diospolis Parva (Flinders Petrie), 81
Direct Historicical Method, 7
Discoveries in the Ruins of Nineveh and Babylon (Layard), 53
Donnan, Chris, **173**
Dorpfeld, Wilhelm, 47, 66, 99
Douglass, A. E., 73
Drovetti, Bernardino, 30–31, 32, 45, **67**
Druids, 20–21

The Early Mesoamerican Village (Flannery), 171
East Jerusalem, 143
East Turkana, 152, 171, 172
Ecological archaeology, 156
Edfu, 59
Edwards, Emelia, 68, **69**, 71, 98
Egypt, *11*, 45, 58–60, 72, 78–81, 90–93, 126, 130, 133, 134
Egyptologists, 58, 67, 68, 72, 79, 91, 93, 103, 126, 127, 133, 172
Egyptology, 78
El-Kahun, 79
Emeryville, 126
Engendering Archaeology (Conkey, Gero, eds.), 173
Erligang, 164
Esarhaddon's palace, 52
Espíritu Pampa, 69
Ethics of archaeology, 9
Ethiopia, 131, 158, 168
Ethiopian Rift, 159
Europe, *12*

Evans, Arthur John, 72, 80, *94*, **94–97**, 96, 99, 101, 118
Evans, John, 17, *33*, **33–36**, *34*, 36
By the Evidence: Memoirs (Leakey, L.), 150
Excavations at Star Carr (Clark, G.), 155, 156
Excavations at Ur (Woolley), 119
Excavations on Cranborne Chase (Pitt-Rivers), 75, 77

Fayum Depression, 133, *135*, 143
Fiorelli, Giuseppi, 25
Flannery, Kent, 168, **171**
Flinders Petrie, William Matthew, 7, 70, 72, **78–81**, *79*, 91, 126, 133, 141, 167
Florida, 160
Flotation methods, 164, 168, 171
Ford, James A., 73, **127**
A Forest of Kings (Schele, Freidel), 172
Fossey, Dian, 152
Four Hundred Centuries of Cave Art (Breuil), 87
From Amurath to Amurah (Bell), 83

Gamble, Clive, **173**
Gamble's Cave, 148
Gamio, Manuel, **127**
Gardner, Elinor, 133
Garrod, Dorothy, 130, *136*, **136–139**, 156
Garstang, John, 142
Gendrosia, 115
Gero, Joan, **173**
Ghurab, 80
Giza, 59, 72, 78, 79, 172
Global archaeology, 129
Godwin, Harry, 154, 155
Goodall, Jane, 152
Gordon Childe, Vere, 73, **121–124**, *124*
Gournia, 99, 99–100, *100*
Gournia, Vasiliki and Other Prehistoric Sites on the Isthmus of Ierapetra, Greece (Hawes, H.B.), 101
Great Basin, 165
Great Basin archaeology, 164
Great Britain, *12*, 145–146
Great Plains, 164
Great Zimbabwe, 72, 130, 132, 133–134, *140*
Greece, *13*
Green, Roger, **170–171**
Grotte de Chauvet, 173
Growth in archaeology, 167
Guatemala, 49, 110, 125, 161
Guibert, Abbé, 86, 87
A Guide to the Northern Antiquities (Thomsen), 27
Guillieron, Emile, 96

Hadrian's Wall, 21, 118
Hamilton, William, **42**
Hamoudi, Sheikh, 119
Handbook of South American Indians (Willey, ed.), 160
Haram esh Sharif, 61–62
Harappa, 146
Harrappa, 115

Hatshepsut's mortuary temple, 59, 91, 127
Haury, Emil, **164**
Haven, Samuel, 47, **67–68**
Hawass, Zahi, **172**
Hawes, Charles Henry, 100
Hawes, Harriet Boyd, 72, **98–101**, *99*
Hawkes, Christopher, **164**
Hazar Merd cave, 138
Heizer, Robert, **165**
Herculaneum, 16, 22–24
Hetepheres' tomb, 126
Hewitt, Edgar, 102–103, 110
Higgs, Eric, **164**
High-technology science, 7–8, 168
Higham, Charles, *166*, 168, **171–172**
Hincks, Edward, 56, 57
Hissarlik mound. See Troy
A History of American Archaeology (Willey, Sobloff), 161, 162
History of the Art of Antiquity (Winckelmann), 23, 25
Hodder, Ian, **173**
Hogarth, David, 99
Hohokam culture, 164
Holmes, William H., **69**
Homo ergaster, 151
Homo sapiens sapiens, 136, 138
Hooten, Ernest Albert, 104
Hopi, 104
L'Hôte, Nestor, 58
Hua Fteah, 165
Hudson, Beatrice, *166*
Human cultural evolution, 123
Human evolution, 130
Hume, Ivor Noel, **173**
Huxley, Thomas Henry, 7, 17, 35, **43**

Ice Age, 123, 129, 130, 133, 137, 138, 165
Ice Age archaeology, 87
Ice Age art, 86, 88–89, 172, 173
Igbo Ukwo, 165
Ilios (Schliemann), 65
Incidents of Travel in Arabia Petraea (Stephens), 49
Incidents of Travel in Central America, Chiapas, and Yucatán (Stephens), 49, 50
Incidents of Travel in Yucatán (Stephens), 49, 50
India, 114, 115, 146–147, 159, 170
Indus civilization, 146
Innermost Asia: Detailed Report of Explorations in Central Asia, Ken-su, And Eastern Iran (Stein), 115
The Inscriptions of Copán (Morley), 111
The Inscriptions of Péten (Morley), 111
Instruction of Musketry (Pitt-Rivers), 74, 75
An Introduction to American Archaeology (Willey), 161
Introduction to the Archaeology of Cuzco (Rowe), 165
An Introduction to the Study of Suthwestern Archaeology (Kidder), 103
Invitation to Archaeology (Deetz), 170
Iran, 46, 116, 133

Iraq, 45–46, 83, 115, 138
Iron Age, 108, 129, 145, 146, 164, 165
Iron Age hill forts, 154
Isaac, Glynn, 159, 168, **171**
Ishtar Gate, 126
Israel, 81
Itinerarium Curiosum (Stukeley), 19–20

Jamestown, 173
Jamo, 164
Jefferson, Thomas, **42**, 46
Jennings, Jesse D., **164**
Jericho, 130, 132, 133, 140, 142–143
Jerusalem, 61–63, *141, 142*, 143
Jewry Wall, 141
Johanson, Don, 168, **172**, *173*
Jordan, 133

Kalambo Falls prehistoric site, 131, 158
The Kalambo Falls Prehistoric Site (Clark, JD),
    159
Karnak, 30, 59
Kenya, 130, 148
Kenyon, Dame Kathleen, 130, 139,
    140–143, *141*, 145
Kerma, 126
Kharga Oasis, 134
Khorsabad, 45, 52–53, 56, 68
Khotan Empire, 114
Kidder, Alfred Vincent, 7, 73, *102*, **102–105**,
    105, 110, 111, 126–127, 161
Kikuyu people, 148–149
Kirch, Patrick, **173**
Kivik burial mound, *38*
Knossos, 95–97
Koldeway, Robert, **126**
Kossina, Gustaf, **126**
Koster, 170
Kroeber, Alfred, **126–127**
Kuyunjik mounds, 46, 52

Laetoli hominid prints, 151–152
de Landa, Diego, **41**
Landscape archaeology, 130
Langdon, Stephen, 85
Lapita culture, 170
Lartet, Edouard, 87, 88
Lawrence, T. E., *117*, 118
Layard, Austen Henry, 7, 46, **51–54**, *52, 54*,
    56, 118
Le Cotte de St. Brelade cave, 165
Le Moustier, 88
Leakey, Louis S. B., and Mary D., 130–131,
    148–152, *149, 151, 157*, 159, 167
Leakey, Richard, 152, **172**
Legislation to protect archaeological sites,
    170
Lenormant, Charles, 58
Lepsius, Karl Richard, 45, **68**, 71
Lewis-Williams, David, 173, **173**
Libby, Willard, 8
Linear A, Linear B, 95–96
London's Roman wall, 75
Lovelock Cave, 165

Lubbock, Sir John, 27
Lucy, 168, 172, *173*
Luxor, 30, 59, 60, 92, 133
Lydney, 145
Lyell, Sir Charles, 35

Machu Pichu, 47, 69
MacIver, Randall, 134
Maes How, *122*
Magdalenian culture, 88
Maiden Castle, *128*, 144, 145–146, *147*, 157,
    164
Malawi, 159
Mallowan, Max, 119, 147
Malta, 133, 137
Mal'ta, 164
Mammoth Cave, 171
Management of archaeological sites, 169
Manners and Customs of the Ancient Egyptians
    (Wilkinson), 67
Man's Place in Nature (Huxley), 43
Marcus, Joyce, 168
Mariette, Auguste, 45, 58, **58–60**, 60, 78
Marret, R. R., 137
Martin's Hundred, 173
Maudsley, Alfred P., 73, **125–126**
Maya, 47, 48, 49–50, 67, 73, 105, 109,
    110–112, 125–126, 130, 161–162, 164,
    169, 172
McAdams, Robert, **170**
McBurney, Charles, **165**
McEnery, Father James, 35
McGown, Theodore, 138
Merekete's household, 127
Meroitic civilization, 118
Mesapotamia, 82, 83–85
Mesoamerican civilization, 171
The Mesolithic Age in Britain (Clark, G), 154,
    155
The Mesolithic Settlement of Northern Europe
    (Clark, G), 155
Mesopotamia, 126, 170
Method and Theory in American Archaeology
    (Willey, Phillips), 160, 161
Methods and Aims in Achaeology (Flinders
    Petrie), 80, 81
Mezhirich, 172
Middle Zabezi Valley, 159
Minoan civilization, 72, 94, 98
Moche civilization, 173
Moche Lords of Sipán, 169, 173
Mohenjo-daro, 115, 146
Mongolia, 115, 127, 164
Montelius, Oscar, 17, 28, 40, 73, *106*,
    106–108, *108*, 122, 125
Morley, Sylvanus Griswold, 73, 103, 105,
    109–112, *110*
de Mortillet, Gabrielle, 87, 88
The Most Ancient East (Gordon Childe),
    123
Mosul, 45–46, 51, 68
Mount Carmel caves, 130, 136, 138–139
Mualia, Famaanu, *166*
Müller, Sophus, 108, **125**

Multidisciplinary archaeology, 169
Mulvaney, John, 168
Mumbwa Cave, 158
Mummies, 79, 80, 172
Murder in Mesopotamia (Christie), 119
Mycenae, 66, 95
Mycenae (Schliemann), 65

Nai, Xia, **164**
Naqada cemeteries, 80
*Narrative of the Operations and Recent
    Discoveries within the Pyramids, Temples,
    Tombs, and Excavations in Egypt and Nubia*
    (Belzoni), 31
Native Americans, 46–47, 68, 73, 102,
    103–104, 165
The Native Races (Bancroft), 109
Naukratis, 79
Naville, Edouard, 91
Neander Valley, 17
Neanderthal people, 17, 88, 126, 137–139,
    164
Near East, 172
Nelson, Nels, 103
"New archaeology," 165, 168, 170
New Light on the Most Ancient East (Gordon
    Childe), 123
New York, 165
Newberry, Percy, 91, **126**
Niebuhr, Carsten, **42**
Nigeria: Its Archaeology and early History
    (Shaw), 165
Nile, 81, 103
Nile Delta, 79
Nile Valley, *11*, 118, 130
Nimrud, 47, 52, 55, 56
Nineveh, 45–46, 51, 52–53, 55, 56, 68
Nineveh and Babylon (Layard), 54
Nineveh and Its Remains (Layard), 53
Njoro River Cave, 149
North Africa, *12*
North America, 8–9, *10*, 162, 164, 165
North American archaeology, 105, 165, 168
Nubia, 126
Nyerup, Rasmus, 16, 27, **43**

Okladnikov, Aleksei Pavlovich, **164**
Old Kingdom tombs, 133
On Old Routes of Western Iran (Stein), 116
Oldowan culture, 151–152
Olduvai Gorge, 131, 148, 149–152
*Olduvai Gorge: A Report on the Evolution of
    the Hand-Axe Culture in Beds I-IV* (Leakey,
    L.), 150
Olduvai Gorge: My Search for Early Man
    (Leakey, M.), 151
*Olduvai Gorge:, Vol. 3: Excavations in
    Beds I and II, 1960-1963* (Leakey, M.),
    151
Ole Worm's Museum of Curiosities, 8
Olorgesaillie, 149, 171
Olympia, 68, 71
Oppert, Jules, 57
Origin of Species (Darwin), 7, 36, 75

Pachacamac, 126
Pacific Ocean cultures, 173
Pacific prehistory, 170
Pakistan, 146
Palace and Mosque at Ukhaidir (Bell), 83
Palace of Knossos, 72
Palace of Minos, 36, 72, 94, 96, 96–97, 99
The Palace of Minos at Knossos (Evans, A.J.), 95, 97
Palenque, 49–50, *172*
The Paleolithic Societies of Europe (Gamble), 173
Palestine, 143
Parkington, John, 168
Peacock's Farm, 154, *154*
Pecos Pueblo, 73, 102, 103–104, *105*
Persia, 115–116
"Persian Cuneiform Inscriptions at Behistun" (Rawlinson), 56
de Perthes, Jacques Boucher, 17, 35, **43**
Peru, 73, 126, 130, 160, 165, 167, 173
Péten, 161–162
Petra, 48, 49
Petrie, William Matthew Flinders, *see* Flinders Petrie, William Matthew
The Phenomenon of Man (de Chardin), 127
Phillips, Philip, 160–161
Photography, 7, 77
Phylakopi, 172
Piecing Together the Past (Gordon Childe), 123, 124
Piette, Edouard, 87, 88
Piggott, Stuart, 129, **164–165**
Pitt-Rivers, General Augustus Lane, 7, *70*, 71, *74*, **74–77**, 78, 129, 145
Pollen analysis, 129, 154, 155
Pompeii, 16, 22–25
Post-processual archaeology, 169, 173
Potassium-argon dating, 150, 168
La Préhistoire (Breuil), 87
Prehistoric and Roman Wales (Wheeler), 145
Prehistoric archaeology, 73, 87–89
Prehistoric art, 89
Prehistoric Cultures of the Horn of Africa (Clark, J. D.), 158, 159
Prehistoric Europe: the Economic Basis (Clark, G.), 155
Prehistoric Settlement Patterns in the Virú Valley, Peru (Willey), 161
Prehistory, 133
The Prehistory of European Society (Gordon Childe), 123, 124
Prehistory of Southern Africa (Clark, J. D.), 159
The Prehistory of Southern Africa (Clark, J. D.), 159
Prestwich, Joseph, 36
The Primeval Antiquities of Denmark (Worsaae), 37, 39
Processual archaeology, 168–169
Proconsul africanus, 149
Proskouriakoff, Tatiana, 164
Pueblo Bonito, 73

Pulak, Äemal, 171
Pumpelly, Raphael, 102
In Pursuit of the Past (Binford), 170
Putnam, Frederick Ward, 102, 109
Pyramid of Kephren, 31–32
The Pyramid Survey 1880-82 (Flinders Petrie), 79
Pyramids, 132, 172
Pyramids and Tombs of Egypt (Flinders Petrie), 78, 81

Qinshihuangdi's terra-cotta regiment, 169
Qurna, 30, 31

Radiocarbon dating, 8, 130, 133, 156, 168
Ramses II, 30, *32*
Rassam, Hormuzd, 46, **68–69**
Rawlinson, Henry Creswicke, 46, 53, 55–57, *56*
Reck, Hans, 148
Redfield, Robert, 105
Reflections on the Imitation of Greek Works in Painting and Sculpture (Winckelmann), 23
Reisner, George A., 103, 104, **126**
Relacion de las Cosa de Yucatán (de Landa), 41
Relics of saints, 9
Renfrew, Colin, 168, **172**
Report on the Mound Explorations of the Bureau of Ethnology (Thomas), 68
Rich, Claudius, **43**
Roman cemetery at Hawara, 79
Roman sites, 130, 141
Roman towns, 129
Rosetta Stone, 45, 67
Rowe, John, **165**
The Ruins of Desert Cathay (Stein), 114, 115
Rusinga Island, 149

Sabloff, Jeremy A., 162
Sabratha, 141
Sahara, 159
Salvage archaeology, 164, 165, 169
Samaria, 140
Samothrace, 71
San Cristobal Pueblo, 103
San hunter-gatherer art, 173
Sand-Buried Ruins of Khotan (Stein), 115
Sanders, William, 162
Sankalia, Hasmuk, **170**
Saqqara, 58–59
Sargon II's palace, 46, 68
de Sarzac, Ernest, 69, **69**
Scandinavia, 125, 155
Schele, Linda, 169, **172**
Schliemann, Heinrich, 7, 47, *61*, **64–66**, 95
Schliemann, Sophia, 99
Scientific archaeology, 71–73
Seagar, Rodney, 101
Sennacherib's palace, 53–54
Seti I's tomb, 31, 32
Settlement archaeology, 130
Shaw, Thurstan, **165**
Shipwreck excavations, *171*
Silk Road, 73, 114, 115

Skara Brae, 122
Skull 1470, 172
In Small Things Forgotten (Deetz), 170
Smith, George, 46
Snaketown, 164
Social Evolution (Gordon Childe), 123
Society of Antiquaries of London, 19
Soffer, Olga, **172**
Solutrean culture, 88
Somalia, 131, 158
Somme Valley, 17
South Africa, 167
South America, *10*, 73, 162
Southeast Asia, 168
Southern Africa, 158
Southwest archaeology, 102–104
Southwest Asia, *13*
Squier, Ephraim, 46, **68**
Stanwick Iron Age hill fort, 147
Star Carr hunting camp, 129, *153*, 155–156, 167
Stein, Sir Aurel, 73, **113–116**
Stephens, John Lloyd, 7, 47, 48, *48*, **48–50**, 162
Still Digging: Leaves from an Antiquary's Notebook (Wheeler), 145
Stone Age, 108, 123, 124, 125, 127, 129, 130, 131, 133, 134, 138, 148–149, 155, 158–159, 164
Stone Age archaeologists, 72
Stone Age archaeology, 87, 88, 126, 157
The Stone Age Cultures of Kenya Colony (Leakey, L.), 148, 150
The Stone Age Cultures of Northern Rhodesia (Clark, JD), 158, 159
The Stone Age of Mount Carmel (Garrod, Bate), 139
Stonehenge, 16, 18–20, *41*, *43*, 78, 169
Stonehenge, A Temple Restored to the British Druids (Stukeley), 19
Stonehenge (Stukeley), 20
Stratified occupation mounds, 127
Strong, William Duncan, 160, **164**
Struever, Stuart, **170**
Study of Archaeology (Taylor), 165
Stukeley, William, 16, **18–21**, *20*
"The Subdivisions of the Upper Paleolithic and Their Significance" (Breuil), 88
Sumerian civilization, 69
The Survey of Western Palestine (Warren), 63

Taklamakan Desert, *113*
Tanis, 79
Taxila, 146
Tayler, Walter W., **165**
Teamwork archaeology, 169
Tell el-Hesi, 81
Tent Work in Palestine (Warren), 63
Teotihuácan, 127, *127*
Thailand, 171
Theban necropolis, 126
Thomas, Cyrus, **68**, 73
Thompson, Edward H., 109, 163, **163**
Thompson, J. Eric, **164**
Thomsen, Christian Jurgensen, 16, 17, **26–28**

The Thousand and One Churches (Bell, Ramsey), 83
A Thousand Miles up the Nile (Edwards), 70
Three Age System, 16, *26*, 26–28, 37, 39, 40
Tiglath-Pileser's palace, 52
Tikal, 111
Tobias, Philip, 151
The Tomb of Tut.ankh.Amen (Carter, Mace), 93
Tozzer, Alfred Marsten, 109, 110, 161
Travels (Bartram), 42
Tree-ring dating, 8, 73, 168
Tropical Africa, 131, 132, 134–135, 168
Troy, 7, *14*, 47, 64, 65–66
Troy and Its Remains (Schliemann), 65
Tulum, 50
Turville-Petre, Francis, 137
Tutankhamun's funerary feast, 127
Tutankhamun's tomb, 72, 81, 90, 92–93, 133

Uaxactún, 111
Uhle, Max, **126**
Uluburun, 169, 171
Undeground Jerusalem (Warren), 63
Underwater archaeology, 171
Upper Nile, 159

The Upper Paleolithic Age in Britain (Garrod), 137, 139
Upper Zambezi Valley, 131
Ur, 72, 84–85, 116, 117, 119–120, *120*
Ur of the Chaldees (Wooley), 120
Ur Royal Cemetery, 119–120
Urban Revolution, 123, 124
Uxmal, 50

Valley of the Golden Mummies, 172
Valley of Mexico, 168
Valley of Oaxaca, 168
Van Giffen, Albert E., **127**
Ventris, Michael, 97
Verulamium, 140, 145
Vilcabamba, 69
Voyage dans le Haute Egypte (Mariette), 59

Ward-Perkins, John, 141
Warren, Charles, 46, **61–63**, *62*, 81
Watson, Patty Jo, **171**
Welsh archaeology, 145
What Happened in History (Gordon Childe), 123
Wheeler, Sir Mortimer, 71, 77, 128, 129, 130, 131, 140–141, **144–147**, 157, 164, 170
White, Marion, **165**

White, Tim, 168, 172
Wilkinson, John Gardner, 45, **67**
Willey, Gordon R., 73, 129–130, **160–162**, *161*, 167
Williamsburg, 173
Winckelmann, Johan Joachim, 16, **22–25**
Winlock, Herbert E., **127**
Woodbury, Richard, 160
Woolley, Sir Leonard, 72–73, 78, 84–85, 93, 116, *117*, **117–120**
Wor Barrow ditch excavations, 76, 76–77
World prehistory, 139
World Prehistory (Clarke), 130, 155, 156
Worsaae, Jacob Jens A., 16–17, *22*, *24*, 28, **37–40**, *106*

Yaxchilán, 164

Zambesi River, 158
Zapotecs, 168
Zarzi cave, 138
Zettupeh Cave, 137–138
Zimbabwe. See Great Zimbabwe
The Zimbabwe Culture: Ruins and reactions (Caton-Thompson), 133
Zinjanthropus boisei 131, 150–151, 159

Picture Credits

Brian Fagan is a professor of anthropology at the University of California, Santa Barbara. He is internationally known for his more than forty books on archaeology, among them *The Adventure of Archaeology*, *The Rape of the Nile*, *The Oxford Companion to Archaeology*, *Eyewitness to Discovery*, and *Ancient North America*. He is the general editor of the Oxford University Press series *Digging for the Past*, which explores archaeological sites around the world.